Letter to the Tribulation

Letter to the Tribulation

A Chronological Retelling of the Book of Revelation

by Matthias Key

King James Version

D2D edition

Letter to the Tribulation
A Chronological Retelling of
the Book of Revelation
(KJV D2D edition)

Published by Matthias Key

ISBN-13 KJV D2D paperback edition: 979-8-9921331-8-9
ISBN-13 KJV e-book edition: 979-8-9921331-5-8

Cover artwork:
• van der Wolf, Jan, *A spiral staircase in a white room with wood floors*, https://www.pexels.com/photo/a-spiral-staircase-in-a-white-room-with-wood-floors-27548308/, free to use for commercial purposes.
• Musely royalty-free AI image generator, *Glowing futuristic key hovering vertically over processor*, https://musely.ai/tools/ai-non-copyright-image-generator, free to use for commercial purposes.

First Edition Published in 2025
Second Edition Published in 2026

Psalm 119:18 Open thou mine eyes, that I may behold wondrous things out of thy law.

Revelation chronology key

Verse(s)	Section(s)
1:1-6	K00
1:7	K38
1:8-20	K00
2:1-7	K06
2:8-11	K07
2:12-17	K08
2:18-24	K09
2:25	K09, K13
2:26	K46
2:27	K42
2:28	K46
2:29	K09, K13
3:1-6	K10
3:7-9	K11
3:10-11	K11, K13
3:12	K47
3:13	K11
3:14-22	K12
4:1-11	K14
5:1-7	K00
5:8	K00, K14
5:9-10	K14
5:11-14	K00
6:1-2	K16
6:3-4	K21
6:5-8	K25
6:9-11	K26
6:12-17	K27
7:1-8	K18
7:9-17	K26
8:1-6	K28
8:7-9	K29
8:10-11	K30
8:12-13	K31
9:1	K15, K32
9:2-11	K32
9:12-21	K33
10:1-11	K00
11:1-2	K18
11:3	K19,K34
11:4-6	K19
11:7-10	K34
11:11-13	K35
11:14-19	K36
12:1	K03
12:2	K04
12:3-4	K01, K04, K15
12:5	K05, K42
12:6	K18
12:7-10	K15
12:11	K26
12:12	K15
12:13-17	K18
13:1-2	K21
13:3-10	K23
13:11-18	K24
14:1-3	K43
14:4	K18
14:5	K43
14:6	K41
14:7	K41, K42
14:8	K21
14:9-11	K42
14:12-13	K24
14:14-18	K36
14:19	K38
14:20	K40
15:1	K36
15:2-4	K43
15:5-8	K36
16:1-11	K37
16:12-16	K38
16:17-21	K39
17:1	K02, K17, K20
17:2	K20
17:3-5	K17
17:6	K20
17:7-11	K02
17:12-13	K21
17:14	K38
17:15	K17
17:16-17	K21
17:18	K17
18:1-5	K21
18:6-7	K20
18:8	K20, K21, K25
18:9-10	K22
18:11	K21
18:12-13	K20
18:14-16	K21
18:17-20	K22
18:21-24	K20
19:1-4	K22
19:5-10	K48
19:11-14	K38
19:15	K38, K42
19:16-19	K38
19:20	K40
19:21	K38
20:1-2	K42
20:3	K42, K45
20:4	K24, K43
20:5	K43, K46
20:6	K44, K46
20:7-10	K45
20:11-15	K46
21:1-3	K47
21:4-7	K49
21:8	K46
21:9-21	K47
21:22-27	K49
22:1-5	K49
22:6-21	K50

Churches, Seals, Trumpets, and Vials

Contents

A letter to the tribulation

Hello. My name is Matthias Key. I am writing to you from the year 2024. I am writing especially to you people of the future, who find yourselves in years of food shortages, famines, and worldwide war. There are millions of people dying, worse than World War I or World War II. You have a government with global aspirations and an extreme leader. Are you in the most difficult period of human history? Could it be the End? Yes, it could be.

I am named after Matthias, the last of the twelve apostles, who took the place of Judas Iscariot. He was one of the disciples who followed Jesus Christ during all three years of his intensive ministry in Israel two thousand years ago. According to the Christian Bible, Matthias and many others saw Jesus die a criminal's death on the cross. They saw him again three days later after he was resurrected from the dead. After forty more days they watched him ascend up to heaven in a cloud. And almost all the apostles accepted death at the hands of their enemies, rather than forsake their risen Lord.

The Jewish, Christian and Muslim traditions all talk about an extreme seven-year period on earth at the end of our era. This comes from the book of Daniel in the Jewish Old Testament, the book of Revelation in the Christian New Testament, and the Muslim traditions about the life of Muhammad known as the *hadiths*. All three religious traditions agree that the seven years are not just a time of political upheaval, but have a spiritual dimension that has eternal consequences.

The Christian version of this seven-year period is commonly called the *tribulation*. The second half of the seven years will be particularly terrifying. It is known as the *great tribulation*.

It is amazing that you have found my book, because I have no doubt it is officially banned in your time. You live in a surveillance state. Government systems are in place to detect anyone who accesses the book and will track you down. My prayers go with you that almighty God in heaven will protect you until you have fully read this, and take it to heart. Then he will see you through the ultimate consequences the authorities can inflict on you.

Your government is pushing a pseudo-religious agenda of its own. Are you wondering if there is any substance behind this agenda? Some of the Christian church buildings are open still, with worship services going on occasionally. The people meeting there seem to be Christian by religion, but they and their pastors and priests have done a lot of things out of character to accommodate the government. They may not be of much help to answer your questions about what's really going on. If you check more carefully, many of the Christian believers have disappeared, and every Christian group that used to gather at homes has stopped meeting. There are different people who live there now. You may have been told that those missing were extreme Christians that were arrested one particular day across the world for subversive activity, and sent to long-term re-education camps. The official media might also explain that, at the same time, tremendous sonic booms occurred around the world, along with highly unusual atmospheric activity. The Christian religious tradition has ancient prophecies about this day! In this book you will read what really happened to them.

One reason why Christians are so convinced about the truth of the Bible is that many of its prophecies came true in the first coming of the savior Jesus Christ. They also recognize that many biblical prophecies are still waiting to be fulfilled. The Book of Revelation in the New Testament, which was written after Jesus ascended into heaven, contains much about the end times.

Revelation is a history of the future like no other book, because it is inspired by almighty God himself. It is the telling of a long vision that came to John, another of the twelve apostles. John was deep in worship when Jesus showed him these things of the future. Prophetic visions and dreams were regarded with great significance by both Jews and Christians. Records of them are scattered throughout the Bible. Individual Muslims have an even higher opinion of dreams, and try to find divine guidance for their everyday lives from them. The vision of Revelation is possibly the most fantastic one ever recounted.

Here in my book, I will explain Revelation chronologically, in consecutive periods of time, touching on all of human history after God created Adam and Eve. The time sections will be designated K00 through K50. (If you are here mainly to find out about the infamous mark of the beast, or the meaning of the number 666, jump straight to section K24, "*The false prophet upholds the beast.*" For the battle of Armageddon, go to section K38, "*The second coming of Christ, and the sixth plague: the battle of Armageddon*").

I plan a second book where I will go back and repeat most of Revelation, this time adding in a parallel column with Muslim hadiths that line up with many Revelation sections. I will have further commentary that brings Revelation into sharper focus in view of the hadiths. Along the way I will mention the authors that inspired me toward this sharper interpretation.

Even though Revelation comes from the Christian scripture, many Muslims do not realize its prophecies are foundational to their own end-time traditions. In my future book, I hope to show how the predictions in the hadiths of an end-time leader called the Mahdi are echoes and mirror images of the prophecies of Revelation. The hadiths are more difficult to understand than Revelation, because they are not all given in one source document. They were relayed by many different associates of Muhammad and not combined into one authoritative book. Revelation, on the other hand, is from one author, John, and is the last book of the New Testament. It is part of the holy inerrant word of God, accepted as fully authoritative by Bible believing Christians. Revelation is quoted in the hadiths, so it is respected by Muslims as a holy writing. Many Muslims will admit that Revelation is part of the *Injil*, their version of the New Testament. The hadiths were recorded over 500 years after Revelation. What was happening during those 500 years that resulted in the hadiths? How is it that they are surprisingly similar to Revelation? In my future book I will discuss that. An understanding of Revelation is thus the key to understanding the true meaning and purpose of the hadiths. We shall see how the content of the hadiths regarding the end times is a paradoxical but amazing confirmation of the prophecies of Revelation.

In my time there are significant worldwide happenings. The world is trending in a direction as far away from the God of the Bible as possible. Those of us who follow Christ should be immeasurably grateful that God has saved us. But we should be on guard for our children, our friends and our nations, that they not be taken captive by the lies of this world. These lies are forerunners of the great deceptions that will come in the tribulation and the last days. While the church is still on earth, we should find ways to bring the good news of Christ to minds that seem closed. We can invite people to escape from the coming tribulation by putting their faith in Christ, now, instead of delaying to see what happens.

As the end draws closer, I believe that God is giving us who seek discernment an improved view ahead of the fulfillment of prophecy. There will be greater clarity as the day draws near (2 Peter 1:19). All of this compels me to bring this chronological retelling of the book of Revelation to you who live in the future, and find yourselves living through the tribulation.

In the worldwide flood of Noah's day, only the eight members of his family were rescued by God. They obeyed him and built the ark that survived the flood. There is definitely a parallel between Noah's flood and the great tribulation.

Most people will not survive the great tribulation either. Revelation predicts that at least 50% of everyone on earth will die, by the sword, hunger, fire, and war. But it also predicts that before their death many Jews and gentiles will repent of their rebellion against God almighty. Their number will include Muslims, globalists, Marxists, Hindus, Buddhists, atheists, agnostics, animists, and even regular attenders at registered churches. Instead, they will put their trust in God's son Jesus Christ to be their Savior and Lord. They will spend eternity with him in the new heaven and the new earth.

My prayer is that this book will persuade you to be one of those saved during the tribulation. Please, accept God's gift. If you do, eternal life awaits you. Beware, lest you be one of the tribulation's victims, and you spend eternity apart from God.

A chronological retelling of the book of Revelation

Revelation was written around the year 95 CE by John, the last surviving apostle, from the Greek island of Patmos in the Aegean Sea. He had been exiled there as an elderly man in his 80's as punishment for his Christian faith, under the reign of the Roman Emperor Domitian. Revelation was a long letter circulated to seven churches in the Roman province of Asia, a region in western-central Asia Minor (today's Turkey).

John wrote a letter since he was unable to leave the island to visit the churches. A storm of persecution was about to come upon them, and at least one man - probably a pastor - had already been martyred (see verse 2:13 in section K08).

Most of John's vision details events during the seven-year end-time period popularly known as the tribulation. Revelation is therefore more than a letter to the seven churches, or a book to all the churches of the church age.

Revelation is God's letter to the tribulation.

My book will be a chronological retelling of Revelation, complete with commentary that will hopefully shed much insight on the timeline.

The major characters are Christ the Messiah, the two witnesses, and their adversaries Satan, the woman of Babylon, the beast, and the false prophet. The title of antichrist is nowhere explicitly used, but obvious implications from the rest of the Bible are that the beast is the antichrist. We will talk about this when the character of the beast comes on the scene. (In my second book I will visit the question: where will the beast and the false prophet come from?) The groups of people mentioned in Revelation are the Jews, the gentiles, and countless martyrs who are targeted and killed for their new found faith in the

Messiah. The church faithful only appear in beginning and end chapters of the book – this offers an amazing clue to their whereabouts during the tribulation that comes in between.

In my commentary of the different sections, I will explain how to interpret difficult passages and symbolism in the most literal and non-contradictory way. The principal of scripture interpreting scripture will always be our guide.

Ever since Revelation was written, there has been great disagreement about what it means. Many have argued that it is an *apocalypse*, expressed in extravagant dreamlike motifs. They say it is mostly symbolic, from which timeless spiritual lessons can be derived. They dwell on how the vision is structured around the trials of the seven seals, the seven trumpets, and the seven vials. They do not agree whether these series of sevens are repeats of one another.

There is a large group of Christians who believe that Revelation is foremost a *prophecy* from the God of Heaven. This mode of expression is called *apocalyptic prophecy*, and is present in Revelation and much of the Old Testament book of Daniel. These Christians also believe that Revelation is meant to be taken literally wherever possible, unless obvious symbolic language is being used. It is a prediction of future events, events that have eternal consequences for each and every person on earth, living and long dead. If you agree that the book of Genesis starts with six literal twenty-four hour days of creation, you should agree that the appearance in Revelation of angels, Satan, demons, the beast, and the false prophet, are not pointers to some parallel spiritual concepts to be interpreted allegorically. Instead, they are God's creatures, real characters interacting with us here on earth, bound in time the way we are.

Some interpreters choose to emphasize certain passages of the book, or make some sections allegorical, in order to make a preconceived point. That can be a shortcoming. These writers may seem plausible, but their interpretation starts to ring hollow when you try to fit the other sections and verses into their framework. I don't want to do that. In fact, I will not skip any section or verse of the book.

Premillennial interpreters of Revelation believe that the second coming of Christ will happen *prior to* his millennial kingdom on earth (see K38). Among these interpreters, there is a difference of opinion as to when he will rapture the believers of the church age to heaven. I will be following the majority pretribulational premillennial approach. *Pretribulational* means that the rapture is expected *prior to* the tribulation (see K13).

I will further take the view that the seventh seal contains the seven trumpets, and the seventh trumpet contains the seven vials. However, an apocalypse is not necessarily given in a time-ordered sequence. I will look to extract the timeline of what is described, and will point out when seals, trumpets, or vials are cross-linked to others. Thus, in my presentation you will often see verses appearing out of the order they were written. In this way, I will help you understand how the different motifs in Revelation are repetitive and intertwined.

I will use the King James Version (KJV) translation of the Bible. It uses older English words and idioms, but the advantage is that almost all Christians hold it in high respect.

Mine will be a retelling of Revelation in the most consistent chronological order possible, by individual verse. This will help you to understand the trials that you are going through in your future time, and how you can ultimately be delivered from them by our almighty God in heaven.

The seven seals, then seven trumpets, then seven vials, are the spine of the book of Revelation. When they are treated in consecutive order, it becomes evident where to wrap the other verses of John's spiral vision around the spine. That is the key to unravelling the timeline of the entire book.

By this method, I will reorganize the book into time sections in chronological order designated K00 through K50. Section K00 is an introduction. K01 is the beginning of the timeline, and is about Satan being cast out of heaven, and the fall of Adam and Eve into sin. K02 is on the spirit of Babel in the seven empires of the Old Testament, K03 God founding the nation of Israel, and so forth. We finally get to K49 about the river of eternal life proceeding from the new Jerusalem. K50 will be concluding revelations and exhortations that are in the book.

Every verse of Revelation will be found in one of those time sections.

The apostles of Jesus were looking for fulfillment of prophecies from the Old Testament in their own time when they walked with Jesus. It was only after he died, rose from the dead and ascended to heaven, that they realized many of the prophecies had a double fulfillment – with more events to happen when Jesus returns someday from heaven to earth.

Such double fulfillments also occur within Revelation. You will see the verses for them in more than one section. They are indicated by a double dagger mark ‡ that points to the other section(s) where they occur, for example 12:3‡[K04,K15]. Sometimes it is an entire verse that has the double or triple fulfillment. Other times this happens when there are two or three parts to the verse and only one part is applicable to the section. The portion that is relevant to the section under consideration will be in regular font, and the portion belonging to elsewhere in the timeline will be in italics. For example, in this verse from K04, the dragon ready to devour the child is the portion that is relevant to K04:

> 12:4‡[K01,K15] *And his tail drew the third part of the stars of heaven, and did cast them to the earth:* and the dragon stood before the woman which was ready to be delivered, for to devour her child as soon as it was born.

My section commentaries will explain each case.

Before the table of contents of my book there is an index of all the verses of Revelation, which gives the sections where each is found.

My source on pretribulational interpretation is the classic textbook *The Revelation of Jesus Christ* written in 1966 by John F. Walvoord, former Chancellor of Dallas Theological Seminary. For prophecies outside of Revelation, I refer to *Major Bible Prophecies* written in 1991, also by Dr. Walvoord. My apologies if you find direct quotations from Walvoord which I neglected to designate.

Several generations of eschatology teachers matured their views before the 1948 independence of Israel. Walvoord was among them. His biblical scholarship from the 1960's was certainly of the highest standard. In the decades that followed, students of prophecy understand more and more how significant was the marker that God put down in history with that 1948 event. I hope to build on that understanding.

God gave John the vision of Revelation in scenes of supreme assurance, and in words that are divinely inspired. They promise God's people the ultimate triumph and reward. We begin with the verses of chapter 1.

Koo

John is called to receive this apocalyptic prophecy

1:1 The Revelation of Jesus Christ, which God gave unto him,
to shew unto his servants things which must shortly come to
pass; and he sent and signified it by his angel unto his
servant John:
1:2 Who bare record of the word of God, and of the
testimony of Jesus Christ, and of all things that he saw.
1:3 Blessed is he that readeth, and they that hear the words
of this prophecy, and keep those things which are written
therein: for the time is at hand.
1:4 John to the seven churches which are in Asia: Grace be
unto you, and peace, from him which is, and which was, and
which is to come; and from the seven Spirits which are
before his throne;
1:5 And from Jesus Christ, who is the faithful witness, and
the first begotten of the dead, and the prince of the kings of
the earth. Unto him that loved us, and washed us from our
sins in his own blood,
1:6 And hath made us kings and priests unto God and his
Father; to him be glory and dominion for ever and ever.
Amen.
1:8 I am Alpha and Omega, the beginning and the ending,
saith the Lord, which is, and which was, and which is to
come, the Almighty.
1:9 I John, who also am your brother, and companion in
tribulation, and in the kingdom and patience of Jesus Christ,
was in the isle that is called Patmos, for the word of God,
and for the testimony of Jesus Christ.
1:10 I was in the Spirit on the Lord's day, and heard behind
me a great voice, as of a trumpet,
1:11 Saying, I am Alpha and Omega, the first and the last:
and, What thou seest, write in a book, and send it unto the
seven churches which are in Asia; unto Ephesus, and unto
Smyrna, and unto Pergamos, and unto Thyatira, and unto
Sardis, and unto Philadelphia, and unto Laodicea.
1:12 And I turned to see the voice that spake with me. And
being turned, I saw seven golden candlesticks
1:13 And in the midst of the seven candlesticks one like unto
the Son of man, clothed with a garment down to the foot,
and girt about the paps with a golden girdle.

1:14 His head and his hairs were white like wool, as white as
snow; and his eyes were as a flame of fire;
1:15 And his feet like unto fine brass, as if they burned in a
furnace; and his voice as the sound of many waters.
1:16 And he had in his right hand seven stars: and out of his
mouth went a sharp twoedged sword: and his countenance
was as the sun shineth in his strength.
1:17 And when I saw him, I fell at his feet as dead. And he
laid his right hand upon me, saying unto me, Fear not; I am
the first and the last:
1:18 I am he that liveth, and was dead; and, behold, I am
alive for evermore, Amen; and have the keys of hell and of
death.
1:19 Write the things which thou hast seen, and the things
which are, and the things which shall be hereafter;
1:20 The mystery of the seven stars which thou sawest in my
right hand, and the seven golden candlesticks. The seven
stars are the angels of the seven churches: and the seven
candlesticks which thou sawest are the seven churches.
5:1 And I saw in the right hand of him that sat on the throne
a book written within and on the backside, sealed with seven
seals.
5:2 And I saw a strong angel proclaiming with a loud voice,
Who is worthy to open the book, and to loose the seals
thereof?
5:3 And no man in heaven, nor in earth, neither under the
earth, was able to open the book, neither to look thereon.
5:4 And I wept much, because no man was found worthy to
open and to read the book, neither to look thereon.
5:5 And one of the elders saith unto me, Weep not: behold,
the Lion of the tribe of Juda, the Root of David, hath
prevailed to open the book, and to loose the seven seals
thereof.
5:6 And I beheld, and, lo, in the midst of the throne and of
the four beasts, and in the midst of the elders, stood a Lamb
as it had been slain, having seven horns and seven eyes,
which are the seven Spirits of God sent forth into all the
earth.
5:7 And he came and took the book out of the right hand of
him that sat upon the throne.
5:8‡[K14] And when he had taken the book, the four beasts and
four and twenty elders fell down before the Lamb, having
every one of them harps, and golden vials full of odours,
which are the prayers of saints.
5:11 And I beheld, and I heard the voice of many angels
round about the throne and the beasts and the elders: and

the number of them was ten thousand times ten thousand,
and thousands of thousands;
5:12 Saying with a loud voice, Worthy is the Lamb that was
slain to receive power, and riches, and wisdom, and
strength, and honour, and glory, and blessing.
5:13 And every creature which is in heaven, and on the earth,
and under the earth, and such as are in the sea, and all that
are in them, heard I saying, Blessing, and honour, and glory,
and power, be unto him that sitteth upon the throne, and
unto the Lamb for ever and ever.
5:14 And the four beasts said, Amen. And the four and
twenty elders fell down and worshipped him that liveth for
ever and ever.
10:1 And I saw another mighty angel come down from
heaven, clothed with a cloud: and a rainbow was upon his
head, and his face was as it were the sun, and his feet as
pillars of fire:
10:2 And he had in his hand a little book open: and he set his
right foot upon the sea, and his left foot on the earth,
10:3 And cried with a loud voice, as when a lion roareth: and
when he had cried, seven thunders uttered their voices.
10:4 And when the seven thunders had uttered their voices, I
was about to write: and I heard a voice from heaven saying
unto me, Seal up those things which the seven thunders
uttered, and write them not.
10:5 And the angel which I saw stand upon the sea and upon
the earth lifted up his hand to heaven,
10:6 And sware by him that liveth for ever and ever, who
created heaven, and the things that therein are, and the
earth, and the things that therein are, and the sea, and the
things which are therein, that there should be time no
longer:
10:7 But in the days of the voice of the seventh angel, when
he shall begin to sound, the mystery of God should be
finished, as he hath declared to his servants the prophets.
10:8 And the voice which I heard from heaven spake unto me
again, and said, Go and take the little book which is open in
the hand of the angel which standeth upon the sea and upon
the earth.
10:9 And I went unto the angel, and said unto him, Give me
the little book. And he said unto me, Take it, and eat it up;
and it shall make thy belly bitter, but it shall be in thy mouth
sweet as honey.
10:10 And I took the little book out of the angel's hand, and
ate it up; and it was in my mouth sweet as honey: and as
soon as I had eaten it, my belly was bitter.

> 10:11 And he said unto me, Thou must prophesy again before many peoples, and nations, and tongues, and kings.

John begins his letter (1:1) by giving all credit to Jesus the anointed one (*Messiah* in Hebrew, *Christ* in Greek). He is the one who revealed these things which will come. John recognizes that Jesus is also using his servants the angels to convey much of the vision.

He is writing to the seven churches of Asia (1:4-5). The seven spirits which John sees before God's throne are seven angels. He praises Jesus as the one who loved us and washed us from our sins in his own blood. By giving his life on the cross of Calvary, Christ substituted his perfect sinless life in our place. Those who put their faith and trust in him can therefore be accepted before the perfect and righteous God of Heaven.

You will notice that we skip verse 1:7, which says:

> 1:7 Behold, he cometh with clouds; and every eye shall see him, and they also which pierced him: and all kindreds of the earth shall wail because of him. Even so, Amen.

Even though this verse is in chapter 1, it is an anticipation of the battle of Armageddon, which is identified by that name in chapter 16, and described in detail in chapter 19. We therefore will place 1:7 in section K38 *The second coming of Christ, and the sixth plague: the battle of Armageddon*. There we will collect all the verses about that battle.

John hears Jesus announce that he is the Alpha and Omega (1:8), the beginning and end of all things.

Then John refocuses back on himself, and uses the word *tribulation* for the first time (1:9). With this word he recognizes the trials coming upon the seven churches, who are beginning to experience persecution for their faith.

He tells us that his vision took place on the Lord's Day (1:10-13), a Sunday when he was worshipping God when exiled on the small island of Patmos. The vision begins with a dreamlike voice like a trumpet. Then he receives a commission to watch carefully and write all that he sees into a book. When he looks for the voice, he sees seven golden candlesticks. They symbolize the seven churches. He then sees the son of man. This was Jesus' favorite title for himself in the New Testament gospels of Matthew, Mark, Luke, and John.

Jesus is holding seven stars (1:16), which are, according to 1:20, the seven angels of the seven churches.

We will now leave John's introduction and jump to chapter 5, where the vision circles back to the scene of John's commissioning to write the book. (That is why here in section K00, we are including these verses of chapter 5 after the verses of chapter 1).

A strong angel issues the challenge (5:2): "who is worthy to open the book by loosening its seven seals?" The book in question is this book of Revelation being given to John.

The strong angel takes the book (5:8). Then many angels and elders fall down before the Lamb. The *Lamb of God* is another title for Christ used throughout the Bible.

We skip ahead a couple of verses (5:11) to see that a much larger multitude of angels and elders is praising the Lamb with worship. (We will find the two verses that we skipped, 5:9-10, in section K14).

Much further, in chapter 10, the vision circles back once more to John's commissioning. A mighty angel, probably the same strong angel of 5:2, comes down from heaven with a little book open in his hand. This again is the book about to be transmitted to John through the vision.

"There should be time no longer" (10:6), in other words no delay, to announce the end of the age. God will cast aside mankind's foolishness in attempting to create a universe out of resident forces apart from the Almighty. This is in fulfillment of God's word to the Old Testament prophets.

John is instructed (10:10) to eat the little book. It is sweet in his mouth because it is God's word of grace, but bitter in his stomach because divine punishment will be poured out.

This completes our first section, K00. I have numbered it as double zero because this is an introduction.

Now we begin our timeline of Revelation. But where to begin? Most commentators go on immediately to chapters 2 and 3 that describe the seven churches of John's time. I will surprise you and reach far ahead into the vision to chapter 12. In that place there are two verses that bring the main antagonist into action, and tell us the role he and his followers played shortly after the origin of the human race.

K01

Satan and the devils rebel against God and are cast out of heaven

> 12:3‡[K04,K15] And there appeared another wonder in heaven;
> and behold a great red dragon, *having seven heads and ten*
> *horns, and seven crowns upon his heads.*
> 12:4‡[K04,K15] And his tail drew the third part of the stars of
> heaven, and did cast them to the earth: *and the dragon stood*
> *before the woman which was ready to be delivered, for to*
> *devour her child as soon as it was born.*

The chronology of Revelation does not begin after the introduction of the book. Interestingly enough, it starts much later in the middle of John's vision, inside a long parenthetical section (12:1-14:20) which occurs between the seventh trumpet and the first vial that John saw.

The first part of verse 12:3 and the first part of 12:4 are referring to an event of cosmic proportions that occurred not long after God created Adam and Eve, the first man and woman. The great red dragon who had his place in heaven is expelled, along with the third part of the stars of heaven. This is the rebellion of a third of the angels against God led by their leader, Satan, whom the Bible also names as Lucifer. This is the fall of Satan and the origin of the devils.

We know more about this from two passages in the Old Testament:

> Ezekiel 28:11 Moreover the word of the LORD came unto me,
> saying,
> 28:12 Son of man, take up a lamentation upon the king of
> Tyrus, and say unto him, Thus saith the Lord GOD; Thou
> sealest up the sum, full of wisdom, and perfect in beauty.
> 28:13 Thou hast been in Eden the garden of God; every
> precious stone was thy covering, the sardius, topaz, and the
> diamond, the beryl, the onyx, and the jasper, the sapphire,
> the emerald, and the carbuncle, and gold: the workmanship
> of thy tabrets and of thy pipes was prepared in thee in the
> day that thou wast created.

28:14 Thou art the anointed cherub that covereth; and I have
set thee so: thou wast upon the holy mountain of God; thou
hast walked up and down in the midst of the stones of fire.
28:15 Thou wast perfect in thy ways from the day that thou
wast created, till iniquity was found in thee.
28:16 By the multitude of thy merchandise they have filled
the midst of thee with violence, and thou hast sinned:
therefore I will cast thee as profane out of the mountain of
God: and I will destroy thee, O covering cherub, from the
midst of the stones of fire.
28:17 Thine heart was lifted up because of thy beauty, thou
hast corrupted thy wisdom by reason of thy brightness: I will
cast thee to the ground, I will lay thee before kings, that they
may behold thee.
28:18 Thou hast defiled thy sanctuaries by the multitude of
thine iniquities, by the iniquity of thy traffick; therefore will
I bring forth a fire from the midst of thee, it shall devour
thee, and I will bring thee to ashes upon the earth in the
sight of all them that behold thee.
28:19 All they that know thee among the people shall be
astonished at thee: thou shalt be a terror, and never shalt
thou be any more.

Isaiah 14:12 How art thou fallen from heaven, O Lucifer, son
of the morning! how art thou cut down to the ground, which
didst weaken the nations!
14:13 For thou hast said in thine heart, I will ascend into
heaven, I will exalt my throne above the stars of God: I will
sit also upon the mount of the congregation, in the sides of
the north:
14:14 I will ascend above the heights of the clouds; I will be
like the most High.
14:15 Yet thou shalt be brought down to hell, to the sides of
the pit.

Satan and the devils, along with the rest of the angels, were spirit beings created by God on the first of the six days of creation. Those days are described in Genesis 1, the first chapter of the Old Testament. Before their fall, the devils along with the righteous angels had free access to heaven. Afterward, their obsession became to torment men and women on earth. They only returned to heaven when specially summoned by God, for example when Satan appeared before God to discuss the righteousness of Job (Job 1:6).

Satan's first act on earth was to transform himself into a serpent, and he appeared in this guise to Eve. He deceived her and tempted her to eat of the tree of Good and Evil, explaining that she would become like God. Adam followed her into sin. They did not become like God, instead they learned evil. This original sin permanently stained Adam, his wife, and all his descendants, including you and me. The human race was created to be immortal. Created in perfection, but no longer perfect, God sentenced Adam and Eve to eventually die. So, all of us die a physical death, because we share in the sin and rebellion of our original ancestors.

Why did Satan and the devils turn against God? And why did Satan tempt Adam and Eve into sin? A typical answer is because Satan was filled with the sin of pride. He then wanted to recruit humankind as his followers to share in his fall. My answer is that it was not pride, but jealousy of Christ, and of all human beings created in his image, that spurred Satan on to his eternal mission to destroy both Jesus and all mankind. (Please see Appendix A *Why Satan Hates Christ*.)

We will consider the italicized parts of 12:3 and 12:4 in sections K15 and K04.

Next, we will reach further ahead into the vision to chapter 17. In that place there are verses which are an overarching summary of the vastness of human history, from the time after Noah's flood, to the casting of Satan into hell at the end of days.

K02

The spirit of Babel in the empires of the Old Testament period and the coming tribulation

> 17:1‡[K17,K20] And there came one of the seven angels which had the seven vials, and talked with me, saying unto me, Come hither; I will shew unto thee *the judgment of* the great whore that sitteth upon many waters.
> 17:7 And the angel said unto me, Wherefore didst thou marvel? I will tell thee the mystery of the woman, and of the beast that carrieth her, which hath the seven heads and ten horns.
> 17:9 And here is the mind which hath wisdom. The seven heads are seven mountains, on which the woman sitteth.
> 17:10 And there are seven kings: five are fallen, and one is, and the other is not yet come; and when he cometh, he must continue a short space.
> 17:11 And the beast that was, and is not, even he is the eighth, and is of the seven, and goeth into perdition.
> 17:8 The beast that thou sawest was, and is not; and shall ascend out of the bottomless pit, and go into perdition: and they that dwell on the earth shall wonder, whose names were not written in the book of life from the foundation of the world, when they behold the beast that was, and is not, and yet is.

We skip to later in John's vision, when the seven vials have been completed. Here is where we are given the incredible back story of the prostitute, one of the main characters of the letter. The King James version uses the very direct word "whore" for this woman. We know from verses 17:4-5 K17 that this is the woman of Babylon.

She sits on many waters. She also sits on seven mountains. The vision of seven mountains immediately gives way to one of seven kings - five are already done their rule, one is reigning in the time of John, and one is yet to come.

We also see a fantastical beast, who is carrying the woman (17:7). He is inspired by Satan, so his spiritual origin is the bottomless pit. He is tied to the seven kings, yet he is one of them in some manner, and will reappear as an eighth king. His eternal destiny will be perdition, or hell.

The main clue to understanding this is 17:10, where we have five kings that are *fallen*, and one who *is*. This is a direct echo of Daniel 2, written after 600 B.C., where Daniel explains to King Nebuchadnezzar of Babylon the dream that the king had of another beast. That beast had a head of gold, chest and arms of silver, middle and thighs of bronze, and legs partly of iron and partly of clay. Daniel interprets the dream in terms of empires of worldwide power that will soon succeed Babylonia. Within a few hundred years after Daniel it became obvious that those prophesied kingdoms came to be Medo-Persia, Greece and Rome.

All these are not regular kingdoms, but are empires. They have the compulsion to conquer other nations, expand over awesome amounts of territory, and rule over many people groups.

From his vantage point, John saw Rome as the empire that *is* of his day. Viewing backwards in time, Greece, Medo-Persia, and before them Babylonia were empires already in the past. Two more kingdoms of great power existed before then: Assyria and Egypt. Those were the five kingdoms that are *fallen*. All five were crucial in the history of Israel, God's chosen people. Egypt enslaved the Israelites, and they needed to be rescued by God through the Exodus and the parting of the Red Sea. Assyria took the ten northern Israelite tribes captive – they ended up as the ten lost tribes of Israel. Babylon took the two southern tribes captive for 70 years. Medo-Persia was the only empire benevolent to the Jews, allowing them to return and rebuild their temple on a smaller scale in Jerusalem. Greece then came and during its rule desecrated the temple with unholy sacrifice which Daniel prophesied as "the abomination that causes desolation." We shall see another such abomination of even greater magnitude during the tribulation (13:15 K24). Rome was the empire of John's day, that demolished the temple completely. Every single one of these empires had jurisdiction over Jerusalem at some point during the time of the Old Testament. That is important in understanding the future political environment of the tribulation. Jerusalem, and not Rome in Italy, should be our focus when we look at the worldwide order established during the tribulation period.

The woman of Babylon ultimately points us to Babel, which was the precursor to all these empires. Babel was the kingdom of Nimrod. It arose in 2200 B.C., less than 200 years after all the people of the world perished under God's judgment in a worldwide flood, except for Noah and his family. Nimrod certainly knew what happened, but he rebelled against following God, and was the first to aspire to rule all peoples. He and his followers showed their intent by forcing their famous tower of Babel up to the highest heaven their bricks could reach.

The original model for Revelation's woman of Babylon is probably Semiramis, the wife of Nimrod. According to extra biblical records, she was a high priestess of idol worship. She gave birth to a son whom she claimed was conceived miraculously. His name was Tammuz. He appears in Babylonian mystery religions as a savior of his followers. The Babylonian mysteries were the origin of virgins dedicated to religious prostitution, which appeared in many religions. We see in Tammuz and Semiramis the working of Satan to manufacture an impostor "seed of the woman." These two were Satan's attempt to force a false fulfillment to the promise that God made after Satan tempted Adam and Eve into sin:

> Genesis 3:15 And I will put enmity between thee and the woman, and between thy seed and her seed; it shall bruise thy head, and thou shalt bruise his heel.

But God's answer was to judge Babel by miraculously casting down its tower and splitting the people concentrated there into different languages. They then turned on one another, and dispersed to the far corners of the earth. They brought with them different versions of the syncretistic religion that Babel was formulating. The ones that went to China and to India and beyond largely lost touch with the others on the far side of the mountains. Yet Hindu India has a faint memory of Noah's true God in their creator god Prajapati, named after Noah's son Japheth. And China preserves the knowledge of Noah in their alphabet, which has characters that clearly depict the flood event and God's grace toward Noah's family.

The spirit of Babel is the spirit of godlessness, worshipping idols of one's own choosing. It is a systemic rebellion against God that operates spiritually, politically, and personally. This I believe is the deeper meaning of this section.

The harlot is the spirit of empire.

Many writers focus in on the seven mountains on which the woman is sitting. They equate them to the seven ancient hills of Rome, and then use that idea to predict Rome in Italy as the capital of the world government of the tribulation. I think it would be better to see those mountains in terms of the seven continents of the world. The many waters that she sits upon are the seven seas. That is an indication of the worldwide influence of the harlot and the spirit of Babel throughout human history.

The other main character of this section is the beast. He also represents empire, Satan's preferred form of tyranny to control people. We will find out that the woman and the beast use each other, and that the beast is deferential to the woman until halfway through the tribulation period. Here is what we learn about the beast in this section:

- There will be a seventh kingdom coming after Rome the sixth kingdom. (17:10)
- The beast is "of the seven" kings and will also be an eighth. So, he will be an eighth king who was somehow operative in all seven kingdoms, or possibly he will be king of both the seventh and eighth kingdoms. (17:11)
- In between the seventh and eighth kingdom the beast will be eclipsed. (17:8)

We will have more to say about the different kingdoms of the beast when we talk about the hadiths in my second book.

This section then plunges ahead to far after the tribulation is finished, when the beast is cast into hell (17:8, which will be fulfilled in section K40). This is observed with bitterness by his followers. In their joint rebellion they will follow him to hell also (20:15, 21:8 K46). They will not share the everlasting heavenly future of those whom God has written into his book of life.

As you can see, behind this section is a sweep of most of human history. We will now proceed to a more granular account of individual historical events.

K03

God founds the nation of Israel

> 12:1 And there appeared a great wonder in heaven; a woman clothed with the sun, and the moon under her feet, and upon her head a crown of twelve stars.

In God's historical plan, he knows there will be a succession of kingdoms who embrace the spirit of Babel and lead their people in opposition to him. His antidote to this was evident soon after Babel. It occurred early in the history of the first empire, Egypt.

This verse in Revelation about a great wonder in heaven describes a woman with a crown of twelve stars. Twelve is the number of tribes of Israel. In Genesis, Jacob had twelve sons who became these tribes. God gave Jacob the new name of Israel. One of his sons was Joseph, whom God used in a miraculous way to deliver his parents and brothers, as well as the entire nearby nation of Egypt, from a seven-year famine.

In Genesis 37:9, Joseph had a prophetic dream leading up to the events of the famine. In it he saw that "the sun and the moon and the eleven stars made obeisance to me." At the time of the dream, it was unclear how it would come true. But during the famine, his father Jacob, his mother Rachel, and his eleven brothers did indeed bow down to him when they saw him many years later, and recognized that God had transformed him from a household slave into the prime minister of Egypt. The twelve sons of Jacob went on to become an entire nation.

Here in Revelation, John has the same imagery in his own prophetic vision. The woman clothed with the sun, the moon under her feet, and a crown of twelve stars, is Israel, God's chosen people. Israel has always represented truth to the world and its spirit of rebellion against God. That spiritual rebellion is a spiritual famine. God would use Israel in a miraculous way to eventually bring his son Jesus Christ into the world. He will become the true king for all those who put their trust in him, and will bring them the water of everlasting life. The coming of Jesus into the world will be the subject of the next section.

K04

Satan attempts to kill the baby Jesus through King Herod

> 12:2 And she being with child cried, travailing in birth, and pained to be delivered.
> 12:3‡[K01,K15] And there appeared another wonder in heaven; and behold a great red dragon, *having seven heads and ten horns, and seven crowns upon his heads.*
> 12:4‡[K01,K15] *And his tail drew the third part of the stars of heaven, and did cast them to the earth:* and the dragon stood before the woman which was ready to be delivered, for to devour her child as soon as it was born.

In these verses we are told that the woman with the crown of twelve stars, whom we have identified as Israel, will give birth to a child.

The Old Testament of the Bible has many prophecies about the birth of one who would free God's people. He would deliver them from their earthly oppressors, from Satan the evil one, and most importantly from their sins against God, so that they could enter into God's eternal presence. This man was described as the anointed one (in Hebrew the *Messiah*, in Greek the *Christ*).

The prophet Isaiah prophesied the birth of this Messiah, the son of God, in words that Satan found to be a mortal threat to his plan for universal domination:

> Isaiah 9:6 For unto us a child is born, unto us a son is given: and the government shall be upon his shoulder: and his name shall be called Wonderful, Counsellor, The mighty God, The everlasting Father, The Prince of Peace.

Isaiah's words ultimately came true in the birth of Jesus, as recorded in the New Testament book of Matthew:

> Matthew 1:20 But while he thought on these things, behold, the angel of the Lord appeared unto him in a dream, saying, Joseph, thou son of David, fear not to take unto thee Mary thy wife: for that which is conceived in her is of the Holy Ghost.

> 1:21 And she shall bring forth a son, and thou shalt call his
> name Jesus: for he shall save his people from their sins.
> 1:22 Now all this was done, that it might be fulfilled which
> was spoken of the Lord by the prophet, saying,
> 1:23 Behold, a virgin shall be with child, and shall bring
> forth a son, and they shall call his name Emmanuel, which
> being interpreted is, God with us [Isaiah 7:14].
> 1:24 Then Joseph being raised from sleep did as the angel of
> the Lord had bidden him, and took unto him his wife
> 1:25 And knew her not till she had brought forth her
> firstborn son: and he called his name Jesus.

The baby here in Revelation 12:2 is this Jesus - born of the virgin Mary, a daughter of Israel. He was conceived not by Joseph, Mary's betrothed, but by the Holy Spirit of God.

Jesus, the son of God, also has the title Emmanuel, "God with us". In the birth of Jesus, we see all three persons of the triune God: God the Father, God the Son, and God the Holy Spirit. This is the Christian mystery: one God in three persons, God three in one.

In section K01 we already identified the great red dragon as Satan. There we talked about the italicized part of 12:4 where he was cast out of heaven along with all the fallen angels. Here in the second part of 12:4 he stands before the woman as she is ready to deliver, so that he could devour her child.

The vision is referring to an event soon after the birth of Jesus. Wise men called the *magi*, from a land somewhere far to the east of Israel, were led by a special star in the sky to Jerusalem. There they asked Herod the king where to find the newly born king of the Jews. Herod was startled and asked his advisors whether this was prophesied in the Old Testament. They knew of course from Micah 5:2 that the Messiah was to be born in Bethlehem, the city of David, greatest king of Israel. Herod then sent his soldiers to kill all baby boys age two and under who were in Bethlehem and the surrounding area. He did this with the expectation that he would kill this rival whom he saw as a threat to his throne.

Satan knows the Bible in detail. He knew of this prophecy, but did not know when exactly it would be fulfilled. He was already working in the life of Herod, who was one of the most bloodthirsty kings in Israel's history, ruling with the approval of the Roman empire. Satan inspired Herod to issue his search and destroy order to his soldiers. They slaughtered many innocent babies.

However, God, who arranges all things in advance, sent an angel of the Lord to appear once again in another dream to Joseph. The angel warned him to flee with his family to Egypt. Thus, the baby Jesus was protected from harm.

K05

The incarnation and ascension of Jesus

> 12:5‡[K42] And she brought forth a man child, *who was to rule all nations with a rod of iron:* and her child was caught up unto God, and to his throne.

There is one more look backward to the past in John's vision. It is verse 12:5, which is a panorama of Christ's birth, life on earth, and ascension.

This verse highlights the humanity of Jesus. He was "brought forth a man child" from the woman who had the crown of twelve stars (12:1 K03). In other words, his lineage is from the nation of Israel. In theological terms, this is described by the word *incarnation*, which expresses the idea that the son of God adopted the fallen flesh of sinful man and came to earth as the God-man. The word is a Latin term that literally means "the act of being made flesh." It is used in John 1:14, which says that Jesus "was made flesh and dwelt among us."

Verse 12:5 also highlights Christ's ascension into heaven, which occurred after his life on earth, his death on the cross (Matthew 27:45-54, Mark 15:33-39, Luke 23:44-48, John 19:28-30), and his resurrection (Matthew 28:1-7, Mark 16:1-11, Luke 24:1-12, John 20:1-18). The ascension is described in detail in Acts 1, particularly verses 9 and 10:

> Acts 1:6 When they [the apostles] therefore were come together, they asked of him, saying, Lord, wilt thou at this time restore again the kingdom to Israel?
> 1:7 he said unto them, It is not for you to know the times or the seasons, which the Father hath put in his own power.
> 1:8 But ye shall receive power, after that the Holy Ghost is come upon you: and ye shall be witnesses unto me both in Jerusalem, and in all Judaea, and in Samaria, and unto the uttermost part of the earth.
> 1:9 And when he had spoken these things, while they beheld, he was taken up; and a cloud received him out of their sight.
> 1:10 while they looked stedfastly toward heaven as he went up, behold, two men stood by them in white apparel;

> 1:11 Which also said, Ye men of Galilee, why stand ye gazing up into heaven? this same Jesus, which is taken up from you into heaven, shall so come in like manner as ye have seen him go into heaven.

At the ascension the two angels in white explained that someday Jesus will return from heaven to earth in like manner as when he left, in a cloud. That will be the second coming of Christ (1:7 K38).

Finally, verse 12:5 also underscores the divinity of Christ. After his ascension he was "caught up unto God, and to his throne." Then he sat down at the right hand of God the Father, as explained in Mark's mention of the ascension:

> Mark 16:19 So then after the Lord had spoken unto them, he was received up into heaven, and sat on the right hand of God.

We will encounter the italicized portion of 12:5 in section K42, which will occur after Christ returns at his second coming. At that time, he will exert his rule by putting the rebels of the tribulation to death with "a rod of iron." But there is much to happen going forward, from the time that John received his vision, until the second coming.

Now that we have dealt with past historical events that are mentioned in various places in Revelation, I will pick up where most commentators begin, with John's letters to the seven churches of Asia.

K06

The church of the apostles
30 to 98 CE (death of the apostle John)

> 2:1 Unto the angel of the church of Ephesus write; These
> things saith he that holdeth the seven stars in his right hand,
> who walketh in the midst of the seven golden candlesticks;
> 2:2 I know thy works, and thy labour, and thy patience, and
> how thou canst not bear them which are evil: and thou hast
> tried them which say they are apostles, and are not, and hast
> found them liars:
> 2:3 And hast borne, and hast patience, and for my name's
> sake hast laboured, and hast not fainted.
> 2:4 Nevertheless I have somewhat against thee, because thou
> hast left thy first love.
> 2:5 Remember therefore from whence thou art fallen, and
> repent, and do the first works; or else I will come unto thee
> quickly, and will remove thy candlestick out of his place,
> except thou repent.
> 2:6 But this thou hast, that thou hatest the deeds of the
> Nicolaitans, which I also hate.
> 2:7 He that hath an ear, let him hear what the Spirit saith
> unto the churches; To him that overcometh will I give to eat
> of the tree of life, which is in the midst of the paradise of
> God.

After the resurrection and ascension of Jesus, his apostles and first generation of disciples spread throughout the world to bring the good news of forgiveness of sins, and salvation through the cross of Christ. They established churches from Israel to Ethiopia to Spain to Scotland to Ukraine to India, and many places in between.

John in his old age had a special burden for the seven churches of the Roman province called Asia, located in today's western Turkey. He wrote each of them an individual letter, in words inspired by Christ, and joined the letters together with an account of his vision. The letters take up chapters 2 and 3 of Revelation. He addressed them in this order: to the church of Ephesus, Smyrna, Pergamos, Thyatira, Sardis, Philadelphia, and Laodicea.

The letters give words of encouragement, admonishment, promise and hope. To some of the churches there are also words of prophecy. Most commentators interpret each letter separately in terms of each church's situation in John's day.

Commentators note the fact that the seven churches, in the order they are addressed, happened to be geographically adjacent to one another. They form a gentle arc on a circular road connecting the most populous part of the province of Asia.

I will follow a minority of expositors, who in addition believe the seven churches represent the chronological development of church history over the past two thousand years, viewed prophetically. Each church is a symbol of a consecutive time period covering hundreds of years. The words addressed in the time of John to the individual congregations, also echo down the corridors of time to reflect the status of the church at large in different time periods.

This is an example of how some biblical prophecies address more than one future time period. The view of the prophet looks ahead, but his vantage point has difficulties with focus. When you look at a beautiful mountain scene, it is hard to distinguish separate mountain ranges, one behind another, since you are not flying above them. In a similar way, words of prophecy can gaze ahead but not unravel multiple times that might be in view. We who are here two thousand years after John have the benefit of hindsight, and can have better understanding of how to untangle prophetic words. With our ability to look back instead of forward, we can confirm that his prophecy has taken place in the seven time periods of church history prior to our time. This gives us assurance that his prophecy regarding the tribulation period and millennial kingdom will indeed take place in the time ahead of us.

The first of the seven letters is addressed to the church at Ephesus. Over the decades there were some preachers who came to the Ephesian believers advertising themselves as apostles of Christ, but who were also mixing into their teaching non-biblical doctrines. But the Ephesians were careful to distinguish the truth, out of their desire to follow Christ and live the new life that he gave them. Jesus commends them for this. They also opposed the works of the Nicolaitans. Those were followers of Nicolas, one of the first seven deacons in Acts 6. He was a false believer who became apostate. His teaching was like the Old Testament teaching of Balaam in Numbers 25:1-3 and 31:16 (see also Revelation 2:14 in section K08). The Nicolaitans were involved in immorality that led the church into sensual temptation. Their teaching perverted God's grace and forgiveness, and replaced freedom in Christ with license to sin.

However, through all this the church at Ephesus was starting to forget their first love. Their passion for Christ was transforming into cold, mechanical orthodoxy. Their doctrinal and moral purity were no substitute for their relationship with Jesus. In the close of the letter, Jesus encourages them to overcome, and he will grant them to eat of the tree of life in the eternal paradise to come.

The church at Ephesus is symbolic of the entire apostolic age, which began with the resurrection of Christ in 30 CE, and closed with the death of John the last living apostle in 98 CE. We know from other writings in the New Testament that numerous other churches responded with joy to the good news of Jesus. Then many of them were tempted to accommodate the sexual lifestyle of the Roman empire all around them, as in the Corinthian church that was rebuked by Paul in his letters to them. There were others who tried to blend the teachings of new life in Christ with a rationale to continued sinful behavior contrary to God's standard of righteousness. This was a constant trial for first century Christians, that we can still learn from.

In this letter to Ephesus, Jesus called the church back to a passionate relationship with him. He does the same to us today.

K07

The persecuted church
98 to 313 (Constantine's edict of Milan)

> 2:8 And unto the angel of the church in Smyrna write; These
> things saith the first and the last, which was dead, and is
> alive;
> 2:9 I know thy works, and tribulation, and poverty, (but thou
> art rich) and I know the blasphemy of them which say they
> are Jews, and are not, but are the synagogue of Satan.
> 2:10 Fear none of those things which thou shalt suffer:
> behold, the devil shall cast some of you into prison, that ye
> may be tried; and ye shall have tribulation ten days: be thou
> faithful unto death, and I will give thee a crown of life.
> 2:11 He that hath an ear, let him hear what the Spirit saith
> unto the churches; He that overcometh shall not be hurt of
> the second death.

John wrote the second letter of the series to the church at Smyrna. He was writing during the rule of the Roman emperor Domitian, 90 to 96 CE. Under his rule both Jews and Christians were persecuted in Rome and Asia Minor for refusing to offer incense to the genius of emperor. There was a group of Jews who did offer incense however, and they reported the Smyrna church to the Roman authorities. Jesus, through John, encourages the church to be faithful unto death, and promises they will receive the crown of life.

John foretold that Smyrna would have ten days of tribulation soon. But his message was also to the broader church in the decades to come.

There was an earlier persecution under Nero, who made Christians the scapegoats for his burning of Rome (64). Both apostles Peter and Paul met their deaths at that time.

At the time of John's writing, Smyrna was beginning to experience the persecution which became recurring in different parts of the Roman empire over the next two hundred years.[1] Under emperor Trajan (98-117) Christians and other groups were executed if their allegiance was found to be suspect. Hadrian (117-138) continued that policy. Bishop Polycarp, the most famous son of Smyrna, was martyred under Antoninus Pius (155). Marcus Aurelius (161-180) blamed Christians for natural disasters. Justin Martyr suffered martyrdom in Rome in his time.

In the succeeding years the persecution intensified. Septimus Severus (202-211) made conversion to Christianity forbidden under penalty of death. Maximus (235-236) ordered Christian clergy to be executed. Worse came under Decius (249-251). He ordered that all should make an offering to the gods and the genius of the emperor at least once a year. This launched the first empire-wide persecution. Origen died then after suffering torture. Many lapsed in their faith, and the issue of whether they could be reconciled to the church became a controversy known as Donatism.

Emperor Valerian (257-260) confiscated the properties of Christians, and believers were not allowed to assemble. At that time Cyprian bishop of Carthage was martyred. Under Diocletian (303-305), churches were destroyed, scriptures burned, civil rights of Christians suspended, and sacrifices to the gods required. That was when Saint Nicholas suffered imprisonment.

The centuries of troubles finally ended when Constantine converted to Christianity and became emperor. He issued the edict of Milan (313), which allowed freedom of worship. Christians were now free to worship and evangelize.

Smyrna was the church in suffering. No word of rebuke given is given them. The trials they endured and fervency for the Lord Jesus kept them from any impurity or compromise with evil.

Later in 330, Constantine transferred the capital of the Roman empire from Rome in Italy to the city of Byzantium on the Bosphorus strait. He

---

[1] Steven Flick, Persecution of the Early Christian Church, https://christianheritagefellowship.com/persecution-of-the-early-christian-church/, July 15, 2021.

designated this new capital as the 'New Rome'. It became known as Constantinople, and also as the Second Rome, and became the seat of the ecumenical patriarch of the Eastern Orthodox Church. We will encounter this city when I examine the Muslim hadiths in my second book. In our time we know it as Istanbul.

K08

Church and state
313 to 610 (Muhammad's revelation)

> 2:12 And to the angel of the church in Pergamos write; These
> things saith he which hath the sharp sword with two edges;
> 2:13 I know thy works, and where thou dwellest, even where
> Satan's seat is: and thou holdest fast my name, and hast not
> denied my faith, even in those days wherein Antipas was my
> faithful martyr, who was slain among you, where Satan
> dwelleth.
> 2:14 But I have a few things against thee, because thou hast
> there them that hold the doctrine of Balaam, who taught
> Balac to cast a stumblingblock before the children of Israel,
> to eat things sacrificed unto idols, and to commit fornication.
> 2:15 So hast thou also them that hold the doctrine of the
> Nicolaitans, which thing I hate.
> 2:16 Repent; or else I will come unto thee quickly, and will
> fight against them with the sword of my mouth.
> 2:17 He that hath an ear, let him hear what the Spirit saith
> unto the churches; To him that overcometh will I give to eat
> of the hidden manna, and will give him a white stone, and in
> the stone a new name written, which no man knoweth
> saving he that receiveth it.

Pergamos in the first century was epitomized by the serpent god Aesculapius, who was worshipped by some residents. This is the likely reason why John mentions they were dwelling "where Satan's seat is." The Christian believers there held on to their faith in Jesus, though they were threatened by violent opponents in the city. Their brother Antipas (2:13) was a recent martyr.

The church also was hearing teachings of sexual compromise and promotion of impure religious practices from the Nicolaitans (already mentioned in 2:6 K06), similar to Balaam of the Old Testament (Numbers 25:1-3 and 31:16). Jesus through John warns the Pergamos followers to repent of these teachings. If they do, they will be given a new name in heaven (2:17).

Pergamos was the church in compromise. As Balaam sold his prophetic gift for money, and as the Nicolaitans were morally corrupt, so the future church after Constantine would have its conscience blurred. The centuries of persecution were replaced by a period in which the church was favored by the government. Many people joined the church merely because it was the popular thing to do, not because of new life in Christ. They could advance their standing. There was obvious compromise between church and state.

The church struggled with various heresies, most of them about the nature of Christ. The church met these heresies with biblically oriented statements of doctrine. For example, the Arians borrowed pagan philosophy and said that the Son was not as eternal as the Father. In defense of the biblical teaching, Athanasius insisted that the Son was as truly God as the Father, based on Colossians 1:19 and many other passages:

> Colossians 1:19 For it pleased the Father that in him [Christ] should all fulness [of God] dwell.

The council of Nicaea in 325 agreed with Athanasius, and stated that true biblical belief was in "one Lord Jesus Christ, the Son of God, the only-begotten of the Father, of the substance of the Father; God of God and Light of Light; true God of true God; begotten, not made, of the same substance as the Father, by whom all things were made, in heaven and on earth."

But the controversies took their toll. There were even wars fought between Arian and orthodox Christian nations. The experiments with departure from biblical doctrine, and compromise with pagan lifestyle, were confusing to many. It opened the gates to a new self-styled prophet in Arabia named Muhammad. In 610 he proclaimed that Allah was the true God. More on that topic when we visit the hadiths in my second book.

K09

False teaching corrupts the church
610 to 1054 (the Eastern and Roman church split)

2:18 And unto the angel of the church in Thyatira write;
These things saith the Son of God, who hath his eyes like
unto a flame of fire, and his feet are like fine brass;
2:19 I know thy works, and charity, and service, and faith,
and thy patience, and thy works; and the last to be more
than the first.
2:20 Notwithstanding I have a few things against thee,
because thou sufferest that woman Jezebel, which calleth
herself a prophetess, to teach and to seduce my servants to
commit fornication, and to eat things sacrificed unto idols.
2:21 And I gave her space to repent of her fornication; and
she repented not.
2:22 Behold, I will cast her into a bed, and them that commit
adultery with her into great tribulation, except they repent
of their deeds.
2:23 And I will kill her children with death; and all the
churches shall know that I am he which searcheth the reins
and hearts: and I will give unto every one of you according
to your works.
2:24 But unto you I say, and unto the rest in Thyatira, as
many as have not this doctrine, and which have not known
the depths of Satan, as they speak; I will put upon you none
other burden.
2:25‡[K13] But that which ye have already hold fast till I come.
2:29‡[K13] He that hath an ear, let him hear what the Spirit
saith unto the churches.

Jesus praises the church at Thyatira for their love, their service, their faith, and their patience.

Despite these commendable things, the church was guilty of terrible sin. They were under the influence of a woman prophetess, whose name was perhaps not really Jezebel. But she was a lot like the woman of that name who was married to the ancient King Ahab. She led him and the northern ten tribes of Israel astray in the worship of the false god Baal (1 Kings 16-19). She was responsible for the killing of Naboth and the possession of his vineyard for her husband (1 Kings 21). She killed most of the prophets of the Lord and did what she could to kill the prophet Elijah (1 Kings 19:2).

The Jezebel of Thyatira was urging the church-goers to accommodate the unbelievers around them and their pagan worship of idols. This meant participating in sacrilegious feasts by eating food sacrificed to idols, and taking part in the sexual immorality of their festivals. In promoting these behaviors, this prophetess was fulfilling the role of the historic Jezebel.

Christ predicts judgment on this new Jezebel's followers (2:22-23). Each one will be given according to their works.

Thyatira was the church tolerating apostasy. It foreshadowed the church of the Middle Ages, which detracted from Christ by exalting Mary to the plane of a female deity. In that period the church became corrupt. The Roman Catholic church of the west taught that intercession to God should be made through Mary and through dead saints who were officially canonized by the church. Apart from the intercession of Mary and the saints there could be no salvation. Idols in the form of religious statues were introduced. The Eastern Orthodox church defended the veneration of icons of their own numerous saints. Possession of icons was valued more than studying scripture. The two churches officially separated in the year 1054 over a little understood doctrine known as the *Filioque* "and from the Son" clause. (In the late 6th century, some Catholic churches added those words to the description of the procession of the Holy Spirit within the trinity, in what many Eastern Orthodox Christians at a later stage argued was a violation of Canon VII of the council of Ephesus.) This was a suitable excuse for separation, given their geographical distance and disagreement about the pope in Rome being the highest earthly spiritual authority.

All this was representative of the way that churches of both east and west had drifted from their joy in Christ. The church experienced spiritual depravity. The biblical teaching of the all-sufficient work of Christ's death on the cross, and justification by faith in his name, was largely lost.

At the same time, Islam was experiencing great expansion, from Arabia to Spain to Pakistan.

In this letter to Thyatira and its warning of punishment on those who fall into licentious behavior, we skipped 2:26, 2:27 and 2:28. Those verses look forward far in time when Christ will come back to earth to rule with a rod of iron, and when the church saints will be present overlooking the judgment of the unbelievers. Those topics will be included in our discussions of the sentence of death issued to the tribulation rebels in section K42, and the great white throne judgment in K46.

K10

The dead church
1054 to 1517 (Martin Luther's 99 theses)

> 3:1 And unto the angel of the church in Sardis write; These
> things saith he that hath the seven Spirits of God, and the
> seven stars; I know thy works, that thou hast a name that
> thou livest, and art dead.
> 3:2 Be watchful, and strengthen the things which remain,
> that are ready to die: for I have not found thy works perfect
> before God.
> 3:3 Remember therefore how thou hast received and heard,
> and hold fast, and repent. If therefore thou shalt not watch, I
> will come on thee as a thief, and thou shalt not know what
> hour I will come upon thee.
> 3:4 Thou hast a few names even in Sardis which have not
> defiled their garments; and they shall walk with me in
> white: for they are worthy.
> 3:5 He that overcometh, the same shall be clothed in white
> raiment; and I will not blot out his name out of the book of
> life, but I will confess his name before my Father, and before
> his angels.
> 3:6 He that hath an ear, let him hear what the Spirit saith
> unto the churches.

The small community of Christians in Sardis lived among idolaters who worshiped the mother goddess, Cybele. There was a temple in the city erected to her honor. Her worship was of the most debasing character, and orgies like those of Dionysus were practiced in the festivals.

The message addressed to the angel of the church of Sardis does not have any words of commendation, as the other churches were given. The church had a reputation in the area as being spiritual and having a ministry. But from the divine standpoint, it was a church that only had an appearance of being alive.

This is a message that Christians of my time should be careful of. Churches are often full of activity. Pastors speak much of Christ in their sermons. However, they do little to disciple believers on how to live lives that follow God's standard of righteousness. This is so much necessary in a world that is going from extreme to extreme on how to disobey God's commandments and make him irrelevant.

The letter to Sardis anticipates the church of the Middle Ages before the Protestant Reformation.

During the period 1054 to 1517, there were various innovations put forward in western Europe's Roman Catholic Church, which did not have any basis in the Bible.[2] In 1079, celibacy of the priesthood was decreed by Pope Gregory VII. In 1090 the rosary, a mechanical praying with beads, was invented by Peter the Hermit. In 1184 the inquisition was first instituted by the council of Verona. In 1190, the sale of indulgences was begun, which promised people relief from spending time in purgatory their death. (The non-biblical doctrine of purgatory was established earlier by Pope Gregory I in 593). In 1215 the doctrine of transubstantiation, the physical transformation of the cup and the bread of the Eucharist sacrament into real blood and flesh of Jesus Christ, was proclaimed by Pope Innocent III. In 1220 the adoration of the wafer (bread) was decreed by Pope Honorius III. In 1229, the Bible was forbidden to layman, and placed on the index of forbidden books by the Council of Valencia. In 1414 the cup was forbidden to the people at communion by the Council of Constance. In 1439, purgatory was proclaimed as a dogma by the council of Florence. In 1439 the doctrine of seven sacraments was affirmed.

In eastern Europe and the Middle East, the Orthodox Church went through two traumatic events in this period.

In the year 1453, after a thousand years of existence, the capital Constantinople of the Eastern Roman empire finally fell to attacking Muslim Ottoman armies. Constantinople as a center of the church lost a significant part of its influence. One positive consequence was that many biblical Greek scholars became refugees and fled to western Europe, where their knowledge of the original Greek language of the New Testament helped spark the Reformation.

---

[2] Lorraine Boettner, *Roman Catholicism*, Presbyterian and Reformed Publishing Co, Philipsburg NJ US, 1962, pp7-8.

Far to the north, Moscow had been founded in the twelfth century and become capital of a small state that started its own quest for dominance, by conquering other nations around it. After the fall of Constantinople, Ivan III the ruler of Muscovy began calling himself Caesar, or "Tsar and Autocrat" of Russia. According to Russian rulers that succeeded him, the center of the Eastern Orthodox Church was now Moscow, the Third Rome. This remains true for many Russians. The Orthodox Church found itself in a lethal embrace with the autocratic state. The character of the Russian state as an intimidating great power was established, and extends to my time.

Sardis is the church that was dead. That was also true of the church of the Middle Ages. It was a great mass of Christendom, and had a name that it supposedly lived by. But most people did not have a relationship with Christ. The warning of 3:3 is that they need to wake up. Otherwise, they will be no better off than unbelievers who are not prepared for the return of Christ. He will come like a thief in the night.

Only a small number of believers in the Middle Age church trusted in Christ alone as Savior, and took their stand for true biblical righteousness.

This was the situation when Martin Luther nailed his 99 theses, which opposed the corrupt practices of the Roman Catholic Church, onto the door of the castle church at Wittenberg.

K11

Church of the Reformation
1518 to 1682 (founding of modern Philadelphia)

> 3:7 And to the angel of the church in Philadelphia write;
> These things saith he that is holy, he that is true, he that
> hath the key of David, he that openeth, and no man shutteth;
> and shutteth, and no man openeth;
> 3:8 I know thy works: behold, I have set before thee an open
> door, and no man can shut it: for thou hast a little strength,
> and hast kept my word, and hast not denied my name.
> 3:9 Behold, I will make them of the synagogue of Satan,
> which say they are Jews, and are not, but do lie; behold, I
> will make them to come and worship before thy feet, and to
> know that I have loved thee.
> 3:10‡[K13] Because thou hast kept the word of my patience, I
> also will keep thee from the hour of temptation, *which shall
> come upon all the world, to try them that dwell upon the
> earth.*
> 3:11‡[K13] *Behold, I come quickly:* hold that fast which thou
> hast, that no man take thy crown.
> 3:13 He that hath an ear, let him hear what the Spirit saith
> unto the churches.

We now come to a church which is faithful to Christ and the word of God. The letter addressed to the church of Philadelphia is almost entirely a word of praise. This church took full advantage of the open door that God gave them to have a close relationship with Christ. They made a public declaration of their trust in him, and never denied his name or obscured it. Jesus encourages them that he will give them victory over their opposition, those of the synagogue of Satan. Some of their opponents will come to faith and bow down at the feet of the Lord. Their conversion and faith will lead to life everlasting.

Jesus also promises to deliver these faithful ones from the coming hour of temptation. He addresses this to the church of the small town of Philadelphia of the Roman province of Asia, but then shifts the promise to the church throughout the world. This is why we have italicized sections of verses 3:10-11. Those sections are a promise of the rapture, which will be the deliverance of the entire believing church before the end-time tribulation begins. We will discuss the rapture in section K13.

We will encounter the verse that we skipped, 3:12, in K47, when we talk about the future new Jerusalem.

As with the letters to the other churches of the province of Asia, this one to Philadelphia looks ahead to a future time, the Protestant Reformation. Martin Luther helped to launch the Reformation by challenging the Roman Catholic Church. He showed the way by returning to the Bible, God's written word, as the sole authority. Countless other reformers picked up this rallying cry of *Sola Scriptura*, "scripture alone."

New churches were founded across many countries. They discarded the human traditions that had encrusted the life of the Roman Catholic church. This included Lutherans following the teaching of Luther, Reformed and Presbyterians following John Calvin, and Baptists following John Smyth, Thomas Helwys and others. People were hungry to know Christ, and wanted to know how to live by the word of God.

A man who wanted to read the Bible no longer needed to be ordained as a priest and learn Latin, needed to read the Roman Catholic Vulgate version of the Bible. Now both men and women could read the Bible in their own native tongue, translated directly from the original languages Hebrew and Greek. They no longer had to rely on uneducated priests to explain scripture. Entire countries pledged themselves to follow God's standards of righteousness. The Holy Spirit raised up preachers, teachers, and translators. Great multitudes of people became disciples of Christ.

It was a time of revival like no other in history. Countries whose rulers were beholden to the Roman Catholic Church launched wars to retain religious supremacy in western Europe. But thousands of people fought them in this hour of temptation, and gave their lives in the determination to keep to the word of God alone, *Sola Scriptura*.

It is difficult to say when the Protestant Reformation came to a close. We will choose 1682, the founding of the modern city of Philadelphia. Its settlement was part of a migration of English Protestant believers who were seeking freedom of religion in a distant land. They and other earlier European settlers of America, such as the pilgrims and puritans of Massachusetts, had the goal of establishing a biblical commonwealth inspired by their Christian faith. This was the Judeo-Christian underpinning of a great nation, the United States, which lasted for several centuries before it discarded its spiritual moorings.

K12

The lukewarm church of the modern age
1682 to present

3:14 And unto the angel of the church of the Laodiceans
write; These things saith the Amen, the faithful and true
witness, the beginning of the creation of God;
3:15 I know thy works, that thou art neither cold nor hot: I
would thou wert cold or hot.
3:16 So then because thou art lukewarm, and neither cold
nor hot, I will spue thee out of my mouth.
3:17 Because thou sayest, I am rich, and increased with
goods, and have need of nothing; and knowest not that thou
art wretched, and miserable, and poor, and blind, and naked:
3:18 I counsel thee to buy of me gold tried in the fire, that
thou mayest be rich; and white raiment, that thou mayest be
clothed, and that the shame of thy nakedness do not appear;
and anoint thine eyes with eyesalve, that thou mayest see.
3:19 As many as I love, I rebuke and chasten: be zealous
therefore, and repent.
3:20 Behold, I stand at the door, and knock: if any man hear
my voice, and open the door, I will come in to him, and will
sup with him, and he with me.
3:21 To him that overcometh will I grant to sit with me in my
throne, even as I also overcame, and am set down with my
Father in his throne.
3:22 He that hath an ear, let him hear what the Spirit saith
unto the churches.

The last letter is written to the church at Laodicea. That city had a profitable economy based on the production of wool cloth. It was destroyed by an earthquake in 60 CE, but was able to rebuild with no outside help.

Laodicea's material well-being was lulling its church to sleep spiritually. The letter to them has no words of praise. Instead, the church is rebuked for being neither cold nor hot (3:15-16). Its people had been touched by the gospel, but it is not evident that they are truly devoted to Christ. It would be better even if they were cold, with no pretense of putting their trust in God. He has turned many such cold hearts to repent and flame with zeal for him.

Jesus also tells them to anoint their eyes (3:18). By this he is saying they lack spiritual insight. Both pastor and people seem to be blind to the things of God. The Spirit has left the church.

Once again, this letter to a church in a small city of the first century is a prophetic cry reaching deep into the future. It is an uncanny description of the church at large of the last three hundred years.

Our modern era began after the Reformation. In 1687, there appeared the book *Mathematical Principles of Natural Philosophy* by Isaac Newton. It laid down the postulates of classical mechanics, which explain gravity and the motion of planets. Modern physics was born. Many of the early scientists were, like Newton, strong believing Christians. They were seeking to explain the universe based on their belief that God was truthful and reliable, and had a purpose for all things.

But the modern era was also the time of the Enlightenment. This was a movement that made humanism, the study of man, the center of all things. Over time humanism superseded theology, the study of God. Society in many countries was pulled in this direction and became agnostic, then proceeded toward atheism.

Despite this pull, there were times of revival when great numbers turned to Christ. In the 1730s, British evangelist George Whitefield traveled through the American colonies preaching the Bible. The response became known as the Great Awakening. Thousands of people pledged themselves to Jesus Christ in repentance and asked for forgiveness. In the first half of the 1800s there was a second Great Awakening in the United States. Many more converted to Christ.

But afterward there were few awakenings. Instead, a phenomenon known as the burnt-over district started to occur, beginning in the 1820's in western New York state. People became numb to revivalist preaching. Christians also started splitting into many separate church denominations. Some of them had distinctives that were decidedly unbiblical. The Mormons were such a group, founded by Joseph Smith and later led by Brigham Young. They believe Jesus Christ was not God from before time began, but that he progressed to deity in the spirit world.[3] Most of them migrated to Utah, and practiced polygamy for some decades until that practice was stopped by the United States government.

In Europe, the Enlightenment led many scientists to wonder whether God was active in the universe. They started to question the need to appeal to a god as initiator or sustainer of all things. Instead, they worked out a narrative that seemed to explain all things by natural causes alone. In 1859 Charles Darwin wrote his book *On the Origin of Species*, which launched the science of evolution. But the premises of evolution are not falsifiable, which means that there is no set of tests that can be devised to verify the truths that it claims. Therefore, evolution is in reality a pseudo-science. It is a religion or belief system, without appearing as such. Many of the new type of scientists used selective evidence to claim that the world was millions of years old. Later they settled on billions. They ridiculed the book of Genesis and its account of a young earth, and ignored scientific evidence that supports divine creation only thousands of years in the past. The influence of Christians on science was dying out.

In the political sphere, this was matched by activists who promised heavenly things in this world, and dispensed with the idea of afterlife. The chief was Karl Marx, who wrote *The Communist Manifesto* in 1848. His idea of paradise was to liquidate the oppressors, defined as the upper and middle classes. The proletarian working class would then establish by force a just and this-worldly society, forever. His book spawned many isms: communism, socialism, statism, collectivism, globalism, and in my day, critical race theory. They can all be seen as a Judeo-Christian offshoot.

In answer to all this, most of the church walked away from a literal interpretation of Genesis, and tried to accommodate the new evolutionary thinking. Their answer to progressivism and socialism in

---

[3] Justin Taylor, *The 8 Beliefs You Should Know about Mormons When They Knock at the Door*, August 18, 2017, https://www.thegospelcoalition.org/blogs/justin-taylor/the-8-beliefs-you-should-know-about-mormons-when-they-knock-at-the-door/, accessed January 21, 2023.

the early 1900's was to reset the gospel message of redemption from sin. In its place they adopted a new "social gospel" oriented toward redistribution of wealth. The eternal standing of every person before God was no longer the main burden of the churches. A non-biblical Christ was preached.

In Germany, evolutionary science, and its credo of survival of the fittest, was blended with politics to produce national socialism, popularly known as Nazism. They held that Jews were the scapegoats for the world's problems. Their "final solution" was to exterminate them. Churches around the world were largely silent. But Dietrich Bonhoeffer, a Lutheran pastor, described the temptation that national socialism posed for churches in his book *The Cost of Discipleship*, written in 1937. He lamented that Christian churches were no longer preaching about the price that Christ paid with his blood to save us from our sin. They were not discipling believers and challenging them to leave sinful ways behind and obey Jesus. Instead, they were offering cheap grace, which requires no life commitment from Christians.

Bonhoeffer was hanged by Nazi executioners. His prophetic words were little heeded by the church in the decades that followed. Churches in Europe and America ignored or compromised with godless movements in their countries. In doing so they could retain their standing with governments. Tax breaks in some countries kept money contributions flowing from their membership. Many churches became ingrown and deemphasized evangelistic outreach to non-Christians. Professional pastors fell into a rhythm of preaching biblical passages without reference to current events. It was easier to leave the application of their messages up to the imagination of their listeners. Wealthy megachurches became popular as gathering places for many, who felt assured by messages of cheap grace.

If he were still alive, Bonhoeffer would see that most of the church of my day has thrown away God's prophetic gift to engage with the world, and has stopped seeking out the lost. When the church stops engaging society with the message of the kingdom of God, the world starts accelerating its escape from God. This brings on societal decay, and a conscious rejection of God's commandments.

The United States saw this in the legalization of abortion in 1973. Later, traditional biblical marriage solely between a man and a woman was rejected. Same-sex unions were enshrined in law as an alternative. Sexual sin became desirable as a mode of expression. Pseudo-scientific confusion between sex and gender turned into the promoted "woke" practice of transgenderism. Surgical mutilation of under-age boys and girls produced a generation of neutered mutants. The response of much of the church was to preach that God is loving and forgiving for everyone, no matter what their behavior. The message of God giving his son to die on the cross for our sins against the Almighty is being lost.

The last three hundred years are certainly a history of a church becoming lukewarm.

However, one great and pleasing accomplishment in God's eyes is the advancement of missions around the world. The good news of Jesus Christ was spread by many missionaries to dozens of countries within the last three hundred years.

The Christian message was embraced by millions, in countries that formerly had few Christians, such as China, the former Soviet Union, South Korea, Brazil, Chile, Mexico, Nigeria, Uganda, Iran, Columbia, Algeria. Believers in those nations now outnumber Christians in Europe and America. In countries that persecute Christians, they gather in house churches. Pastors who are arrested are replaced by someone else within each gathering. These churches operate on a non-professional basis, at the intersection between biblical belief and persecution. They know that prison is possible any day. They are an inspiration for everyone who believes in Christ.

This is in fulfillment to Christ's challenge in Matthew 24:14:

> Matthew 24:14 And this gospel of the kingdom will be proclaimed throughout the whole world as a testimony to all nations, and then the end will come.

The success of the missionary endeavor is indeed a sign that the end is near.

Unfortunately, the phenomenon of the burnt-over district was encountered by many missionaries when they tried to bring the gospel back to Europe, now in the grip of leftists. It had been the birthplace of the Reformation. This is true in other areas, such as Canada, and Turkey (previously the staunchly Christian area of Asia Minor). Once the biblical message of salvation has transformed a certain land, most of its descendants choose to reject what their ancestors embraced.

We will see during the tribulation period God will overcome the phenomenon of the burnt-over district. Many from those countries will accept Christ.

Laodicea was the lukewarm church satisfied with itself, comfortable within its economic status. It is a sad picture of the professing church in the modern world, those who participate in outer religious worship without inner reality. What Laodicea truly needed, and what the church of my day needs, is something we cannot buy. They need someone, not something. Despite our condition, Jesus invites us to hear him knocking, and asks us to open the door to our lukewarm hearts. The Son of God invites us to fellowship with him.

K13

The rapture and judgment of the church saints

2:25‡[K09] But that which ye have already hold fast till I come.
3:10‡[K11] Because thou hast kept the word of my patience, I also will keep thee from the hour of temptation, which shall come upon all the world, to try them that dwell upon the earth.
3:11‡[K11] Behold, I come quickly: hold that fast which thou hast, that no man take thy crown.
2:29‡[K09] He hath an ear, let him hear what the Spirit saith unto the churches.

At the time that I write this to you, the good news of Jesus Christ has been proclaimed to almost all the peoples of the world. How will the end then come? A careful reading of the Bible shows that it will come in stages. The first stage involves believers in Christ who belong to his church.

In the book of Revelation, the word church, so prominent in chapters 2 and 3 (sections K06 through K12), will not occur again until the end of our timeline in verse 22:16 (section K50). The church is hinted at near the end of this gap as the wife of the Lamb, in 21:9 K47 and 19:7 K48. But the church is out of the picture during the tribulation and the millennial kingdom. Saints who come to know the Lord in these times are described as saved Israelites or saved gentiles, but never as the church or body of Christ. It seems that God somehow completes his work for the New Testament church, comprised of Jews and gentiles saved in the two thousand years after Christ's resurrection, and then the tribulation begins. In the tribulation and millennial kingdom times, he then institutes a non-church program for Israel and the gentiles, even though the means of salvation through the sacrifice of Christ is the same for all who ever lived.

So, what happens to the church?

The answer is that it disappears in an event prophesied in the Bible, known as the *rapture*. (The English word rapture derives from the Latin verb *rapere* meaning to carry off, or to catch up).

At the time the rapture happens, the worldwide government has not been established. But many elements of worldwide control are in place, including power over the information and media space and the news that is allowed to be officially disseminated to the people of the world. The analysts of future government anti-disinformation ministries will be familiar with the concept of the rapture. They could prepare a coordinated public relations contingency plan to explain the event in a way that fits their agenda. They may tell you as an indisputable fact that only Christians who were extremists were carried off in a coordinated worldwide raid, arrested collectively for subversive activity, and sent to long-term re-education camps. They will also have video reenactments that show tremendous sonic booms at the same time, along with highly unusual atmospheric activity. They are counting on these lies to be accepted as truth, especially by those labeling themselves as Christians, but who still remain on earth after the event. (I will discuss those people in section K18).

Those analysts are calculating their narrative based on these prophetic Bible passages outside the book of Revelation:

> 1 Thessalonians 1:10 Await His Son from heaven, whom He raised from the dead—Jesus our deliverer from the coming wrath.
> 5:9 For God hath not appointed us to wrath, but to obtain salvation by our Lord Jesus Christ.
> 5:2 For yourselves know perfectly that the day of the Lord so cometh as a thief in the night.
> 4:15 For this we say unto you by the word of the Lord, that we which are alive and remain unto the coming of the Lord shall not prevent [precede] them which are asleep.
> 4:16 For the Lord himself shall descend from heaven with a shout, with the voice of the archangel, and with the trump of God: and the dead in Christ shall rise first:
> 4:17 Then we which are alive and remain shall be caught up together with them in the clouds, to meet the Lord in the air: and so shall we ever be with the Lord.
>
> 1 Corinthians 15:51 Behold, I shew you a mystery; We shall not all sleep, but we shall all be changed,

> 15:52 In a moment, in the twinkling of an eye, at the last
> trump: for the trumpet shall sound, and the dead shall be
> raised incorruptible, and we shall be changed.
> 15:53 For this corruptible must put on incorruption, and this
> mortal must put on immortality.
>
> John 5:28 Marvel not at this: for the hour is coming, in the
> which all that are in the graves shall hear his voice,
> 5:29a And shall come forth; they that have done good, unto
> the resurrection of life.[4]

These verses describe a "last trump" event, where all the church believers, both alive and dead, who put their complete trust in Christ, will be safeguarded from the wrath of the tribulation. They will suddenly be caught up with Jesus in the air. The dead, even those whose dust has been scattered throughout the earth, will be resurrected and will rise first. Then the living will also rise to meet Jesus in the clouds. They will be *translated* from earth to heaven – "translation" here is a theological concept meaning that their natural bodies will be morphed into glorified bodies that can never die, similar to the resurrected bodies of the dead.

Who are these believers? They belong to the church, which is the body of New Testament followers of Christ, both gentiles and Jews, founded on the day of Pentecost (Acts 2). Jesus, in his love for the church, brings them home to heaven, so that none of them would experience the extreme trials of the tribulation.

The Bible does not enumerate events that precede the rapture. This is why the rapture is deemed to be *imminent* – it comes unexpectedly, like a thief in the night (1 Thessalonians 5:2, quoted above). Even Jesus, the divine son of God, does not know the exact time of the rapture. He is satisfied that only God the Father has set that time:

> Matthew 24:36 But of that day and hour knoweth no man,
> no, not the angels of heaven, but my Father only.
> 24:37 But as the days of Noah were, so shall also the coming
> of the Son of man be.

---

[4] John 5:29b continues *"and they that have done evil, unto the resurrection of damnation."* This is another case of double fulfillment of prophecy, John 5:29a will be fulfilled at the rapture, 5:29b at the great white throne judgment (see K46).

> 24:38 For as in the days that were before the flood they were eating and drinking, marrying and giving in marriage, until the day that Noe entered into the ark,
> 24:39 And knew not until the flood came, and took them all away; so shall also the coming of the Son of man be.

There is no prophecy of scripture involving God's supernatural intervention that we can point to as a direct sign that the rapture will soon occur. Otherwise, the rapture would not be imminent. Any likely events that might happen before the rapture would therefore have to be of a non-supernatural nature.

This means that some prophesied end-time events, such as Ezekiel 38-39, cannot be precursors of the rapture, but must happen between the rapture and the tribulation.

The first promise of the rapture came before the apostles wrote any of their letters or gospels. It came from the Lord Jesus himself at the Last Supper, before he was betrayed and put on trial. Jesus said:

> John 14:3b I will come again, and receive you unto myself; that where I am, there ye may be also.

On another occasion, prior to the Last Supper, he said these words of a much different nature about his return:

> Matthew 24:27 For as the lightning cometh out of the east, and shineth even unto the west; so shall also the coming of the Son of man be.

Jesus said he would come back, but these two contrasting passages indicate two separate returns.

His first return will be the rapture and will be unexpected. It will be signaled with the sounding of a trumpet. Jesus will then descend from heaven, and take the church believers from earth with him back to heaven. They will then be in the Father's house. After the rapture, a short period of indefinite length occurs, to be followed by the tribulation. The detailed timeline of Revelation then kicks in, with the tribulation that lasts seven years.

Later, at the end of the seven years, Christ returns a second time from heaven to earth with definite timing. This return is commonly called the second coming. It is signaled with lightning shining across the world. Christ's immediate task is the defeat of the antichrist (19:15 K38). He then remains on earth for a thousand years in his millennial kingdom (20:6 K44). Unlike the rapture, at the second coming there is no possible way to fool people into thinking that Jesus has not come.

The book of Revelation's purpose is not to describe the rapture. Instead, it relates the second coming of Christ and many other events. But the rapture is hinted at in the verses at the top of this section. Verse 2:25 exhorts the church of Thyatira to persevere until the rapture happens. Verse 3:10-11 promises the church of Philadelphia that Jesus will preserve them from the tribulation, the hour of trial that will come upon the whole world. He will accomplish this via the rapture. Finally, the words of 2:29 - "let him hear what the Spirit saith unto the churches" - applies the promise of the rapture to all the churches.

In the biblical timeline of history, the rapture is actually the third time that dead people are resurrected and receive glorified bodies that will live forever. (See Appendix E *List of the Resurrections*). Christ's was the first resurrection. The second occurred in connection with this, according to a passage in Matthew 27:

> Matthew 27:50Jesus, when he had cried again with a loud voice, yielded up the ghost.
> 27:51 And, behold, the veil of the temple was rent in twain from the top to the bottom; and the earth did quake, and the rocks rent;
> 27:52 And the graves were opened; and many bodies of the saints which slept arose,
> 27:53 And out of the graves after his resurrection, and went into the holy city, and appeared unto many.

The sequence of events seems to be that the tombs are broken open at the death of Jesus. Then after his resurrection these special saints rose from the dead to appear in in Jerusalem.

This second resurrection event shows that God's power over life and death does not narrow down to one moment at the end of history. It is a display of his glorious sovereignty that he chooses to resurrect whom he will at different times. The rapture is the time of resurrection for all believers of the New Testament church age. By this he lovingly safeguards them from the awful trials of the tribulation period.

The rapture event is coupled with the withdrawal of the Holy Spirit from active intervention in the world. The Holy Spirit of God is the third person of the Trinity. God's Holy Spirit, living in the heart of every believer, plus his providential power among unbelievers in the world, are the ultimate restrainers of sin. Another name for God's providential power is common grace. This restraint will not be lifted as long as the Holy Spirit indwells the church. It would therefore require the removal of the church, the Holy Spirit, as well as common grace, before the man of lawlessness, the antichrist, will be revealed:

> 2 Thessalonians 2:6 And now ye know what withholdeth [is holding him back] that he might be revealed in his time.
> 2:7 For the mystery of iniquity doth already work: only he who now letteth [holds it back] will let [continue to do so], until he be taken out of the way.
> 2:8 And then shall that Wicked [lawless one] be revealed, whom the Lord shall consume with the spirit of his mouth, and shall destroy with the brightness of his coming.

We will meet the antichrist, known as the beast in the book of Revelation, in verse 6:2 (section K16).

Before the rapture, the natural bodies of the multitudes of dead believers have decayed long ago or been scattered to the winds. But they are still alive in their souls, bodiless, in an intermediate state. 1 Corinthians 15:51-53 (see above) tells us that at the rapture they will be resurrected with new glorified bodies. Those who are alive in body will also be caught up to Christ in the air, and their bodies will also be transformed from corrupted to glorified, from mortal to immortality.

The rapture event also includes the judgment of all New Testament era believers before the throne of God. (See Appendix F *Judgments before the throne of God*). They are not judged for their own works, for based on them they would be condemned:

> Romans 3:23 For all have sinned and fall short of the glory of God.

Instead, they are judged according to their faith in Jesus Christ, who gave himself as an atoning sacrifice for all who put their trust in him:

> 1 John 4:10 Herein is love, not that we loved God, but that he loved us, and sent his Son to be the propitiation for our sins.

Both the living and the dead arrive in heaven in body and in soul.

K14

Scene in heaven after the rapture

4:1 After this I looked, and, behold, a door was opened in heaven: and the first voice which I heard was as it were of a trumpet talking with me; which said, Come up hither, and I will shew thee things which must be hereafter.
4:2 And immediately I was in the spirit: and, behold, a throne was set in heaven, and one sat on the throne.
4:3 And he that sat was to look upon like a jasper and a sardine stone: and there was a rainbow round about the throne, in sight like unto an emerald.
4:4 And round about the throne were four and twenty seats: and upon the seats I saw four and twenty elders sitting, clothed in white raiment; and they had on their heads crowns of gold.
4:5 And out of the throne proceeded lightnings and thunderings and voices: and there were seven lamps of fire burning before the throne, which are the seven Spirits of God.
4:6 And before the throne there was a sea of glass like unto crystal: and in the midst of the throne, and round about the throne, were four beasts full of eyes before and behind.
4:7 And the first beast was like a lion, and the second beast like a calf, and the third beast had a face as a man, and the fourth beast was like a flying eagle.
4:8 And the four beasts had each of them six wings about him; and they were full of eyes within: and they rest not day and night, saying, Holy, holy, holy, Lord God Almighty, which was, and is, and is to come.
4:9 And when those beasts give glory and honour and thanks to him that sat on the throne, who liveth for ever and ever,
4:10 The four and twenty elders fall down before him that sat on the throne, and worship him that liveth for ever and ever, and cast their crowns before the throne, saying,
4:11 Thou art worthy, O Lord, to receive glory and honour and power: for thou hast created all things, and for thy pleasure they are and were created.
5:8‡[K00] And when he had taken the book, the four beasts and four and twenty elders fell down before the Lamb, having every one of them harps, and golden vials full of odours, which are the prayers of saints.

> 5:9 And they sung a new song, saying, Thou art worthy to
> take the book, and to open the seals thereof: for thou wast
> slain, and hast redeemed us to God by thy blood out of every
> kindred, and tongue, and people, and nation;
> 5:10 And hast made us unto our God kings and priests: and
> we shall reign on the earth.

This is the scene in heaven after the rapture.

The twenty-four elders (4:4) are representatives of all the church saints who are now in heaven. They have on their heads crowns of gold, the crowns of victors. God has promoted all the saints to be kings and priests (5:10). They stand in worship and celebration around God the Father who sits on his throne.

Before the throne are seven lamps burning with fire, which are the seven spirits of God (4:5). They are representative of the Holy Spirit.

The four living creatures (4:6) are different aspects of divine majesty. The lion is nobility and omnipotence. The calf is patience and continuous labor. The man is intelligence and rational power. The eagle is sovereignty and supremacy.

The twenty-four elders fall down before the Lamb (5:8). A book appears on the scene, with many seals (5:9), which will turn out to be seven in number. Only the Lamb is worthy to open the seals of the book, because he was the one who died, and yet lives. With his own blood he paid the redemption price for believers of all nations, and freed them from their slavery to sin. Only he could make it possible for them to stand before God and be welcomed into heaven. The Lamb is obviously Jesus Christ, God's son.

The opening of the first seal will inaugurate the tribulation on earth. But before that, God's chief antagonist must get into position.

K15

Satan cast down to earth following the rapture

12:3‡[K01,K04] And there appeared another wonder in heaven;
and behold a great red dragon, having seven heads and ten
horns, and seven crowns upon his heads.
12:7 And there was war in heaven: Michael and his angels
fought against the dragon; and the dragon fought and his
angels,
12:8 And prevailed not; neither was their place found any
more in heaven.
9:1‡[K32] *And the fifth angel sounded,* and I saw a star fall from
heaven unto the earth: *and to him was given the key of the
bottomless pit.*
12:4‡[K01,K04] And his tail drew the third part of the stars of
heaven, and did cast them to the earth: *and the dragon stood
before the woman which was ready to be delivered, for to
devour her child as soon as it was born.*
12:9 And the great dragon was cast out, that old serpent,
called the Devil, and Satan, which deceiveth the whole
world: he was cast out into the earth, and his angels were
cast out with him.
12:10 And I heard a loud voice saying in heaven, Now is come
salvation, and strength, and the kingdom of our God, and the
power of his Christ: for the accuser of our brethren is cast
down, which accused them before our God day and night.
12:12 Therefore rejoice, ye heavens, and ye that dwell in
them. Woe to the inhabiters of the earth and of the sea! for
the devil is come down unto you, having great wrath,
because he knoweth that he hath but a short time.

At the beginning of our timeline we already encountered the dragon of verses 12:3 and 12:4 in section K01. The dragon was Satan leading the rebellion of a third of the angels in heaven against God. Before their fall, these angels had free access to heaven. Afterward, now devils, they spend much of their time on earth tormenting men and women, and tempting them to sin against God.

After his fall, we know that God summoned Satan back to heaven on at least one occasion. One we know of is in Job 1. At this audience before God, Satan declared that Job was faithful only because of all the blessings that he received. In answer to his challenge, God removed those blessings, proved Job's faithfulness, then restored him to have even more than he was given beforehand.

Here in section K15, we encounter 12:3 and 12:4 again, in another case of double prophecy. At this time, which happens immediately after the rapture, Satan and the devils are in heaven. That would be by God's design. A war ensues. The archangel Michael and the righteous angels fight against Satan, and he and his followers are cast out of heaven again. This time it is permanent (9:1, 12:4).

Undoubtedly, the reason for the war was the rapture. The timing of the rapture came as a surprise to everyone, including Satan. His anger boiled over as a consequence of seeing so many people saved by Christ his enemy. This was all part of God's eternal plan, as prophesied by Daniel, more than five hundred years before Christ:

> Daniel 12:1 And at that time shall Michael stand up, the great prince which standeth for the children of thy people: and there shall be a time of trouble, such as never was since there was a nation even to that same time: and at that time thy people shall be delivered, every one that shall be found written in the book.

Now that the New Testament believers had been resurrected to heaven, it was not possible for Satan and the fallen angels to ever again visit or be summoned there. Satan's ability to accuse the believers in heaven, as he has been doing through previous ages, is terminated. The newly resurrected ones have salvation from sin. They will also never be subject to future temptation by their accuser. All the new inhabitants of heaven rejoice that their home has been forever purified from contact with the fallen angels.

Satan and his hosts are excluded from heaven, but their temporary dominion over earth continues. The primary field of operation for them becomes the earth. Satan has prepared for this for hundreds of years. He is reading the same Bible that we have. It seems that he has contingencies for various scenarios, to try to counteract God's decreed plan. This explains the particular virulence and suddenness of events that follow. One of his contingencies is to identify and prepare a suitable candidate among men who will take on the role of the beast.

The seven-year tribulation will begin in the next section. There are indications from other books of the Bible that it does not start immediately after the rapture. However, the happenings between the rapture and the tribulation are not discussed in Revelation.

A grave warning is issued – woe to those remaining on earth, for the accuser of all mankind is cast down from heaven to operate among them. Satan knows that his time is short (12:12), but he believes that he can ultimately win out against God with his schemes. He will establish an eighth and final godless empire, that culminates the line of the kingdoms of 17:10-11 K02. As we get into the tribulation, we will see that these schemes involve the seven heads and ten horns of the dragon, and the seven crowns upon his head (12:3). These heads and horns signify that he will operate through human beings as his surrogates, chief among them is the beast, who in turn comes to power with the aid of the woman of Babylon. Billions of people will follow them. We know that the beast will identify with Satan, because he also will be seen to have seven heads and ten horns (17:3 K17 and 13:1 K21). In section K21, we will examine the meaning of the heads, horns, and crowns.

K16

The rider on the white horse, known as the beast and antichrist, at the beginning of the seven-year tribulation

> 6:1 And I saw when the Lamb opened one of the seals, and I
> heard, as it were the noise of thunder, one of the four beasts
> saying, Come and see.
> 6:2 And I saw, and behold a white horse: and he that sat on
> him had a bow; and a crown was given unto him: and he
> went forth conquering, and to conquer.

After the church has been caught up to heaven, the first seal is opened, inaugurating terrible trials upon the earth. This is the beginning of the great day of God's wrath.

It is the first of seven seals. Out of the seventh will come a series of seven trumpets, and out of the seventh trumpet another series of seven vials or bowls of the wrath of God. As we proceed through them, we will see that it makes sense to see the twenty-one in total as happening chronologically, in the order they are literally given.

With the opening of the first seal, John in his vision hears the noise of thunder. It is a sign of the storm that is coming.

A rider on a white horse is revealed, with a bow to conquer. This is the favorite symbol of John's day for a military conqueror. In 19:11 K38 Christ will come on a white horse heading the armies of heaven that come to earth. But the rider here is someone else. He is the personification of the trial descending upon the earth. He is given the crown of a victor riding in triumph, not the crown of a sovereign. The emphasis is on his victory, not on his authority. We will see as Revelation unfolds that he will be a mighty imperial ruler, who brings under his dominance a vast territory, and his version of peace, order and prosperity. But he will have great difficulties in establishing uniform rule across the globe. Though he is destined to be a world ruler, his victory will only be temporary.

Do we know the identity of the rider? This character reappears in the next section 17:3 K17 as the beast. He will carry the woman, and will rule the world alongside her. He is a pseudo-prince of peace who claims to bring order to a troubled world. But the peace is not real. In actuality the alliance of the woman and the beast brings severe trouble to those who oppose them. They will rule together for three and a half years.

Later in 13:1 K21 the rider on the white horse reappears as the beast out of the sea with ten horns, representing ten kingdoms. In 17:16 K21 the ten horns overthrow the woman and burn her with fire. After that the beast becomes the preeminent world ruler. At that point, the tribulation is superseded by the great tribulation. It will be characterized by continuous war, and will last for the final three and a half years.

In other books of the Bible we read prophecies of a future person who fits the description of this rider and beast.

One prophecy that points to him is the fourth beast with ten horns of Daniel 7:19-21:

> Daniel 7:19 Then I would know the truth of the fourth beast, which was diverse from all the others, exceeding dreadful, whose teeth were of iron, and his nails of brass; which devoured, brake in pieces, and stamped the residue with his feet;
> 7:20 And of the ten horns that were in his head, and of the other which came up, and before whom three fell; even of that horn that had eyes, and a mouth that spake very great things, whose look was more stout than his fellows.
> 7:21 I beheld, and the same horn made war with the saints, and prevailed against them.

The four beasts of this Daniel 7 passage map to the four parts of the statue of Daniel 2, which we saw in K02 was a prophecy of four coming empires. The fourth was the Roman empire. The ten horns of this beast match the ten horns of Revelation's beast (13:1, 17:16 K21). Revelation thus stamps Daniel as a double prophecy with two future fulfillments: the Roman empire that has already come and gone, and the beast with ten subordinates who revive a new Roman empire during the tribulation.

The next prophecy that fits the beast of Revelation is the "prince that shall come" of Daniel 9:26. Many interpreters would say he therefore intends to revive the Roman empire and make it spread across the whole earth during the tribulation period:

> Daniel 9:26 *And after threescore and two weeks shall Messiah be cut off, but not for himself:* and the people of the prince that shall come shall destroy the city and the sanctuary; *and the end thereof shall be with a flood, and unto the end of the war desolations are determined.*

Note that in this passage, there are people of the prince who shall come with him. In my second book, I will talk about who they might be.

Next, the beast is the man of lawlessness of 2 Thessalonians 2:6-8 (see K13). There we were told that he can only appear after the withdrawal of the Holy Spirit from the world.

Finally, the beast is an imitation Christ, what John calls in his biblical letters outside of Revelation an *antichrist*:

> 1 John 2:22 Who is a liar but he that denieth that Jesus is the Christ? He is antichrist, that denieth the Father and the Son.
> 4:3 And every spirit that confesseth not that Jesus Christ is come in the flesh is not of God: and this is that spirit of antichrist, whereof ye have heard that it should come; and even now already is it in the world.
>
> 2 John 7 many deceivers are entered into the world, who confess not that Jesus Christ is come in the flesh. This is a deceiver and an antichrist.

Where does the beast come from? Revelation does not give a physical location, but we are given a spiritual one: at the very beginning of the timeline we were told that the beast "shall ascend out of the bottomless pit" (17:8 K02). This identifies him as a tool of Satan, who is the angel of the bottomless pit (9:11 K32).

All this is sound biblical evidence that the rider on the white horse and beast is *the antichrist*. He is *anti* because he is against Christ. He is *anti* in another way because he seeks to replace Christ as Satan's substitute for God's son. He is *the* antichrist because he not merely another antichrist. He is the final one. He is an impostor, Satan's masterpiece, the counterfeit of all that Christ claims to be. You can find Satan's motivation for molding the character of the antichrist in Appendix A *Why Satan hates Christ*.

K17

The woman of Babylon sitting on the beast at the beginning of the seven-year tribulation

> 17:1‡[K02,K20] And there came one of the seven angels which
> had the seven vials, and talked with me, saying unto me,
> Come hither; I will shew unto thee *the judgment of* the great
> whore that sitteth upon many waters.
> 17:3 So he carried me away in the spirit into the wilderness:
> and I saw a woman sit upon a scarlet coloured beast, full of
> names of blasphemy, having seven heads and ten horns.
> 17:4 And the woman was arrayed in purple and scarlet
> colour, and decked with gold and precious stones and pearls,
> having a golden cup in her hand full of abominations and
> filthiness of her fornication:
> 17:5 And upon her forehead was a name written, MYSTERY,
> BABYLON THE GREAT, THE MOTHER OF HARLOTS AND
> ABOMINATIONS OF THE EARTH.
> 17:15 And he saith unto me, The waters
> which thou sawest, where the whore sitteth, are peoples,
> and multitudes, and nations, and tongues.
> 17:18 And the woman which thou sawest is that great city,
> which reigneth over the kings of the earth.

Immediately after the rider on the white horse inaugurates the seven-year tribulation, the prostitute appears. She is the woman of Babylon. We already met her in section K02. She is the spirit of empire that was the engine behind the successive kingdoms called out by the Old Testament: Egypt, Assyria, Babylon, Persia, Greece, and Rome. Her origin traces back to the original model empire that Nimrod established, which God overthrew at the tower of Babel event.

In K02, I made the case that when we look at the world order established during the tribulation period, Jerusalem should be our focus.

But Daniel's prophecies of the distant future point to a revived Roman empire. Most biblical interpreters reach that conclusion based on two dreams and their divine interpretation. The dream of the statue in Daniel 2 was a prophecy of four coming empires. In Daniel 7, he then had a dream of four beasts. Like the four parts of the statue, the beasts are four future kings (Daniel 7:17). The first three of each series are the ancient Babylonian, Medo-Persian and Greek empires. The fourth empire is characterized by iron in both dreams: strong as iron that crushes in Daniel 2:40; with great iron teeth that breaks in pieces in Daniel 7:7.

The fourth empire of Daniel 2 became the Roman empire of John's day. The fourth beast of Daniel 7 would therefore seem to be the Roman empire also. But the way it is described does not exactly match the empire, now long gone, that we know from our history books. Instead, it is describing a revived Roman empire of the tribulation. We can see that based on the interpretation that God gave for the dream. I have unspiraled the verses of Daniel chronologically to help you see how the events of the dream match up with the events of Revelation:

> Daniel 7:16 I came near unto one of them that stood by, and asked him the truth of all this. So he told me, and made me know the interpretation of the things.
> 7:17 These great beasts, which are four, are four kings, which shall arise out of the earth.
> 7:19 Then I would know the truth of the fourth beast, which was diverse from all the others, exceeding dreadful, whose teeth were of iron, and his nails of brass; which devoured, brake in pieces, and stamped the residue with his feet.
> 7:23 Thus he said, The fourth beast shall be the fourth kingdom upon earth, which shall be diverse from all kingdoms, and shall devour the whole earth, and shall tread it down, and break it in pieces.
> 7:20 And of the ten horns that were in his head, and of the other which came up, and before whom three fell; even of that horn that had eyes, and a mouth that spake very great things, whose look was more stout than his fellows.
> 7:24 And the ten horns out of this kingdom are ten kings that shall arise: and another shall rise after them; and he shall be diverse from the first, and he shall subdue three kings.
> 7:25 And he shall speak great words against the most High, and shall wear out the saints of the most High, and think to change times and laws: and they shall be given into his hand until a time and times and the dividing of time.
> 7:21 I beheld, and the same horn made war with the saints, and prevailed against them.
> 7:26 But the judgment shall sit, and they shall take away his dominion, to consume and to destroy it unto the end.

> 7:22 Until the Ancient of days came, and judgment was given to the saints of the most High; and the time came that the saints possessed the kingdom.
> 7:27 And the kingdom and dominion, and the greatness of the kingdom under the whole heaven, shall be given to the people of the saints of the most High, whose kingdom is an everlasting kingdom, and all dominions shall serve and obey him.
> 7:18 But the saints of the most High shall take the kingdom, and possess the kingdom for ever, even for ever and ever.

Note these direct comparisons between this dream and the great tribulation events that we will be going through later in the chronology of Revelation:

- The fourth beast is said to have ten horns (Daniel 7:20,24), which compares to the ten horns of Revelation 17:3. One of the fourth beast's horns subdues three of the others, leaving seven. This compares to the seven heads of 17:3.
- The fourth beast makes war on the saints and seems to prevail against them (Daniel 7:21). This compares with 13:7 K23.
- Then his kingdom will be taken away and he will be judged (Daniel 7:26). This compares with 19:20 K40.
- God's saints will then be given his kingdom (Daniel 7:22). This compares with the tribulation saints entering into the millennial kingdom in 20:4 K43.
- It is reiterated again that they will be given his kingdom (Daniel 7:27,18). This compares with the entrance of the saints into God's eternal kingdom in 21:3 K47.

We also saw in K16 that Daniel 9:26 speaks of the "prince that shall come," which points to the future beast of the tribulation period.

These many similarities with the rest of Daniel and Revelation lead us to see the fourth beast of Daniel 7 as a revived Roman empire during the future tribulation, established by the woman of Babylon with the aid of the antichrist beast.

The woman is known for promiscuity, fornication, and adultery. They are expressions of defiance against God. Instead of seeking security in him, she seeks it in forbidden unions with numerous others. If not found there, she compensates with easy financial gain through sexual ecstasy instead of hard work.

The woman's illicit relationship at this time is with the beast. She comes to power riding the beast (17:3). Her aim is to establish rule over the world through him, and make it pleasurable in the process. The woman is dressed as a seductress. In her hand is a golden cup, a product of the riches gained from her chosen profession (17:4).

She proudly announces the mystery of the name written on her forehead (17:5). It brazenly advertises her harlotry, and her enticement to fornication and abomination.

Here at the beginning of the seven-year tribulation, the spirit of Babylon is finally successful at achieving a world order. The woman establishes control over nations of many languages and peoples (17:15,18). This empire involves an ideology of immorality, and especially an emphasis on sex, that imposes a stupefying drunkenness as far as spiritual things are concerned.

Most pretribulational commentators count this new kingdom of the woman as the *seventh* king of verse 17:10 in K02. They maintain that the eighth kingdom will come afterward during the second three and a half years. Their viewpoint satisfies the first prophecy that we saw in K02:

- There will be a seventh kingdom coming after Rome the sixth kingdom. (17:10)

They deal with the second prophecy of K02 by designating the beast as the king of both the seventh (jointly with the woman) and eighth kingdoms:

- The beast is "of the seven" kings and will also be an eighth. So, he will be an eighth king who was somehow operative in all seven kingdoms, or possibly he will be king of both the seventh and eighth kingdoms. (17:11)

However, this approach does not explain the third prophecy:

- In between the seventh and eighth kingdom the beast will be eclipsed. (17:8)

In my second book, I will put forward a view that satisfies all three prophecies when I examine Islamic eschatology and the Mahdi. I will present the case that the woman and the beast begin their rule jointly as the *eighth* king. I will then uncover the identity of the missing seventh kingdom.

Do we know the identity of the woman of Babylon?

She represents an entire culture that enforces itself through a politically controlling system, a system that works visibly and invisibly to oppose the commandments of God. It cannot rest until it establishes dominance that will brook no opposition. In Babel and the six historic kingdoms of the Old Testament (K02), the visible role of the woman as political and cultural ruler was held by a succession of leaders. In a similar way, there will likely be one or more top leaders who will be the public face of Babylon to the world during the tribulation.

Instead of asking *who* is the woman, we might ask *where* exactly will her headquarters be? Will it be Babylon, Rome, or some other city?

The grand ancient city of Babylon was capital of the Babylonian empire, located 85 km south of Baghdad. It fell to the Medo-Persians in 539 BCE. It slowly crumbled over centuries of foreign invasions and occupations. A tourist site was recreated there by Saddam Hussein, dictator of Iraq, in the 1970s. Since then, it has been partially destroyed by decades of war. It was designated a UNESCO World Heritage Site in 2019. It's a sad ending to such a fabled city.

The Babylon of Revelation is certainly not referring to some rebuilt city at that original location.

In John's time, Rome was the capital of the Roman empire, which ruled over the Mediterranean Sea basin. It included northern Africa, much of the Middle East, and southern Europe. Of course, Rome itself is in Europe. But it was not always the capital of the empire. During the fourth century the capital of the western half of the empire was moved to Milan, in the fifth it was in Ravenna. A second capital of the eastern empire was founded in Constantinople (today's Istanbul), and stayed as capital till 1453, becoming known as the second Rome. That is when the Roman empire finally ended.

Europe and the western civilization that it founded had almost 2,000 years of strong Christian influence. In the 20th century it moved into a post-Christian age, and dismantled much of its Judeo-Christian basis. The Catholic church headquartered in Rome, and the various Protestant churches, lost their relevance in the culture. In the place of Christianity, the west became obsessed with establishing social conformance, forced redistribution of wealth, neutering religious influence on society in the name of separation of church and state, murder of newborns by abortion, appeasement of dictators, "peace" and "health" at any cost, and sex. Personal freedom had to become subordinate to all these values. God's commandments as found in the Bible certainly are to be overruled. Adultery, death, falsehood, gaining other people's possessions, disrespecting elders - all are preferred when necessary. The ends always justifies the means. God's followers are to be marginalized and persecuted. Antisemitism and anti-Christianity become official policy. After World War II, America and Europe devised worldwide political structures to push this agenda.

The values of this post-western civilization are eerie premonitions of the values of the women of Babylon, which I will discuss in more detail in section K20.

The likely capital of the revived Roman empire is therefore the future capital of post-Christian Europe - be it Rome, Istanbul, Brussels, or some other city. It will be one main city in the geography of the tribulation. The other will be Jerusalem.

If the tribulation occurs near my time, it may become obvious that the woman of Babylon is the spirit of the post-western civilization that has dispensed with God. It now finds a way to establish its new values across the world by making an alliance with the beast, who is the antichrist. The harlot seeks to gain mastery from her European headquarters, and the beast from Jerusalem. They find common ground in that they both oppose the commandments of almighty God in heaven. They seek to negate his offer of forgiveness of sins by the sacrifice of his son Jesus Christ. But we will see that the apparent harmony between the two tribulation allies will not last.

K18

Preservation of a portion of the nation Israel through the tribulation

12:13 And when the dragon saw that he was cast unto the earth, he persecuted the woman which brought forth the man child.
12:6 And the woman fled into the wilderness, where she hath a place prepared of God, that they should feed her there a thousand two hundred and threescore days.
12:14 And to the woman were given two wings of a great eagle, that she might fly into the wilderness, into her place, where she is nourished for a time, and times, and half a time, from the face of the serpent.
12:15 And the serpent cast out of his mouth water as a flood after the woman, that he might cause her to be carried away of the flood.
12:16 And the earth helped the woman, and the earth opened her mouth, and swallowed up the flood which the dragon cast out of his mouth.
12:17 And the dragon was wroth with the woman, and went to make war with the remnant of her seed, which keep the commandments of God, and have the testimony of Jesus Christ.
7:1 And after these things I saw four angels standing on the four corners of the earth, holding the four winds of the earth, that the wind should not blow on the earth, nor on the sea, nor on any tree.
7:2 And I saw another angel ascending from the east, having the seal of the living God: and he cried with a loud voice to the four angels, to whom it was given to hurt the earth and the sea,
7:3 Saying, Hurt not the earth, neither the sea, nor the trees, till we have sealed the servants of our God in their foreheads.
7:4 And the number of them which were sealed: and there were sealed an hundred and forty and four thousand of all the tribes of the children of Israel.
7:5 Of the tribe of Juda were sealed twelve thousand. Of the tribe of Reuben were sealed twelve thousand. Of the tribe of Gad were sealed twelve thousand.

> 7:6 Of the tribe of Aser were sealed twelve thousand. Of the tribe of Nepthalim were sealed twelve thousand. Of the tribe of Manasses were sealed twelve thousand.
> 7:7 Of the tribe of Simeon were sealed twelve thousand. Of the tribe of Levi were sealed twelve thousand. Of the tribe of Issachar were sealed twelve thousand.
> 7:8 Of the tribe of Zabulon were sealed twelve thousand. Of the tribe of Joseph were sealed twelve thousand. Of the tribe of Benjamin were sealed twelve thousand.
> 14:4 These are they which were not defiled with women; for they are virgins. These are they which follow the Lamb whithersoever he goeth. These were redeemed from among men, being the firstfruits unto God and to the Lamb.
> 11:1 And there was given me a reed like unto a rod: and the angel stood, saying, Rise, and measure the temple of God, and the altar, and them that worship therein.
> 11:2 But the court which is without the temple leave out, and measure it not; for it is given unto the Gentiles: and the holy city shall they tread under foot forty and two months.

The government of the woman and the beast, which now claims to rule the entire world, makes it a top priority to persecute Christ followers and other non-conformists. How could this be, when all the believers were raptured sometime before, and all nations of the world give formal allegiance to the woman and the beast? Revelation is silent on this topic. But we can make some logical deductions.

The ones who are least compliant at this time are Jewish people. They are the most threatened. The woman of this section represents Israel, the one which "brought forth the man child" (12:13). It is the nation that gave birth to God's promised Messiah, Jesus the Christ. Israel has always been targeted by Satan because she is chosen of God and is central to the overall purpose of God for time and eternity. Now with the woman and the beast in power, the Jewish people face the worst persecution in their history.

At the end of this section we see a mention of the temple in Jerusalem (11:1-2). John is told to measure the inner court of the temple. This refers to the Holy Place and the Holy of Holies, where Jewish priests have jurisdiction. We also see that the outer court of the temple comes under the world government's control, and will be trodden underfoot by non-Jews for the forty-two months (three and a half years), the first half of the tribulation period.

There is no such temple in my time, or realistic plans underway to build one. I surmise that the temple's construction must therefore have started after the rapture and before the tribulation, spearheaded by a movement of Orthodox Jews. Ever since the last temple was destroyed in 70 CE, some Orthodox have longed for the temple to be rebuilt, and the Old Testament sacrificial system to be reestablished. God permits the temple to be rebuilt after the rapture, because the church is gone and the Messiah has not yet returned. Having the temple rebuilt is a comfort to the Jewish people in this terrible time.

The official arrangement to partition the temple district between Jews and non-Jews would be part of the prophesied seven-year treaty granted to Israel by the beast, who is also the prince of Daniel 9:27:

> Daniel 9:27 And he [the prince] shall confirm the covenant with many for one week: *and in the midst of the week he shall cause* the sacrifice and the oblation *to cease, and for the overspreading of abominations he shall make it desolate, even until the consummation, and that determined shall be poured upon the desolate.*

The *week* here is the seven-year tribulation period. When we align this with Revelation, we see the treaty was put in place with Israel as soon as the woman and beast come to power. It is a treaty unequalled in history, that promises peace in the Middle East, to be enforced by the new worldwide government. For the first time in the modern era, it seems to many that Israel will find rest. Unfortunately, this rest turns out to be an illusion.

Indeed, a treaty that seems to establish permanent peace in the Middle East will be of such historic significance that the woman and the beast can use it as irresistible leverage to establish their ascendancy over all the nations. Through it they can implement their new layer of hard authority over the entire world.

The temple or tabernacle will be mentioned just once more in Revelation, in 13:6 K23. That is where the second part of Daniel 9:27 will be fulfilled: the beast will renege on the treaty halfway through its promised time, he will desecrate the temple, and the second three-and-a-half year period of the great tribulation will begin.

In the book of Romans, the Bible foretells another movement of Jews in the last days. They will come to realize they cannot be saved by carrying out the Old Testament temple sacrificial ritual. Instead, they will embrace Jesus as their Messiah:

> Romans 11:25 For I would not, brethren, that ye should be ignorant of this mystery, lest ye should be wise in your own conceits; that blindness in part is happened to Israel, until the fulness of the Gentiles be come in.
> 11:26 so all Israel shall be saved: as it is written, There shall come out of Sion the Deliverer, and shall turn away ungodliness from Jacob:
> 11:27 this is my covenant unto them, when I shall take away their sins.
> 11:28 concerning the gospel, they are enemies for your sakes: but as touching the election, they are beloved for the father's sakes.

In these conditions of an antisemitic world government, and after "the fulness of the Gentiles be come in" to heaven by the rapture, these Jews know they have nowhere to go but to *Yeshua haMashiach*.

God responds by bringing a remnant of them into relative safety for the first three and a half years, spelled out as a thousand two hundred and threescore days (12:6). Twelve thousand from each of the twelve tribes of Israel are sealed as servants of God, 144,000 in total (7:4).[5] God will provide them with special protections:

- They will be delivered from "the face of the serpent" (12:14).
- They will be rescued from a mysterious flood that will be sent by the serpent (12:15-16, Revelation is silent on details regarding this flood).
- They will be preserved from continuous war waged by Satan on the remnant (12:17).
- As the sealed ones, they will survive with their lives through the tribulation.

They are named by tribe. God will name them, even though Jewish genealogies are almost all lost, and the ten northern tribes can no

[5] The tribes of Dan and Ephraim are omitted from this listing, perhaps because they were connected with idolatry in Israel (1 Kings 12:25-33). But Ephraim is covered here under the tribe of Joseph his father, and Dan is named in the future distribution of land on the eternal new Earth in Ezekiel 48:2.

longer be traced after they went into Assyrian captivity in 722 BCE. Their assignment to tribe must therefore be done by divine guidance.

In verse 14:4 we also learn that the 144,000 sealed ones have kept themselves from sexual relations with women. This means they are likely younger men, who have taken a vow to devote themselves solely to God in the midst of the oversexualized culture inspired by the woman of Babylon. They started following Yeshua after the rapture, and probably adopted their purity vow in answer to the intensifying persecution of God's followers. They are similar to the Nazirites of the Old Testament, who vowed to totally abstain from alcohol and grapes, from shaving their head and from contact with corpses (Numbers 6:1-21). The most famous men who took the Nazirite vow were Samuel (see the book of 1 Samuel) and Samson (Judges 13-16).

The 144,000 dedicated Jewish evangelists and their testimonies about the good news of Jesus will not be silenced. The Old Testament prophet Zechariah prophesied about these 144,000 Jewish evangelists bringing people to Christ in the end time:

> Zechariah 8:20 Thus saith the LORD of hosts; It shall yet come to pass, that there shall come people, and the inhabitants of many cities:
> 8:21 And the inhabitants of one city shall go to another, saying, Let us go speedily to pray before the LORD, and to seek the LORD of hosts: I will go also.
> 8:22 Yea, many people and strong nations shall come to seek the LORD of hosts in Jerusalem, and to pray before the LORD.
> 8:23 Thus saith the LORD of hosts; In those days it shall come to pass, that ten men shall take hold out of all languages of the nations, even shall take hold of the skirt of him that is a Jew, saying, We will go with you: for we have heard that God is with you.

The witness of the Jewish evangelists will persuade many non-Jews to follow Christ, even if it costs them their life.

They will also lead many other Jews to recognize sorrow for Christ, whom their religious leaders crucified two thousand years ago. And God will turn their sorrow into everlasting life. The same prophet Zechariah looked ahead to this happening:

> Zechariah 12:8 In that day shall the Lord defend the inhabitants of Jerusalem; and he that is feeble among them at that day shall be as David; and the house of David shall be as God, as the angel of the Lord before them.
> 12:10 And I will pour upon the house of David, and upon the inhabitants of Jerusalem, the spirit of grace and of supplications: and they shall look upon me whom they have pierced, and they shall mourn for him, as one mourneth for his only son, and shall be in bitterness for him, as one that is in bitterness for his firstborn.

Tragically, most tribulation Jews who come to faith in Yeshua, but who are not of the 144,000 sealed ones, will be martyred. This includes Jewish women who come to faith, and many of the men.

With regards to the non-Jewish gentile population of the world, I believe many will not believe the official media narrative, and will question what really occurred to the Christians who disappeared. Rumors will spread about the rapture that happened. People ask one another how to verify the event, and what to do. The witness of the Jewish evangelists, access to the Bible and books about it like the one you are reading now, become key. Modern governments have technology that is capable of tracking this non-conformance. It is dangerous to access this information, even more dangerous to be in contact with a Jewish follower, but it will be much worse to comply with the authorities blindly into the tribulation. Many around the world will pray on their knees and cry out for Christ to save them. I hope that you will be one of them.

As soon as the worldwide government of the woman and the beast takes power, they will press to stamp out this movement to Christ. Despite their efforts, a great multitude of gentiles will be saved to eternal life, though they be put to death physically. They become a martyred throng in heaven. God uses the 144,000 sealed ones of Israel as a channel of witness to them. That is in keeping with his purposes for the Jewish nation.

Tragically, the government's cover story about the rapture event could be acceptable to the vast majority of people. But if you believe yourself to be a Christian, and you hear their explanations about the rapture, you should really ask yourself, "why wasn't I taken away, too?" God's answer is that the ones he took away were also sinners, just like you:

> Romans 3:23 For all have sinned, and come short of the glory of God.

But they are sinners who repented of their sins. He wants you to repent also, confess your own sins, and ask for forgiveness in the name of Christ. You will experience the time of tribulation, but God will then save you. Indeed, he will give you the unexpected blessing that those who were raptured will not have – you will become one of the citizens of the thousand-year millennial kingdom, which I will describe in detail in section K44.

K19

The two witnesses come before the great tribulation begins

> 11:3‡K34 And I will give power unto my two witnesses, and they shall prophesy a thousand two hundred and threescore days, clothed in sackcloth.
> 11:4 These are the two olive trees, and the two candlesticks standing before the God of the earth.
> 11:5 And if any man will hurt them, fire proceedeth out of their mouth, and devoureth their enemies: and if any man will hurt them, he must in this manner be killed.
> 11:6 These have power to shut heaven, that it rain not in the days of their prophecy: and have power over waters to turn them to blood, and to smite the earth with all plagues, as often as they will.

Some months before the end of the first three and a half years, two strange characters appear. We know they are in Jerusalem, because later in 11:8 K34 their location is described as the place where Jesus was crucified.

They are described as witnesses, who shall prophesy for 1,260 days (11:3). They will be active during most of the great tribulation.

God gives them unusual perseverance for such a length of time. This resolve comes from aspects of their character: they are like two candlesticks (lampstands) and two olive trees (11:4). This symbolism comes from the Old Testament prophet Zechariah. When he was shown two olive trees and two lampstands, God told him what they stood for:

> Zechariah 4:12 And I answered again, and said unto him, What be these two olive branches which through the two golden pipes empty the golden oil out of themselves?
> 4:14 Then said he, These are the two anointed ones, that stand by the Lord of the whole earth.

The two stand as lampstands. They shine light on the true things of God. That matches their description as witnesses for him. They are fueled by olive oil, representing God's Holy Spirit. They are two in number, because:

> 2 Corinthians 13:1b In the mouth of two or three witnesses shall every word be established.

The government takes extreme actions against them. But God gives them miraculous power to oppose the beast. They are able to respond to the agents sent against them by literally speaking fire to consume them (11:5). Undoubtedly they demonstrate this power, as did the Old Testament prophet Elijah, who on two occasions called fire from heaven upon companies of fifty soldiers sent to arrest him (2 Kings 1:9-15).

The two witnesses also demonstrate the ability to stop rain from falling upon the earth (11:6a), as proof that the government does not have power over climate change which it claims to have. This is again like Elijah, who prayed that Israel would not have rain for three and half years (James 5:17). Elijah displayed God's power over the false god Baal, whom the Israelites were worshiping. Curiously this is the same length of time that the two witnesses minister to the world in Revelation.

They also show their power to bloody entire bodies of water (11:6b), as would happen if wounded armies were drowning in the seas.

Finally, they are able to send unexpected plagues upon the earth (11:6c). This is like Moses, who was sent by God to free the Israelites from their slavery in Egypt under Pharaoh. He would not listen to Moses' repeated requests, so God through Moses turned the water of the Nile to blood. He sent the Egyptians plagues of frogs, gnats, flies, cattle sickness, boils, hail, locusts, darkness, and the death of all their firstborn. There is evidence that many Egyptians, when they experienced these plagues, threw off their own slavery to Pharaoh and joined the Jews in the exodus across the Red Sea.

These striking similarities convince many commentators that the two witnesses of Revelation are Elijah and Moses, returned to earth in the end times. Both were very unusual: Elijah never died, and Moses' body was never found. Both were present with Jesus at his transfiguration (Matthew 17).

Others contend that the two witnesses are two prophets who will be raised up from among the Jews who turn to Christ in the time following the rapture. In either case, the two witnesses are a continuing obstacle to the plans of the woman and the beast. Their government propagandists have great difficulty explaining their activity, or trying to hide it from the population of the world they are trying to control.

When the two are shown on worldwide television or internet, they are always clothed in sackcloth (11:3). Even this garb is a witness. It directs people to realize they need to repent and turn back to God because of approaching judgment. This is reminiscent of the response of the people of the evil city of Nineveh to the Old Testament prophet Jonah:

> Jonah 3:4 And Jonah began to enter into the city a day's journey, and he cried, and said, Yet forty days, and Nineveh shall be overthrown.
> 3:5 the people of Nineveh believed God, and proclaimed a fast, and put on sackcloth, from the greatest of them even to the least of them.
> 3:6 For word came unto the king of Nineveh, and he arose from his throne, and he laid his robe from him, and covered him with sackcloth, and sat in ashes.
> 3:7 And he caused it to be proclaimed and published through Nineveh by the decree of the king and his nobles, saying, Let neither man nor beast, herd nor flock, taste any thing: let them not feed, nor drink water:
> 3:8 let man and beast be covered with sackcloth, and cry mightily unto God: yea, let them turn every one from his evil way, and from the violence that is in their hands.
> 3:9 Who can tell if God will turn and repent, and turn away from his fierce anger, that we perish not?
> 3:10 And God saw their works, that they turned from their evil way; and God repented of the evil, that he had said that he would do unto them; and he did it not.

Just as when God sent Moses, Elijah, and Jonah, his purpose in sending the two witnesses is not to destroy, but to give one more opportunity to people to save themselves from Satan, the woman, and the beast. In wearing sackcloth, the witnesses are appealing to others to do the same. They challenge the people of the world to turn back to the almighty God of heaven, like the people of Nineveh and their king did. It is clear from the actions taken against them that the two witnesses are successful in turning many of the tribulation away from Satan and the beast, and toward Jesus Christ, the son of God.

K20

The sins of Babylon subject her to God's wrath

17:1‡[K02,K17] And there came one of the seven angels which
had the seven vials, and talked with me, saying unto me,
Come hither; I will shew unto thee the judgment of the great
whore *that sitteth upon many waters.*
17:2 With whom the kings of the earth have committed
fornication, and the inhabitants of the earth have been made
drunk with the wine of her fornication.
18:12 The merchandise of gold, and silver, and precious
stones, and of pearls, and fine linen, and purple, and silk,
and scarlet, and all thyine wood, and all manner vessels of
ivory, and all manner vessels of most precious wood, and of
brass, and iron, and marble,
18:13 And cinnamon, and odours, and ointments, and
frankincense, and wine, and oil, and fine flour, and wheat,
and beasts, and sheep, and horses, and chariots, and slaves,
and souls of men.
17:6 And I saw the woman drunken with the blood of the
saints, and with the blood of the martyrs of Jesus: and when
I saw her, I wondered with great admiration.
18:24 And in her was found the blood of prophets, and of
saints, and of all that were slain upon the earth.
18:6 Reward her even as she rewarded you, and double unto
her double according to her works: in the cup which she hath
filled fill to her double.
18:7 How much she hath glorified herself, and lived
deliciously, so much torment and sorrow give her: for she
saith in her heart, I sit a queen, and am no widow, and shall
see no sorrow.
18:8‡[K21,K25] Therefore shall her plagues come *in one day,
death, and mourning, and famine; and she shall be utterly
burned with fire:* for strong is the Lord God who judgeth her.
18:21 And a mighty angel took up a stone like a great
millstone, and cast it into the sea, saying, Thus with violence
shall that great city Babylon be thrown down, and shall be
found no more at all.
18:22 And the voice of harpers, and musicians, and of pipers,
and trumpeters, shall be heard no more at all in thee; and no
craftsman, of whatsoever craft he be, shall be found any
more in thee; and the sound of a millstone shall be heard no
more at all in thee;

> 18:23 And the light of a candle shall shine no more at all in thee; and the voice of the bridegroom and of the bride shall be heard no more at all in thee: for thy merchants were the great men of the earth; for by thy sorceries were all nations deceived.

In his vision John sees that God will soon send judgment upon the woman of Babylon, the great whore, because of her wickedness during the first three and a half years of the tribulation (17:1).

We have seen how she represents the spirit of empire. Her signature transgression is sexual sin. The word for fornication in the Greek original text is *porneuo* (17:2), which is the root for *pornography*. She tempts countless people of the nations and their leaders with her adultery and promiscuity. She preaches "free" love, and the sacrifice of unborn babies (the "souls of men" of 18:13) for the sake of convenience, built upon the murder industry of abortion. This culture that promotes adultery expands into adultery that is also spiritual – frivolous relationship with religions that are contrary to God's holy word, or with political ideologies that are substitutes for God. We saw such religious experimentation in kingdoms throughout human history, as explained in section 17:10 K02. There the woman of Babylon first appeared at the tower of Babel event. She then inspired the six kingdoms of the Old Testament and their religious systems. Her alliance with the beast, who we shall see will enforce his own religion, is the last of her frivolous spiritual relationships.

The proper relationship that God wants to have with his people is like a husband to his wife. In the Old Testament he appears as the husband of Israel (Isaiah 54:1-8, Jeremiah 3:14, 31:32). In the New Testament the church is like a virgin destined to be joined her husband Christ (2 Corinthians 11:2).

The woman has deceived the nations of the world into adopting an easy-going lifestyle of adultery in the context of wealth and luxury (17:2). John describes this in terms of the luxuries of his time (18:12-13): precious stones, costly metals, and fine fabrics in magnificent colors. The rich apparel of the tribulation's favored ones is matched by the furnishings of their homes. They also have expensive perfumes and spices, abundance of foods, property in the form of animals, and methods of transportation formerly available only to the wealthiest. In the time that I write to you, all this has increased exponentially with our age of technology. Western civilization has turned away from its Judeo-Christian inheritance to a hedonism fed by technology. By the time of the tribulation this materialism will undoubtedly be an even greater idol in the world. How much easier it is to selfishly indulge in material surplus and sexual licentiousness, with no thought at all about consequences, than to think of the creator God who made us in his image to live lives of righteousness.

This is the treasure of Babylon that will soon be destroyed with fire (18:8 K21).

The sins of fornication and indulgence are certainly not new in this fallen world. In the first half of the tribulation, these are compounded with the systematic and mass persecution of God's people (more "souls of men" in 18:13). The political elites cannot contain their fury at seeing God's followers multiply. After all, this is a post-rapture world that started off with no true Christians, to their great satisfaction. How could it be that, despite constructing a heaven on earth, so many people are turning to Jesus Christ? The work of the 144,000 Jewish evangelists whose lives are safeguarded by God (Zechariah 8:20-23 K18), and most recently the two intrepid witnesses in Jerusalem, has brought this great spiritual harvest of souls.

The new believers are fearless in denouncing the government system, and announcing it will be judged for completely violating God's standards of righteousness. They are also fearless in proclaiming repentance, forgiveness of sins, and the good news of Jesus Christ who paid the price of our sins, that God may take us into his eternal kingdom.

The world government's key pillar of social conformity (see K17) is undermined by these believers on a daily basis. The government structures have no choice but to respond with violent and unsparing persecution, a tyranny so widespread that John describes them as being "drunken with the blood of the saints, and with the blood of the martyrs of Jesus" (17:6).

If the tribulation occurs soon after I write this book, your government may borrow on the techniques that Communist China has used against God's followers. China is a country that has dispensed with traditional religions. It exercises tyranny over its population in order to establish a more perfect Marxist society. Over decades it has limited the size of families and promoted abortions. The Communist party established full control over the country in 1949, and expelled all Christian missionaries. The party thought it had cleansed the country from Christianity. But over the next forty years, more than 100 million Chinese turned to Christ because the truth about him would not die out. They did not believe what the government was telling them. The authorities responded by attempting to register and regulate the churches. They continue to intensify their actions. In my time the Chinese government:

- controls buildings where Christians worship,
- monitors the movement of all people with outdoor and indoor cameras,
- penalizes Christian behavior through a computerized social credit system,
- infiltrates Christian gatherings with paid informers,
- publishes materials that bend biblical teaching in the direction of Marxist thought,
- restricts churches from teaching children about Jesus,
- arrests pastors and Christian leaders arbitrarily,
- sends many Christians to labor camps where they have little means of communication,
- targets Christians in euthanasia campaigns meant to provide organs for harvesting.

Chinese Christians counter this persecution by going underground. They establish home fellowships, disciple one another to obey God's commandments, and learn to follow Christ without the benefit of paid pastors.

Many western countries of my time see the Chinese government as a model to emulate. The woman of Babylon will consolidate the western and communist countries and their ideology, with the goal of remaking the earth into a godless world. Her dictatorship during the tribulation time will intensify the Communist Chinese model with single-minded ruthlessness. It will inspire fear, respect, and a grudging form of admiration (17:6).

In answer to all this, the voice of an angel calls on God to recognize the enormity of these sins of Babylon, and pay her back double. Her self-glorification will be rewarded with torment and sorrow. The one who sits as queen will see sudden destruction in the space of one day (18:6-8). Babylon will fall with great violence, like a millstone sending shock waves upon the sea (18:21). Her fall will be reminiscent of the original Babylon. Belshazzar its king watched as the finger of God wrote condemning words on the wall. Then his empire fell to the Medo-Persians in less than a day (Daniel 5).

When the final Babylon falls, the luxuries and economy of the tribulation world will be constricted immediately. The activity of its factories, the work of its designers, the voices of its entertainers will be stilled. The steady electricity supply of the great cities will cease.

In the next section we will see who makes this happen.

K21

The great tribulation begins
with the beast launching war and the fall of Babylon

6:3 And when he had opened the second seal, I heard the
second beast say, Come and see.
6:4 And there went out another horse that was red: and
power was given to him that sat thereon to take peace from
the earth, and that they should kill one another: and there
was given unto him a great sword.
13:1 And I stood upon the sand of the sea, and saw a beast
rise up out of the sea, having seven heads and ten horns, and
upon his horns ten crowns, and upon his heads the name of
blasphemy.
13:2 And the beast which I saw was like unto a leopard, and
his feet were as the feet of a bear, and his mouth as the
mouth of a lion: and the dragon gave him his power, and his
seat, and great authority.
17:12 And the ten horns which thou sawest are ten kings,
which have received no kingdom as yet; but receive power as
kings one hour with the beast.
17:13 These have one mind, and shall give their power and
strength unto the beast.
17:16 And the ten horns which thou sawest upon the beast,
these shall hate the whore, and shall make her desolate and
naked, and shall eat her flesh, and burn her with fire.
17:17 For God hath put in their hearts to fulfil his will, and to
agree, and give their kingdom unto the beast, until the words
of God shall be fulfilled.
14:8 And there followed another angel, saying, Babylon is
fallen, is fallen, that great city, because she made all nations
drink of the wine of the wrath of her fornication.
18:8‡[K20,K25] Therefore shall her plagues come in one day,
death, and mourning, and famine; and she shall be utterly
burned with fire: for strong is the Lord God who judgeth her.
18:11 And the merchants of the earth shall weep and mourn
over her; for no man buyeth their merchandise any more.
18:14 And the fruits that thy soul lusted after are departed
from thee, and all things which were dainty and goodly are
departed from thee, and thou shalt find them no more at all.
18:15 The merchants of these things, which were made rich
by her, shall stand afar off for the fear of her torment,
weeping and wailing,

> 18:16 And saying, Alas, alas, that great city, that was clothed
> in fine linen, and purple, and scarlet, and decked with gold,
> and precious stones, and pearls!
> 18:1 And after these things I saw another angel come down
> from heaven, having great power; and the earth was
> lightened with his glory.
> 18:2 And he cried mightily with a strong voice, saying,
> Babylon the great is fallen, is fallen, and is become the
> habitation of devils, and the hold of every foul spirit, and a
> cage of every unclean and hateful bird.
> 18:3 For all nations have drunk of the wine of the wrath of
> her fornication, and the kings of the earth have committed
> fornication with her, and the merchants of the earth are
> waxed rich through the abundance of her delicacies.
> 18:4 And I heard another voice from heaven, saying, Come
> out of her, my people, that ye be not partakers of her sins,
> and that ye receive not of her plagues.
> 18:5 For her sins have reached unto heaven, and God hath
> remembered her iniquities.

The second seal begins the second half of the seven-year tribulation. This half is known as the great tribulation, because troubles intensify dramatically. A rider on a red horse is revealed, who unleashes war (6:3-4). The events pictured in the ensuing seals, trumpets, and vials are a concentrated prophecy of this time of great wrath, which must occur before the second coming of Christ.

Who is the rider on the red horse? He appeared previously as the rider on the white horse (6:2 K16), the beast upon whom rode the woman of Babylon (17:3 K17). Together they jointly ruled the world for three and a half years. For the beast this alliance was one of convenience. Now he grabs the mantle of single-handed rule by launching a worldwide war.

This beast is named as such in many verses of chapter 13, which occurs later in John's vision. But to be consistent with the chronological approach, all the verses that refer to the beginning of the great tribulation are gathered in this section. They are from five different chapters.

We are told that the beast originates out of the sea, the place of chaos. He identifies with his mentor Satan, as both are said to have seven heads and ten horns (13:1, also see 12:3 K15). Upon his heads are an unstated name of blasphemy (13:1). The dragon, who is Satan (see

K01), has been grooming this man to become dictator of the world (13:2).

The beast is the antichrist.

The seven heads are the beast and six other kings with whom he has schemed in the previous years for this moment. The six promise their direct allegiance to him, because they detest the woman of Babylon and her methods (17:16). During that time, the beast also usurped the kingships of three other nations. Thus, when he comes on the red horse to launch war, he has ten horns holding the ten crowns of the nations allied with him (17:13). The ten horns represent only seven kings at this point, because the beast has absorbed three of the kingships already. The six remaining vassal kings will be sub-rulers under the new worldwide government to be headed by the beast. He promises them this power, which they receive for the hour of the woman's overthrow (17:12). Such an interpretation is supported in the Old Testament by the prophecy of the last stage of Daniel's fourth kingdom, which is also about the great tribulation:

> Daniel 7:23 Thus he said, The fourth beast shall be the fourth kingdom upon earth, which shall be diverse from all kingdoms, and shall devour the whole earth, and shall tread it down, and break it in pieces.
> 7:24 And the ten horns out of this kingdom are ten kings that shall arise: and another shall rise after them; and he shall be diverse from the first, and he shall subdue three kings.
> 7:25 And he shall speak great words against the most High, and shall wear out the saints of the most High, and think to change times and laws: and they shall be given into his hand until a time and times and the dividing of time.

Daniel 7:25 indicates that the antichrist will rule for a time (year), plus times (two years), and the dividing of time (half a year). This matches the timeline of Revelation.

A political structure for the tribulation period was established in the first seal period. Any government must operate with layers of authority. Even a surveillance state cannot have completely uniform exercise of its power, especially if there are dozens of nations with billions of people it is trying to control. The kings of the world (in our modern day they are presidents) who were in place at the inauguration of the world government would be operating somewhat autonomously under its jurisdiction.

This accounts for the beast's ability to raise up opposition to the woman. It also explains the resistance that the beast then faces as he conducts war over the upcoming years, even from those who do not follow the true God (see K33).

The immediate goal of the beast and the six other kings is the fall of Babylon, whom they have outwardly courted but secretly hated. They do so in the space of one day (18:8) with a well-planned and sudden attack. His coalition of ten nations kill the head ruler or rulers, and eat their remains in a macabre ceremony. They set fire to the woman of Babylon and her domain (17:16, 18:8).

Money makers across the world are devastated, because Babylon's lucrative economic system is mortally crippled as a result of the woman's overthrow (18:15-16). They thereby receive immediate payback for their complete devotion to the wealth of the world, with total disregard of God who is the ultimate source of blessing.

The political and pseudo-religious system of Babylon is judged because she made all nations drink of her obsessions: promiscuity, fornication, and adultery (14:8), which she makes mandatory in her culture. The beast for his own purposes opposes this. His approach to rule will be very different. Though it is the beast, another tool of Satan, who overthrows Babylon, ultimately both the beast and Satan are fulfilling the eternal plan of God. God allows the beast to take over the woman's domain (17:17). It is the almighty's judgment upon the spirit of Babylon that it be destroyed forever (18:21 K20).

After its downfall, Babylon literally becomes the habitation of devils (18:2). Many who live there become demonically possessed. This is another divine judgment stemming from the utter wickedness of its inhabitants. The lands of the world return to their original spiritual state before Judeo-Christian influence came their way.

In my day, human beings experience demonic possession in many areas where Hindus and animists live, where the good news of Jesus Christ was never accepted. They are subject to the spiritual oppression of their hundreds of gods. This affects their day-to-day living, and often results in physical sickness and disease. This can only be overcome by fervent prayer in the name of Jesus.

If you find yourself in the future tribulation dealing with such oppression, you must flee to a far corner of the world, at the edges of the government's reach. Follow God's admonition and "come out of her, my people, that ye be not partakers of her sins, and that ye receive not of her plagues" (18:4-5). Ask others to pray for you in the power of Jesus, the son of God. Otherwise, in the rest of your days on earth you will only experience the coming plagues, especially the greatest earthquake in history that will raze Babylon's capital city to the ground (16:18-19 K39).

For pretribulational commentators who treat the first half of the tribulation as the seventh kingdom of 17:10 K02, this action of the beast in throwing off the woman is the beginning of the eighth and final kingdom. In my second book I will make the case that the prophecies of K02 might be satisfied if the beast's action is a *continuation* of the eighth. There we will also find the possible identity of the missing seventh kingdom. We will also discuss the question, who might the antichrist be?

K22

The smoke of Babylon

> 18:9 And the kings of the earth, who have committed
> fornication and lived deliciously with her, shall bewail her,
> and lament for her, when they shall see the smoke of her
> burning,
> 18:10 Standing afar off for the fear of her torment, saying,
> Alas, alas, that great city Babylon, that mighty city! for in
> one hour is thy judgment come.
> 18:17 For in one hour so great riches is come to nought. And
> every shipmaster, and all the company in ships, and sailors,
> and as many as trade by sea, stood afar off,
> 18:18 And cried when they saw the smoke of her burning,
> saying, What city is like unto this great city!
> 18:19 And they cast dust on their heads, and cried, weeping
> and wailing, saying, Alas, alas, that great city, wherein were
> made rich all that had ships in the sea by reason of her
> costliness! for in one hour is she made desolate.
> 19:1 And after these things I heard a great voice of much
> people in heaven, saying, Alleluia; Salvation, and glory, and
> honour, and power, unto the Lord our God:
> 19:2 For true and righteous are his judgments: for he hath
> judged the great whore, which did corrupt the earth with her
> fornication, and hath avenged the blood of his servants at
> her hand.
> 19:3 And again they said, Alleluia. And her smoke rose up for
> ever and ever.
> 18:20 Rejoice over her, thou heaven, and ye holy apostles
> and prophets; for God hath avenged you on her.
> 19:4 And the four and twenty elders and the four beasts fell
> down and worshipped God that sat on the throne, saying,
> Amen; Alleluia.

In the previous section, the beast and his allies started the great fire of Babylon (17:16 K21). Over a period of days and weeks this will completely burn up the treasures of the woman's capital.

The allies of the woman see the smoke of the burning city, and cry out with the greatest agony and regret. They know that their godless empire of pleasure, luxury, and control is done, never to rise again. How painful is the hour of punishment when it is too late for mercy. Those whose lives are based on trade with Babylon also lament. Their mourning is not for the city. It is because their source of wealth is also at an end.

Christ warned against making the riches of this world into an idol:

> Matthew 6:19 Lay not up for yourselves treasures upon earth, where moth and rust doth corrupt, and where thieves break through and steal:
> 6:20 But lay up for yourselves treasures in heaven, where neither moth nor rust doth corrupt, and where thieves do not break through nor steal:
> 6:21 For where your treasure is, there will your heart be also.

True riches consist of the treasure of faith, devotion, and service for God, which are laid up in heaven.

The fire and smoke are God's righteous judgment on Babylon for the blood of the martyrs. The destruction by fire fatally cripples the city and the woman's world system.

The ones who died in Babylon's persecution (17:6 K20) affirm God's judgment when they see the smoke of the city (19:1-2, 18:20). It burns itself out on earth, but in a spiritual dimension it rises forever and ever, signifying eternal judgment against the woman and her spirit of empire (19:3). Uniting with the martyrs are those who were resurrected to heaven earlier in the rapture: the holy apostles and prophets, martyrs of earlier persecutions, and the entire church as represented by the twenty-four elders (19:4, 4:4 K14). They are joined by the four living creatures, who we saw represent different aspects of divine majesty (4:6 K14).

If we understand the geography of Revelation to have centers at both Jerusalem and the capital of the renewed Roman empire, it is the latter city that is burned. This leaves Jerusalem as the focal point of the great tribulation. The two witnesses are still active there, and special events will soon transpire in the Jewish temple.

K23

The supremacy of the beast

> 13:3 And I saw one of his heads as it were wounded to death; and his deadly wound was healed: and all the world wondered after the beast.
> 13:4 And they worshipped the dragon which gave power unto the beast: and they worshipped the beast, saying, Who is like unto the beast? who is able to make war with him?
> 13:5 And there was given unto him a mouth speaking great things and blasphemies; and power was given unto him to continue forty and two months.
> 13:6 And he opened his mouth in blasphemy against God, to blaspheme his name, and his tabernacle, and them that dwell in heaven.
> 13:7 And it was given unto him to make war with the saints, and to overcome them: and power was given him over all kindreds, and tongues, and nations.
> 13:8 And all that dwell upon the earth shall worship him, whose names are not written in the book of life of the Lamb slain from the foundation of the world.
> 13:9 If any man have an ear, let him hear.
> 13:10 He that leadeth into captivity shall go into captivity: he that killeth with the sword must be killed with the sword. Here is the patience and the faith of the saints.

The antichrist, whom Revelation knows as the beast, has overthrown the woman of Babylon and her closest allies. He now takes on his new role as head ruler of all nations (13:7).

We are told that one of his heads was wounded (13:3). Evidently the wound was inflicted recently in battle. Out of the seven heads, the one mortally wounded was the beast's own, and not one of the six kings allied with him. Despite the wound appearing to be fatal, the beast survives. The news spreads quickly, and his miraculous recovery is taken as evidence of the beast's divine power. This would not be true if the wounded head was one of the allied kings, or if the wounded head merely symbolized just one of the allied nations being wiped out during the day that Babylon was struck down.

People are awestruck. They know that the beast is devoted to the dragon, who both get credit for the miraculous survival. Most begin to worship and devote themselves to the dragon and the beast (13:4). Don't they realize that the dragon is Satan? We know that fact from section K01. Unfortunately, most are deceived into thinking that the dragon and beast are worthy of their loyalty.

The beast not only welcomes this worship, he enforces it and makes it the mandatory world religion (13:8). The dragon takes the position of God, and the beast is the dragon's messiah figure. This was prophesied by Daniel:

> Daniel 11:36 And the king shall do according to his will; and he shall exalt himself, and magnify himself above every god, and shall speak marvellous things against the God of gods, and shall prosper till the indignation be accomplished: for that that is determined shall be done.
> 11:37 Neither shall he regard the God of his fathers, nor the desire of women, nor regard any god: for he shall magnify himself above all.
> 11:38 But in his estate shall he honour the God of forces: and a god whom his fathers knew not shall he honour with gold, and silver, and with precious stones, and pleasant things.
> 11:39 Thus shall he do in the most strong holds with a strange god, whom he shall acknowledge and increase with glory: and he shall cause them to rule over many, and shall divide the land for gain.

Note that the beast does not use his quick defeat of Babylon to declare peace on earth.

Instead, with his supreme power, he and his government start an intense disinformation campaign of blasphemies against the true God, the Bible, the raptured Christians, and the saving news of the gospel (13:5-6).

The beast also blasphemes the tabernacle (13:6), which is another name for the temple of God in Jerusalem (11:1-2 K18). In doing so, and by allowing an image of himself to be worshipped (in the next section K24), the beast manifestly abrogates the seven-year treaty that he and the woman of Babylon made with Israel when they came to power at the beginning of the tribulation (Daniel 9:27 K18). He unilaterally nullifies the treaty that he had solemnly sworn to uphold, even though the treaty period is only halfway done. He thus revokes his earlier agreement that the Jews could worship in the temple they rebuilt. His ostentatious blasphemies are part of his ongoing antisemitic propaganda campaign. He also commands his non-Jewish followers to take full control of Jerusalem, as Jesus predicted would happen:

> Luke 21:24 *And they shall fall by the edge of the sword, and shall be led away captive into all nations:* and Jerusalem shall be trodden down of the Gentiles, until the times of the Gentiles be fulfilled.

He also makes war on the saints scattered across all nations (13:7), thus targeting for death those who have recently decided to trust their eternal lives to Jesus Christ (13:7). From the beginning of time, God predestined them to be saved, by the blood of his son who died on the cross for their sins (13:8b). The almighty encourages them to persevere, by promising that their tormenters who wield the sword against them will have the same done in return (13:10).

A verse that is difficult to understand is the first part of 13:8. It says *all* that dwell upon the earth, except for the tribulation saints, *shall* worship the beast. We will see in upcoming sections (6:8 K25, 9:18 K33) he still has numerous opponents remaining across the world, whom he continues to war against. The word *shall* here tells us that some only half-heartedly worship the beast, others are compelled to worship after he defeats them, others he kills outright. Hopefully many will repent during the wars and turn to Christ.

Christ's millennial reign is still in the future (see K44). This satanic counterfeit of Christ's coming rule is permitted by God in a final display of evil. The antichrist's rule over all nations continues for the three and a half years of the great tribulation (13:5). But the dictatorship of the beast struggles with a prolonged rebellion against its world government. We shall see that it will be Christ who bring the wars to a conclusion at his second coming (19:15 K38). Shortly thereafter he will terminate the reign of the beast (19:20 K40).

K24

The false prophet upholds the beast

13:11 And I beheld another beast coming up out of the earth; and he had two horns like a lamb, and he spake as a dragon.
13:12 And he exerciseth all the power of the first beast before him, and causeth the earth and them which dwell therein to worship the first beast, whose deadly wound was healed.
13:13 And he doeth great wonders, so that he maketh fire come down from heaven on the earth in the sight of men,
13:14 And deceiveth them that dwell on the earth by the means of those miracles which he had power to do in the sight of the beast; saying to them that dwell on the earth, that they should make an image to the beast, which had the wound by a sword, and did live.
13:15 And he had power to give life unto the image of the beast, that the image of the beast should both speak, and cause that as many as would not worship the image of the beast should be killed.
13:16 And he causeth all, both small and great, rich and poor, free and bond, to receive a mark in their right hand, or in their foreheads:
13:17 And that no man might buy or sell, save he that had the mark, or the name of the beast, or the number of his name.
13:18 Here is wisdom. Let him that hath understanding count the number of the beast: for it is the number of a man; and his number is Six hundred threescore and six.
14:12 Here is the patience of the saints: here are they that keep the commandments of God, and the faith of Jesus.
20:4‡[K43] *And I saw thrones, and they sat upon them, and judgment was given unto them:* and I saw the souls of them that were beheaded for the witness of Jesus, and for the word of God, and which had not worshipped the beast, neither his image, neither had received his mark upon their foreheads, or in their hands; *and they lived and reigned with Christ a thousand years.*
14:13 And I heard a voice from heaven saying unto me, Write, Blessed are the dead which die in the Lord from henceforth: Yea, saith the Spirit, that they may rest from their labours; and their works do follow them.

The beast's closest collaborator now comes on the scene (13:11). He is described as another beast. We will meet him again in 16:13 K38, 19:20 K40, and 20:10 K45. There he is identified as *the false prophet.*

Whereas the first beast is a charismatic military-political chief, this second beast is a religious leader. We know this from his title of "prophet." But he is a false one, because he does not speak the word of almighty God in heaven. Instead, his words are motivated by the power of Satan. We also know he is a religious leader from his similarity to a lamb (13:11). In the Old Testament the lamb was the preferred sacrificial animal that Jews brought to the temple in Jerusalem to atone for their sins before God. We will see that the false prophet, unlike Jesus, certainly does *not* offer himself up for the sins of the people.

The false prophet is completely loyal to the beast. He is deputy to him in authority, brings down fire from the sky, and works other signs and wonders by the power of the beast, whose fatal wound is miraculously healed (13:12-13, see 13:4 K23). The only thing we know about the false prophet's past is that he is from the earth (13:11). In my second book, I will discuss his possible identity.

He compels the people to make an image of the beast (13:14). He then is able to animate the image, so that upon examination it seems to be fully alive (13:15). This last miracle is totally persuasive to most people. They join in worshipping the image. It becomes the center of the false worship of the world ruler. This is the well-known "*abomination* that causes desolation" foreseen in the following passage from Daniel, especially Daniel 12:11:

> Daniel 9:27 *And he shall confirm the covenant with many for one week:* and in the midst of the week he shall cause the sacrifice and the oblation to cease, *and for the overspreading of abominations he shall make it desolate, even until the consummation, and that determined shall be poured upon the desolate.*
> 12:11 And from the time that the daily sacrifice shall be taken away, and the abomination that maketh desolate set up, *there shall be a thousand two hundred and ninety days.*

> *12:12 Blessed is he that waiteth, and cometh to the thousand three hundred and five and thirty days.*[6]
> 9:26 *And after threescore and two weeks shall Messiah be cut off, but not for himself:* and the people of the prince that shall come shall destroy the city and the sanctuary; *and the end thereof shall be with a flood, and unto the end of the war desolations are determined.*

Daniel mentions the sacrifice and the oblation (Daniel 9:27). These are the regular liturgical rites that God mandated for the Jewish priests to perform in the Old Testament temple of Jerusalem, to atone for the sins of the people against the Almighty.

The false prophet sets up the image of the beast as counterfeit for the regular worship "in the midst of the week" (Daniel 9:27). That points to immediately after the abrogation of the treaty with the Jews at the midpoint of the seven-year tribulation. The greatest impact is made if he installs the image within the newly built Jerusalem temple, which the beast has commandeered from the Jews by breaking the treaty. We can conjecture that the normal sacrifices of the temple are replaced by the abomination of the animated image of the beast.

When John had this vision, he already knew of a precedent for such an abomination. In 167 BCE, the Greek king Antiochus IV Epiphanies desecrated the temple in Jerusalem. He set up an altar to Zeus, and sacrificed a pig upon it. He also killed many Jews, sold others into slavery, outlawed circumcision, decreed that Jews must sacrifice to pagan gods and eat pig meat. But at the time there was no treaty with Israel for seven years. So that historical event was only a partial foreshadowing of the end-time Daniel's prophecy.

But the prophecy will be fulfilled in its entirety in this section of Revelation. Many of the beast's followers come to Jerusalem to take over the city and the temple, destroying much in the process (Daniel 9:26).

---

[6] Daniel mentions periods of 1,290 and 1,335 days in connection with the great tribulation, instead of the 1,260 days or forty-two months of Revelation. See Appendix B for a plausible explanation that takes all those numbers literally.

The worship of the beast within the holy precincts of the temple of God was also prophesied by the apostle Paul. The antichrist beast's intention is to assume the place of the true God, to become god in his own right:

> 2 Thessalonians 2:3 Let no man deceive you by any means: for that day shall not come, except there come a falling away first, and that man of sin be revealed, the son of perdition;
> 2:4 Who opposeth and exalteth himself above all that is called God, or that is worshipped; so that he as God sitteth in the temple of God, shewing himself that he is God.

Those who refuse to worship the image are targeted for death (13:15). In the next section K25, famine and death will start the *desolation* that will be the consequence of the desecration of the holy temple.

Jesus has already warned the Jews of the future Jerusalem not to try any accommodation with the false prophet. They must flee. And Jesus will save them:

> Matthew 24:15 When ye therefore shall see the abomination of desolation, spoken of by Daniel the prophet, stand in the holy place, (whoso readeth, let him understand:)
> 24:16 Then let them which be in Judaea flee into the mountains:
> 24:17 Let him which is on the housetop not come down to take any thing out of his house:
> 24:18 Neither let him which is in the field return back to take his clothes.
> 24:19 And woe unto them that are with child, and to them that give suck in those days!
> 24:20 But pray ye that your flight be not in the winter, neither on the sabbath day:
> 24:30 And then shall appear the sign of the Son of man in heaven: and then shall all the tribes of the earth mourn, and they shall see the Son of man coming in the clouds of heaven with power and great glory.
> 24:31 And he shall send his angels with a great sound of a trumpet, and they shall gather together his elect from the four winds, from one end of heaven to the other.

Now we come to the infamous mark of the beast (13:16-17).

When the beast came to supreme power riding the red horse (6:4 K21), he destroyed the lucrative economic system of Babylon which he despised. His armies were not successful at immediately subduing all opposition, though, and a protracted war began across the world (13:7-8 K23). In these circumstances, with no working substitute for the old supply chains, there will be severe shortages of all goods. Rationing is unavoidable. In the next section (K25) we will see widespread famine and death among the civilian population.

The beast has no interest in creating a rationing system that we would regard as equitable. He will use rationing as a tool of war. The false prophet, acting as the beast's deputy and minister of religion, implements the mark of the beast system for this purpose. The mark is some kind of token issued only to qualifying beast worshippers. This identification will be necessary to conduct business and to purchase the necessities of life. It is another device to compel people to worship the beast. It will prove useful in blaming Christ followers for shortages, and stirring the people of the world into a frenzy to attack them.

There has been much speculation over the centuries on what the mark may be. The usual candidate is the latest controversial technology that could be used by governments to control people. Such speculation will undoubtedly continue until the rapture occurs. It is thus premature to dwell on this topic. But if you are reading this after the rapture, this subject will become critical. The one clue that we get in 13:16-17 is that the mark will be applied on the right hand or on the forehead, and might also display a special number.

The spiritual purpose of the mark as a means of identification is to easily target new Christ believers for death, those who refuse it. Just as Satan sought to kill the baby Jesus by the hand of King Herod's soldiers, he still wants to eradicate Jews and new Christians here in the tribulation. He thinks that by doing so he can forestall the second coming of Christ and defeat him in advance.

That brings us to the number of the beast, 666 (13:18).

Many have attempted to come up with a mathematical computation that results in this number, with allusions to the Bible. For example, 666 is said to signify "Caesar Nero" in Hebrew קסר נרון (Qsr Nrwn). In the ancient Hebrew alphabet, where decimal numbers were not known, certain round numbers were associated with different letters. This is similar to the way Roman numerals were constructed. When such numbers for Qsr Nrwn are added together, 666 is the total:[7]

ן	ו	ר	נ	ר	ס	ק
50	6	200	50	200	60	100

Total: 666

In 64 CE the emperor Nero set fire to his own capital city of Rome, blamed the Christians for it, and burned them on crosses as punishment. In this interpretation, Nero is the figure behind 666. He will return as the beast in the tribulation to reestablish the Roman empire and persecute the believers on a greater scale.

There are dozens of other calculations like this that refer to other candidates for the beast.

A much better interpretation is to see that the number six in the Bible represents man, his rebellion, imperfection, sin, and weakness. For example, the number six occurs in these biblical contexts:

- Man was created on day six of creation week.
- Men are appointed six days to labor.
- God flooded the whole world when Noah was six hundred years old (Genesis 7:6,11).
- The sixth commandment is "thou shalt not murder" (Exodus 20:13, Deuteronomy 5:17).
- There was darkness over the world at the sixth hour (Hebrew time, after dawn) when Christ was hanging on the cross (Matthew 27:45).[8]

---

[7] Peter Goeman, *The Mark of the Beast, 666, and Nero (Rev 13:18)*, August 1, 2020, https://petergoeman.com/the-mark-of-the-beast-666-and-nero-rev-1318/, accessed April 29, 2022.

[8] *How Long was Jesus on the Cross*, no author, https://www.gotquestions.org/Jesus-on-the-cross.html, accessed September 16, 2022.

- Jesus suffered on the cross for six hours (Mark 15:25, Matthew 27:46-50)

The number six is also how many times Jesus was charged with being a devil:

- Mark 3:22 and Matthew 12:24: "He hath Beelzebub."
- John 7:20: "Thou hast a devil."
- John 8:48: "Say we not well that...Thou hast a devil?"
- John 8:52: "Now we know that Thou hast a devil."
- John 10:20: "He hath a devil, and is mad."
- Luke 11:15: "He casteth out devils by Beelzebub."

In the Greek that John wrote, verse 13:18 gives the number of the beast using the Greek symbols for 600, 60 and 6. (The decimal system that we have was unknown in Greek literature of the New Testament period.)

If we focus on the three sixes, we can see that the number of the beast is the number of man in triplicate. It is a counterfeit trinity. Each digit falls just short of the biblically perfect number seven. Let us consider each digit in turn.

First, Satan has always schemed to take over control of the universe and turn God into a being whose time has passed (see Appendix A). In contrast to the Holy Trinity of the Bible, in the fake 666 trinity Satan takes the place of God the Father.

Second, because of Satan's principled opposition to God having a son (John 3:16), in the tribulation he raises up the beast as the antichrist messiah alternative to Jesus.

The third audacious substitution is the false prophet for the Holy Spirit. The false prophet inspires awe and worship by ostentatiously performing miracles before large numbers of people, presumably with the aid of mass media. In contrast, Jesus did miraculous things, but whenever he was asked to perform a miracle in order to prove his divinity, he refused. For example:

> Mark 8:11 And the Pharisees came forth, and began to question with him, seeking of him a sign from heaven, tempting him.

> 8:12 And he sighed deeply in his spirit, and saith, Why doth this generation seek after a sign? verily I say unto you, There shall no sign be given unto this generation.

Before Jesus went to the cross, he promised the Holy Spirit would come in his place:

> John 16:13 Howbeit when he, the Spirit of truth, is come, he will guide you into all truth: for he shall not speak of himself; but whatsoever he shall hear, that shall he speak: and he will shew you things to come.
> 16:14 He shall glorify me: for he shall receive of mine, and shall shew it unto you.

The Holy Spirit is the third person of the trinitarian God. He is God making a home in the heart of every believer. He operates secretly without conspicuous display:

> 1 Corinthians 3:16 Know ye not that ye are the temple of God, and that the Spirit of God dwelleth in you?

Jesus also sends the Holy Spirit to be our comforter in times of trouble:

> John 14:16 And I will pray the Father, and he shall give you another Comforter, that he may abide with you for ever;
> 14:17 Even the Spirit of truth; whom the world cannot receive, because it seeth him not, neither knoweth him: but ye know him; for he dwelleth with you, and shall be in you.

The Holy Spirit prays for us when we know not what to pray:

> Romans 8:26 Likewise the Spirit also helpeth our infirmities: for we know not what we should pray for as we ought: but the Spirit itself maketh intercession for us with groanings which cannot be uttered.
> 8:27 And he that searcheth the hearts knoweth what is the mind of the Spirit, because he maketh intercession for the saints according to the will of God.

In Satan's trinity, the false prophet does not have such divine power. He has no interest in providing the comfort, secret presence, and compassionate prayers that the Holy Spirit gives to those who believe. His only means of persuasion is to perform impressive miracles. But they cannot give us the peace that God's Holy Spirit gives.

In Revelation, all three members of the unholy trinity are beasts. The beast who is also the angel of the bottomless pit is Satan (9:11 K32, 11:7 K34). The beast out of the sea is the world ruling beast (13:1 K21). And the beast out of the earth is the false prophet (13:11).

Another supporting interpretation of the number 666 is that it represents Satan's goal to overcome his fall from heaven, which took place in verses 12:3-4 of section K01. A third of the angels rebelled alongside him and were also expelled from the presence of the Almighty. This event occurred not long after God created Adam and Eve. If Satan can find a way to be victorious over God and the righteous angels, through the actions of the beast and the false prophet, he will achieve equality and even superiority over God and his son Jesus. Satan therefore aggressively claims 666 as his due, his final intention to cancel his early defeat at the hands of the two-thirds of God's holy angels.

To conclude with a last thought on the number of the beast 666 – it represents the ultimate system that mankind can produce without God, under the influence of his chief adversary. Sinful man's hatred to the Lord Jesus is thus branded three times over with man's number.

The beast, the false prophet, and their new policies for the world government increases the persecution of Christ followers to the most violent level ever. In 14:12 God encourages all his followers who maintain their patience amidst the suffering. He exhorts you to cling to your faith in Christ, and follow the path of discipleship by obeying his commands. Some of you will face martyrdom, and some will go into hiding, face severe hunger and thirst. But your lot is far preferable to those who accept the easy way and worship the beast.

You who are put to death will go through the agony of losing your physical lives. But in 20:4 the promise is that your souls will immediately be taken to heaven, you who will be "beheaded for the witness of Jesus." (I will discuss the significance of the mention of beheading in my second book). You will sit on magnificent thrones prepared by God. You earn this place because you have not worshipped the beast, neither have you received his mark upon your foreheads, nor in your hands. At the end of the great tribulation in section K43, you will receive God's favorable judgment of the righteous. You will be ushered into the millennial kingdom to reign with Christ. As Jesus said in Matthew:

> Matthew 7:14 Because strait is the gate, and narrow is the way, which leadeth unto life, and few there be that find it.
> 5:10 Blessed are they which are persecuted for righteousness' sake: for theirs is the kingdom of heaven.

If you have turned to Christ during the great tribulation, do not be afraid. The words of 14:13 should give you comfort: "blessed are the dead which die in the Lord from henceforth." You will rest from your labors, and your new found faith in Jesus Christ will follow you into the millennium, and then to the new heaven and new earth.

K25

Famine and death upon a fourth of men under the beast's rule

> 18:8‡[K20,K21] Therefore shall her plagues come *in one day,* death, and mourning, and famine; *and she shall be utterly burned with fire:* for strong is the Lord God who judgeth her.
> 6:5 And when he had opened the third seal, I heard the third beast say, Come and see. And I beheld, and lo a black horse; and he that sat on him had a pair of balances in his hand.
> 6:6 And I heard a voice in the midst of the four beasts say, A measure of wheat for a penny, and three measures of barley for a penny; and see thou hurt not the oil and the wine.
> 6:7 And when he had opened the fourth seal, I heard the voice of the fourth beast say, Come and see.
> 6:8 And I looked, and behold a pale horse: and his name that sat on him was Death, and Hell followed with him. And power was given unto them over the fourth part of the earth, to kill with sword, and with hunger, and with death, and with the beasts of the earth.

The war that started with the beast's overthrow of Babylon does not come to a quick conclusion. Despite the rationing system based on the mark of the beast, despite the killing of Jesus followers who are blamed for shortages, war continues. As the conflict mounts, a rider on a black horse appears, who brings famine to those who survived the fire of Babylon (18:8), and to the whole world. This is the third seal (6:5). Then a rider on a pale horse brings death. That is the fourth seal (6:7).

This famine and death are the first plagues sent upon the world as judgment on the godless Babylon system. The abomination of 13:15 K24 now indeed causes *desolation*:

> Daniel 9:27 *And he shall confirm the covenant with many for one week: and in the midst of the week he shall cause the sacrifice and the oblation to cease,* and for the overspreading of abominations he shall make it desolate, even until the consummation, and that determined shall be poured upon the desolate.

A fourth part of all people perish by war and hunger. These are billions of men, women, and children. Out of the world's population at the beginning of the great tribulation, at least 25% have now died.

Many of these are targeted because they turned from the beast and put their trust in Christ. Others die in battle against the beast's armies, or are collateral victims as civilians. Perhaps some are you followers of Jesus who are defending the earthly lives of your families, friends, and homelands. But I think that by this time most of you who have converted to Christ are looking forward to the blessings after martyrdom.

The war continues at such scale, undoubtedly because of substantial military resistance from nations that nominally swore their allegiance to the previous world government, which was jointly ruled by the woman of Babylon and the beast. These resisters do not turn to God, but neither do they worship the beast. How could this be, if Satan has finally achieved his dream of being the ruler of the world?

I have already mentioned how a political structure for the tribulation period was established in the first three and half years, and that the kings (presidents) of the nations who pledged obedience to the woman and the beast at the inauguration of the world government would be operating somewhat autonomously. All of them are rebels against the almighty God of heaven. In this sense they are all inspired by Satan. But they certainly do not agree with one another, and many of them seek to maximize their own glory and power at the expense of the others. They would oppose the woman and the beast in any area they felt they could get away with. They display sinful human nature at its extreme, in this most extreme period of history.

Satan has worked through such leaders throughout time. In just one example, in the 11th century, Mahmud, the Muslim sultan of Ghazni in eastern Afghanistan, made 17 raids deep into India. He slaughtered Hindus, pillaged their cities, destroyed their temples, and carried away the accumulated treasures of centuries. Muslim historian Mahomed Kasim Firishta in the 16th century proudly recorded that by his day over 400 million Hindus had been killed. India's population had dropped catastrophically to only 200 million.

Islam and Hinduism are religions that have persecuted Christians at many times in their history. It can be said that Satan is the spiritual inspiration behind both. Yet they despise each other.

Satan may be the first progenitor of evil, but he is not divine, all-powerful, or present at all times in every place. He cannot know the future. Therefore, he does not have all of eternity planned in advance. Those are all attributes unique to the almighty God of heaven. Satan wishes he had that kind of power. He has to settle for pointing his followers into any convenient direction of rebellion against God. He chooses not to support a single unified movement. His strategy has always been to spawn multiple movements, as long as they oppose the true God of the Bible and his son Jesus Christ. The result is that his confederates sometimes work at cross purposes.

There is a biblical passage that describes this perfectly. Many do not realize this, because it was quoted in a totally different context by Abraham Lincoln before the American civil war of the 19th century. He used it as an illustration of how the institution of slavery was corroding the morals of the United States:

> Mark 3:23 And he [Jesus] called them unto him, and said
> unto them in parables, How can Satan cast out Satan?
> 3:24 And if a kingdom be divided against itself, that kingdom
> cannot stand.
> 3:25 And if a house be divided against itself, that house
> cannot stand.
> 3:26 if Satan rise up against himself, and be divided, he
> cannot stand, but hath an end.

The actual biblical backdrop of this passage was Jesus defending himself against accusations that he was performing miracles by the power of Satan. He spoke these words as a parable. I believe the parable's spiritual interpretation is this: Jesus was contrasting his kingdom, which will stand forever, with that of Satan. Satan's kingdom will not last because of the words Lincoln made famous – a house divided against itself cannot stand.

This explains why the great tribulation, the time when Satan is at the pinnacle of his rule, is a time of continuous war, famine and death. He knows that his kingdom over men and women is flawed with contradiction. But by it he satisfies his goal of eradicating as many billions of people as possible. He is content to have full control over his legions of fallen angels. He believes that by way of the beast and his war, he will find a means to thwart the Almighty's plans. He will then scheme to take over God's place as the effective ruler of the universe.

K26

The martyrs' plea for retribution

6:9 And when he had opened the fifth seal, I saw under the
altar the souls of them that were slain for the word of God,
and for the testimony which they held.
12:11 And they overcame him [the accuser] by the blood of
the Lamb, and by the word of their testimony; and they
loved not their lives unto the death.
6:11 And white robes were given unto every one of them; and
it was said unto them, that they should rest yet for a little
season, until their fellowservants also and their brethren,
that should be killed as they were, should be fulfilled.
7:9 After this I beheld, and, lo, a great multitude, which no
man could number, of all nations, and kindreds, and people,
and tongues, stood before the throne, and before the Lamb,
clothed with white robes, and palms in their hands;
7:10 And cried with a loud voice, saying, Salvation to our
God which sitteth upon the throne, and unto the Lamb.
7:11 And all the angels stood round about the throne, and
about the elders and the four beasts, and fell before the
throne on their faces, and worshipped God,
7:12 Saying, Amen: Blessing, and glory, and wisdom, and
thanksgiving, and honour, and power, and might, be unto
our God for ever and ever. Amen.
6:10 And they cried with a loud voice, saying, How long, O
Lord, holy and true, dost thou not judge and avenge our
blood on them that dwell on the earth?
7:13 And one of the elders answered, saying unto me, What
are these which are arrayed in white robes? and whence
came they?
7:14 And I said unto him, Sir, thou knowest. And he said to
me, These are they which came out of great tribulation, and
have washed their robes, and made them white in the blood
of the Lamb.
7:15 Therefore are they before the throne of God, and serve
him day and night in his temple: and he that sitteth on the
throne shall dwell among them.
7:16 They shall hunger no more, neither thirst any more;
neither shall the sun light on them, nor any heat.
7:17 For the Lamb which is in the midst of the throne shall
feed them, and shall lead them unto living fountains of
waters: and God shall wipe away all tears from their eyes.

The vision now shifts to heaven, with the opening of the fifth seal. There we see arrivals of those whose blood was shed during the tribulation. They are received under the heavenly altar (6:9). This echoes the blood sacrifices of the Old Testament, which were poured out under the altar of the earthly temple.

They are surrounded by the church saints in their glorified bodies, who came to heaven earlier in the rapture (5:9-10 K14). One of the elders, who represent the church (4:4 K14), raises the question, where did these new arrivals come from (7:13)? He then provides the answer.

During the great tribulation, those who refuse to worship the beast, and turn to Jesus Christ instead, are on the high priority list to be hunted down and eliminated. Though they die in body, their souls are taken to heaven. Because of their testimony for Christ, they are given white robes, symbols of righteousness (6:11).

Some of these martyrs are Jews, an unknown number of whom give their lives. They left behind the Jews who refused the offer of salvation, and the 144,000 Jewish evangelists who were sealed in safety for the tribulation (7:3-4, Zechariah 8:20-23 K18). But the vast multitude are gentiles, or non-Jews, from all nations, people groups and languages (7:9). The good news of Jesus Christ is able to transform individual hearts in even the most hardened groups of people. They hold palm branches before the throne of God. This is an echo of how Christ's followers greeted him during his first coming, when he made his triumphal entry into Jerusalem on Palm Sunday the week before he was crucified. The martyrs then join into a heavenly chorus of praise to God and his son (7:10-12).

They achieve victory through Christ, who shed his blood on the cross for them. By his sacrifice, Jesus has washed their robes with his blood, and made them white as snow (7:14). Blood is the symbol of life and salvation in many passages of the Bible:

> Leviticus 17:14a For it is the life of all flesh; the blood of it is for the life thereof.
>
> Hebrews 9:22b without shedding of blood is no remission.

> Romans 5:8 But God commendeth his love toward us, in that, while we were yet sinners, Christ died for us.
> 5:9 Much more then, being now justified by his blood, we shall be saved from wrath through him.

The blood of Christ makes his followers spiritually pure before the Father in heaven. Because of Christ, God accepts the tribulation saints, despite the sins they committed in the past. Jesus' sacrifice nullifies all the accusations Satan makes against them. Their final testimony to the world is this: they trust they will be with Christ forever. They trade death for eternity (12:11).

The martyrs, now in heaven, have not yet received glorified bodies. That will occur later in 20:4 K43. Though they are bodiless souls at this time, they are given white robes (6:11). They as spirit creatures wear them as the two angels did who witnessed to the resurrection and ascension of Jesus at his first coming (John 20:12, Acts 1:10). With these robes they have rest, in a place of prominence and honor before God, serving him continually (7:15). They will always be provided for (7:16). They will be delivered from all the afflictions of their previous life, and Jesus will dwell among them (7:17).

The martyrs then join together to cry out for God to avenge their deaths, and for him to judge their murderers who remain on earth (6:10). Their appeal is in the same spirit as the Psalmist, who frequently called on God to assert holiness and visit judgment on those who revel in sin. Psalm 94 is one example.

> Psalm 94:1 O Lord God, to whom vengeance belongeth; O God, to whom vengeance belongeth, shew thyself.
> 94:2 Lift up thyself, thou judge of the earth: render a reward to the proud.
> 94:3 Lord, how long shall the wicked, how long shall the wicked triumph?
> 94:4 How long shall they utter and speak hard things? and all the workers of iniquity boast themselves?
> 94:5 They break in pieces thy people, O Lord, and afflict thine heritage.
> 94:6 They slay the widow and the stranger, and murder the fatherless.
> 94:7 Yet they say, The Lord shall not see, neither shall the God of Jacob regard it.

> 94:11 The Lord knoweth the thoughts of man, that they are vanity.
> 94:16 Who will rise up for me against the evildoers? or who will stand up for me against the workers of iniquity?
>
> 94:21 They gather themselves together against the soul of the righteous, and condemn the innocent blood.
> 94:22 But the Lord is my defence; and my God is the rock of my refuge.
> 94:23 And he shall bring upon them their own iniquity, and shall cut them off in their own wickedness; yea, the Lord our God shall cut them off.

They now watch for God to act, while they wait for the complete number of tribulation martyrs to join them.

K27

God signals retribution with heavenly omens and earthquake

> 6:12 And I beheld when he had opened the sixth seal, and, lo,
> there was a great earthquake; and the sun became black as
> sackcloth of hair, and the moon became as blood;
> 6:13 And the stars of heaven fell unto the earth, even as a fig
> tree casteth her untimely figs, when she is shaken of a
> mighty wind.
> 6:14 And the heaven departed as a scroll when it is rolled
> together; and every mountain and island were moved out of
> their places.
> 6:15 And the kings of the earth, and the great men, and the
> rich men, and the chief captains, and the mighty men, and
> every bondman, and every free man, hid themselves in the
> dens and in the rocks of the mountains;
> 6:16 And said to the mountains and rocks, Fall on us, and
> hide us from the face of him that sitteth on the throne, and
> from the wrath of the Lamb:
> 6:17 For the great day of his wrath is come; and who shall be
> able to stand?

The sixth seal (6:12) is God's immediate response to the martyrs' plea for retribution. It is an awesome and cosmic response. But incredibly, it is only a preview, and will be followed by more punishments on the antichrist and his supporters: the seventh seal, the seven trumpets and the seven vials. Beginning with the sixth seal, God is undertaking direct intervention into human affairs. The trials up till now of war, famine, death, and martyrdom, have originated in the evil heart of man. Those to come will be authored directly by God as a divine punishment upon those who dare overthrow him.

In the sixth seal, God harnesses his power over the cosmos. He miraculously and suddenly interrupts the predictable behavior of sun, the moon, even the stars of the sky (6:12-14). To the earth he brings an earthquake that moves all mountains and islands (6:12,14).

Please do not think this language is only a metaphor, and should not be taken literally. God is a miraculous God. The Bible records God's words that explain how he supernaturally created the entire universe in six days (Genesis 1). God also miraculously brought forty days of non-stop rain worldwide to judge the people of Noah's time (Genesis 7). There is much evidence put forward by creation scientists that supports both events, despite the scoffing by the secular mainstream.[9]

The earth is the centerpiece of God's creation. It is unique in being the one planet of life. He made the universe as an envelope of glory around this world of human beings created in his image. The same God who is able to create the universe in six days, and bring a worldwide flood upon the earth, can miraculously manipulate the universe at any time of his choosing. The fabric of the universe is now torn at his command – the sun is blackened, the moon becomes as blood, and blazing objects fall from the sky. He thus shows the extent of his aversion to the worst rebellion ever of his image bearers. He limits his anger for now in the physical realm where only atoms and molecules are affected. The lifelessness of the universe beyond earth will not change until he establishes the new heaven and new earth at the end of time (K47).

There is remarkable similarity between the timeline of Revelation and the words spoken by Jesus concerning the end of the age in Matthew 24. Here is the verse of Matthew that summarizes this section:

> Matthew 24:29 Immediately after the tribulation of those days shall the sun be darkened, and the moon shall not give her light, and the stars shall fall from heaven, and the powers of the heavens shall be shaken.

Jesus also spoke of the sun, moon, and stars. He did not mention an earthquake, but does say that "the powers of the heavens shall be shaken" which is strikingly similar.

I provide a complete list of Matthew 24 parallels to Revelation in Appendix C.

To survive these heavenly omens and the earthquake, the unbelievers flee to safety in underground bunkers (6:15). The rebels come from all backgrounds: men and woman, rich and poor, the powerful and the

---

[9] Modern creation science was inaugurated with the book by John C. Whitcomb and Henry M. Morris, *The Genesis Flood: The Biblical Record and its Scientific Implications*, 1961.

ordinary. Perhaps the shelters were prepared beforehand by the worldwide authorities to prepare for extreme war scenarios. Those who go see that the situation exceeds anything expected. They know instinctively that God is beginning his vengeance on them in payment for their defiance. They bitterly cry out, "who is able to stand?" (6:17) because they know it is too late to ask for mercy. They seek escape in death (6:16). However, in this death they will not be annihilated and cease all being. Instead, they will find out that they will spend body and soul in hell for all eternity.

Somehow, the events in sky and on earth are temporary, and do not immediately result in loss of life. Death will resume in the days and months to come. They will make up the "day of wrath" (6:17).

To the people of my time, I appeal to you to repent today and avoid this terrifying future. When God's grace and loving kindness has been spurned, there is nothing more certain than his judgment. But God still beckons:

> Romans 6:23 For the wages of sin is death; but the gift of God is eternal life through Jesus Christ our Lord.

Please accept Jesus Christ as your savior, so that you will not experience the terror of this retribution and the others that follow. By doing so, you will be counted as one of God's children. He will summon you to heaven before these awful events happens, in the rapture (K13). And he will bless you with new life in Christ for the rest of your days in the here and now.

K28

Silence in heaven before the wrath of God

> 8:1 And when he had opened the seventh seal, there was
> silence in heaven about the space of half an hour.
> 8:2 And I saw the seven angels which stood before God; and
> to them were given seven trumpets.
> 8:3 And another angel came and stood at the altar, having a
> golden censer; and there was given unto him much incense,
> that he should offer it with the prayers of all saints upon the
> golden altar which was before the throne.
> 8:4 And the smoke of the incense, which came with the
> prayers of the saints, ascended up before God out of the
> angel's hand.
> 8:5 And the angel took the censer, and filled it with fire of
> the altar, and cast it into the earth: and there were voices,
> and thunderings, and lightnings, and an earthquake.
> 8:6 And the seven angels which had the seven trumpets
> prepared themselves to sound.

At the opening of the seventh seal, there is complete silence in heaven (8:1). The silence is like a courtroom that is hushed before the foreman of the jury pronounces the verdict.

We would expect such silence immediately after the martyrs' plea for retribution, in the fifth seal (6:9 K26). But our guide is the chronological order of the seals, trumpets, and vials. In between that fifth seal and this seventh one, God chose to foreshadow the silence with heavenly omens and the earthquake of the sixth seal (6:12 K27). Through those omens he now has the rapt attention of every creature. That includes all in heaven, and those who have hid themselves on earth.

This is the last of the seven seals. It introduces seven angels who will be bringing the judgments of the seven trumpets (8:2,6).

Trumpets are found in many places of scripture to announce vital occasions. A trumpet was sounded before God summoned Moses to the top of Mount Sinai to receive the ten commandments (Exodus 19:19). The walls of Jericho fell at the sound of trumpets (Joshua 6:20). The rapture of the church believers into heaven was signaled by the sound of the trumpet of God (1 Thessalonians 4:16).

Another angel then stands before the altar in heaven with a golden censer (8:3). At the end of its swinging chains is burning incense within a metallic firepot. Censers were used by the Old Testament Jewish priests for worship in the Jerusalem temple. Censers are also used by priests in churches that follow a liturgical form of worship going back to early centuries of the Christian era. God directed Moses to mix four spices to prepare incense suitable for worship: stacte, onycha, galbanum, and frankincense (Exodus 30:34). The perfumed mixture distributes a fragrant aroma. The wafting smoke is a picture of prayers arising up to heaven. It is a reminder that the prayer of believers has the character of sweet smelling perfume to the Lord. The divinely ordained blend speaks of the perfection of Christ, in whose name believers seal their prayers when they say "in Jesus' name, Amen."

But the angel's offering of incense is not a typical prayer offering. He takes the censer filled with fire and hurls it to the earth (8:5). This results in voices, thunder, lightnings, and an earthquake. This censer offers up judgment. It is in response to the prayers of the tribulation saints (8:4).

K29

God sends hail, fire, and blood

> 8:7 The first angel sounded, and there followed hail and fire
> mingled with blood, and they were cast upon the earth: and
> the third part of trees was burnt up, and all green grass was
> burnt up.
> 8:8 And the second angel sounded, and as it were a great
> mountain burning with fire was cast into the sea: and the
> third part of the sea became blood;
> 8:9 And the third part of the creatures which were in the
> sea, and had life, died; and the third part of the ships were
> destroyed.

At the sounding of the first trumpet (8:7), hail and fire fall from the sky.

The vegetation of the world is massively affected. A third of the trees and all grasses are burnt up. The hail is so devastating that it destroys not only vegetation, but wounds men and beasts caught under it. Thus, the hail gets mixed with blood (8:7). This is an echo of the seventh plague visited upon Egypt before God liberated the Jewish people, the plague of hail and fire (Exodus 9:18-26).

Do we ever thank our God in heaven for plant life on our world? He sustains all animal life by the plants and the trees. Many medicines and foods come from them. They liberate the oxygen that animals need to breathe. The tribulation enemies of God will be surprised that the judgment of the first trumpet takes away this basis for life that they took so much for granted.

At the sounding of the second trumpet (8:8), a great object like a flaming asteroid falls upon the ocean. A third of all ships are destroyed, a third of the seas become blood, and a third of all sea creatures die (8:9). It is likely that the object strikes where maximum damage can occur. This is an echo of the first plague visited on Egypt, which turned the river Nile to blood (Exodus 7:14-24).

At the time Revelation was written, objects like asteroids were unknown. Apophis is an asteroid that comes within the earth's orbit. At 450 meters in length, it would cause massive regional destruction if it were to hit the earth. In 2029, Apophis is calculated to miss earth by only 30,000 kilometers, and will temporarily descend beneath where our geostationary communications satellites are hovering.[10] The object that will strike here in Revelation could be another heavenly object that is supernaturally diverted from its usual course.

[10] Bruce Betts, *Will an Asteroid Hit Earth? Your Questions Answered*, Jun 26, 2018, https://www.planetary.org/articles/will-an-asteroid-hit-earth, accessed May 12, 2022.

K30

God sends wormwood

> 8:10 And the third angel sounded, and there fell a great star
> from heaven, burning as it were a lamp, and it fell upon the
> third part of the rivers, and upon the fountains of waters;
> 8:11 And the name of the star is called Wormwood: and the
> third part of the waters became wormwood; and many men
> died of the waters, because they were made bitter.

The third trumpet (8:10) is a favorite area of speculation in Revelation, because of the mysterious mention of wormwood. The term appears nine times in the Bible: seven times in the Old Testament, and twice here.

Wormwood is a poisonous plant with a bitter taste. It can be consumed in small quantities and has many medicinal benefits and treatments, such as pain relief, reducing arthritic conditions, and treating parasitic infections. In large quantities, wormwood initially causes a hallucinogenic reaction. Higher consumption is extremely toxic, and causes death.

In Russian the word for wormwood is Chernobyl, in Ukrainian it is Chornobyl. This is a combination of the words chornyi (black) and byllia (grass blades or stalks), hence it literally means black grass or black stalks.

On April 26, 1986, one of the reactors at the Chernobyl nuclear power plant in Soviet Ukraine exploded after unsanctioned experiments on the reactor by plant operators were done improperly. The resulting loss of control was the greatest nuclear accident in history. It was caused by design flaws of the reactor which made it prone to thermal runaway. The nearby city of Chernobyl was evacuated nine days after the disaster. Millions of people across Europe were concerned for radioactive fallout for months afterward.

People immediately started to make the connection between that disaster and the third trumpet of Revelation.

There has always been an intense interest in any present or future event which could be identified as a marker or clue that we are approaching the end times. But to do so, you would need to extract a prophecy out of its context. Here is an example of an interpretation based on such cherry picking:

Perhaps the seven trumpets as described in Revelation would not occur in rapid succession at the endtime, but have already begun, starting with the first trumpet prophesying the events of the First World War, and the second trumpet describing the Second World War. The third trumpet is the Chernobyl nuclear disaster. There is backup evidence for this, such as the second trumpet describing a conflict where one-third of the ships were sunk. Coincidentally, in WWII, out of over 100,000 ships from all the nations involved in the conflict, almost exactly one-third were sunk in combat.[11]

Evidence for Chernobyl as the third trumpet is certainly a stretch. Less than 100 deaths were attributed to the accident. Long-term death estimates range from 4,000 for the most exposed people of Ukraine, Belarus, and Russia, to 16,000 cases for Europe, to perhaps 60,000 when including relatively minor effects around the globe.

It is true that people paid attention to the Chernobyl disaster, especially the people of the Soviet Union, who overthrew their communist government just five years later. But that event should focus us on an exponentially greater judgment which will occur during this moment of the three-and-a-half year great tribulation.

The star of the third trumpet (8:10) seems to be another heavenly body from outer space, burning up as it enters the earth's atmosphere. It has a noxious composition that is prone to chemical reaction. It falls upon the rivers and waters, contaminating a third of them (8:11). This results in the worldwide interruption of water supply, and the death of millions.

When the children of Israel were brought out of Egypt, they encountered the bitter waters of Marah (Exodus 15:23-25). God showed Moses a special log, and he threw it into the water. The waters then

---

[11] Bob Downing, *Chernobyl, Wormwood, and Prophecy*, August 2011, http://www.bobdowning.org/2011/08/chernobyl-wormwood-and-prophecy.html, accessed May 13, 2022.

became sweet. Here in Revelation, the wormwood cast into sweet water makes it poison, and many die from drinking it.

This is like the contrast between Christ in his two comings. When he first came in his incarnation, he went to the cross to pay for our sin. He made what is bitter for us into the sweetness of grace and forgiveness. At his second coming, Christ will come in judgment. Whatever sweetness is left is turned to bitter.

How few of us thank God for providing water every day. We take for granted the blessings of water, the beauty of the sea, the majestic flow of great rivers, the pure fountains and springs that abound. They are all gifts from a loving God to an undeserving world. When you see the water withdrawn that you always assumed would be there, you should also think what would happen if God withdrew himself from you.

K31

God darkens the heavens

> 8:12 And the fourth angel sounded, and the third part of the sun was smitten, and the third part of the moon, and the third part of the stars; so as the third part of them was darkened, and the day shone not for a third part of it, and the night likewise.
> 8:13 And I beheld, and heard an angel flying through the midst of heaven, saying with a loud voice, Woe, woe, woe, to the inhabiters of the earth by reason of the other voices of the trumpet of the three angels, which are yet to sound!

Another blessing from God is the light of the sun, moon, and stars. He manifests his eternal power through them. King David wrote:

> Psalm 19:1 The heavens declare the glory of God; and the firmament sheweth his handywork.

The fourth trumpet (8:12) inflicts trial by way of these heavenly objects. A third part of the sun's rays and a third part of the moon's reflections are darkened. A third of the stars stop twinkling. This affects the third part of a day, and the third part of a night.

Many commentators say this could not possibly be taken literally, and is proof that most of Revelation should be interpreted symbolically.

It is impossible to say exactly how God could accomplish this darkening. We must conclude that he overcomes the physical laws of the universe, which he himself instituted, and intervenes to bring about this darkening miraculously.

There are events in the Old Testament where God supersedes the laws of physics. For example, on the first day of creation he said "let there be light" (Genesis 1:3) but he did not create the sun until the fourth day (Genesis 1:16). We can only wonder how this could be. But we can rest in the fact that God is the creator of all physical laws, and has not retreated from the universe. He will overrule them at any time of his choosing to accomplish his will.

In 8:13 the angel proclaims a triple woe upon those remaining on earth. The disruption of light from heaven is a solemn warning of even more severe punishments to come. The enemies of the Lord can no longer ignore the fact that God is dealing with them.

K32

Satan unleashes the demons from their confinement to torment unbelievers for five months

9:1‡[K15] And the fifth angel sounded, and I saw a star *fall from
heaven unto the earth: and to him was given the key of the
bottomless pit.
9:2 And he opened the bottomless pit; and there arose a
smoke out of the pit, as the smoke of a great furnace; and
the sun and the air were darkened by reason of the smoke of
the pit.
9:3 And there came out of the smoke locusts upon the earth:
and unto them was given power, as the scorpions of the
earth have power.
9:4 And it was commanded them that they should not hurt
the grass of the earth, neither any green thing, neither any
tree; but only those men which have not the seal of God in
their foreheads.
9:5 And to them it was given that they should not kill them,
but that they should be tormented five months: and their
torment was as the torment of a scorpion, when he striketh a
man.
9:6 And in those days shall men seek death, and shall not
find it; and shall desire to die, and death shall flee from
them.
9:7 And the shapes of the locusts were like unto horses
prepared unto battle; and on their heads were as it were
crowns like gold, and their faces were as the faces of men.
9:8 And they had hair as the hair of women, and their teeth
were as the teeth of lions.
9:9 And they had breastplates, as it were breastplates of
iron; and the sound of their wings was as the sound of
chariots of many horses running to battle.
9:10 And they had tails like unto scorpions, and there were
stings in their tails: and their power was to hurt men five
months.
9:11 And they had a king over them, which is the angel of the
bottomless pit, whose name in the Hebrew tongue is
Abaddon, but in the Greek tongue hath his name Apollyon.

The first four trumpets inflicted plagues on *natural objects*: trees, grass, sea, rivers, and the lights of heaven. The next two trumpets send plagues directly on *men*.

We encountered the middle part of 9:1 in K15, after the rapture and the withdrawal of the blessings of the Holy Spirit from the world. At that time Satan was permanently expelled from heaven and cast down to earth.

Here in K32, the rest of the verse is fulfilled. It is the fifth trumpet judgment, which follows the darkening of the heavenly objects in the fourth trumpet. God continues his punishments on men by giving Satan the key to the bottomless pit. Satan has desired this key very much, and God finally permits him to have it.

The result is so severe, that in the next section (9:12 K33) it is identified as a woe, the first of three that was previously announced (8:13 K31). The word *woe* in Scripture refers to some great calamity or judgment from God.

When Satan unlocks the pit, it causes an eruption that releases smoke, enough to darken the sun and pollute the air (9:2). This is a tangible sign of the spiritual corruption that comes next, with the release of the locusts (9:3). They are an echo of the locust plague, the eighth one visited on ancient Egypt because it enslaved the Jews, God's chosen people (Exodus 10:4-19).

We can identify who these locusts really are, by the fact that they are coming out of "the bottomless pit" (9:2). The word for this place in the original Greek of the Bible is *abyssos*, or the abyss. It is the abode of wicked angels or demons. We know this from Luke 8:31, one of two verses outside of Revelation where we also find the word. (The other occurrence is in Romans 10:7). It is part of the story of Jesus encountering the demoniac man who was possessed by a legion of evil spirits. Those demons begged him not to send them to the *abyssos*:

> Luke 8:26 And they arrived at the country of the Gadarenes, which is over against Galilee.
> 8:27 And when he [Jesus] went forth to land, there met him out of the city a certain man, which had devils long time, and ware no clothes, neither abode in any house, but in the tombs.

> 8:28 When he saw Jesus, he cried out, and fell down before him, and with a loud voice said, What have I to do with thee, Jesus, thou Son of God most high? I beseech thee, torment me not.
>
> Matthew 8:29 And, behold, they cried out, saying, What have we to do with thee, Jesus, thou Son of God? art thou come hither to torment us before the time?
>
> Luke 8:29 (For he had commanded the unclean spirit to come out of the man. For oftentimes it had caught him: and he was kept bound with chains and in fetters; and he brake the bands, and was driven of the devil into the wilderness.)
> 8:30 And Jesus asked him, saying, What is thy name? And he said, Legion: because many devils were entered into him.
> 8:31 And they besought him that he would not command them to go out into the deep *[the abyssos]*.

The legion of demons, like their master, Satan, are aware that God's word speaks of an appointed time when they will be meet their final destiny. They also knew of the abyss, and were much afraid of it. It seems they were mindful that other demons were already imprisoned there.

After God created Adam and Eve, Satan and a third of the angels rebelled against God and were defeated (section 12:3-4 K01). Then they made their target the earth and the descendants of Adam and Eve. We encounter these demons in many books of the Bible. They are especially prevalent in the four gospels of the New Testament. At that time they were making themselves known and trying to impede Jesus in his earthly ministry. From this we know that not all demons have been imprisoned in the pit, but that many have been very active accomplices of Satan in his earthly schemes.

Jude 6-8 offers a clue as to which demons were imprisoned, whom Satan is eager to release:

> Jude 6 And the angels which kept not their first estate, but left their own habitation, he hath reserved in everlasting chains under darkness unto the judgment of the great day.
> 7 Even as Sodom and Gomorrha, and the cities about them in like manner, giving themselves over to fornication, and going after strange flesh, are set forth for an example, suffering the vengeance of eternal fire.

> 8 Likewise also these filthy dreamers defile the flesh, despise dominion, and speak evil of dignities.

The place of "everlasting chains under darkness [kept] unto the judgment of the great day" is likely the bottomless pit. Jude directly compares the ones dwelling there to the sexually deviant sinners of Sodom and Gomorrah (Jude 7). Jude also compares them to those involved in sexual orgies in his day, as part of the decadence of the Roman empire (Jude 8). These comparisons suggest that these demons were those rebel "sons of God" who somehow had sexual intercourse with women to produce a race of giants in the days before Noah's flood:

> Genesis 6:4 There were giants in the earth in those days; and also after that, when the sons of God came in unto the daughters of men, and they bare children to them, the same became mighty men which were of old, men of renown.

It is with a sense of irony that these demons that Satan liberates from the pit have an affinity with Babylon, whom the beast recently overthrew. They and the woman both have an obsession with the sexualization of everyday life. When he unleashes the demons, Satan is partially turning away from his support for the beast. He is certainly not committed to any consistency of treatment for people who come under his control. He will gladly whipsaw them between opposing ideologies, as long as they point away from God's commandments.

The demons are permitted to torment people, but not to kill them (9:4-5). Those who do not know the Lord Jesus Christ as Savior come under affliction and even demonic possession. The demons inflict severe pain, rather like scorpions (9:10). Their plague will be thorough, like swarms of locusts that strip a land of every green leaf and sprout. Only believers will be safe, because they are sealed and protected by God.

The army of demons is led by a leader whose name, whether in the Hebrew *Abaddon* or the Greek *Apollyon* (9:11), means destroyer. This is another title for Satan. Though at times Satan appears as an angel of light (when inspiring the false prophet, for example), here the mask is stripped away and evil is seen in its true character. Satan and the demons are destroyers of the souls of men.

In contrast to the pain caused by a scorpion, which passes away in a matter of hours, this scourge continues for five entire months (9:5). The ungodly become so tormented in mind and body by the satanic forces, that they wish to commit suicide (9:6). But the demonic grip upon them is intense enough that they will be prevented from doing so (9:4-6). This is a description of severe demonic possession.

The locusts are described in 9:7-10 in unearthly, hallucinogenic terms. The descriptions might be from the point of view of those possessed.

There are countless anecdotes of people who have subjected themselves to demonic oppression, who are observed to have ravings where they experience contact with such unearthly creatures. Such people are past the precipice of insanity.

I would like to help you understand the extended danger that comes with demonic influence. One Christian author who offers excellent biblical guidance based on his own exorcism ministry to those possessed is Ken Gardiner.[12]

I will summarize some of his insights here.

There are actually a small number of people, devoted to Christ, that discover they have psychic abilities. For example, Watchman Nee, a great Christian pastor and teacher of the early 1900's, was able to telepathically discern people's thoughts after just a brief conversation. He thought this would be useful in his ministry. But as he became more experienced, he dared not use this ability, and resisted it with prayer. Also, Dom Robert, who mentored Ken Gardiner, had the psychic ability to 'see' spirits. But whenever he used it to try to deliver people from demonic possession, it conflicted with the workings of the Holy Spirit. Over the years, he learned to lay aside his ability. How to explain such abilities? These seem not to be inspired by Satan. Perhaps God originally gave Adam and Eve some psychic gifts, which then became dormant or misused after the fall into sin.

Another type of psychic phenomenon involves people who can sense impending disasters. However, some seek to enhance this sense by

---

[12] Ken Gardiner, *The Reluctant Exorcist*, Kingsway Publications, Eastbourne, Britain, 2002.

practicing divination, through the interpretation of omens or the aid of spirits. But the Bible strongly warns against divination, because it is not from the Spirit of God (Deuteronomy 18:10). When evil spirits encounter someone who is not walking with Christ, they entice the person away from him with lies. In Acts 16:16-17, the apostle Paul was followed by a slave girl who predicted the future by a such a spirit of divination:

> Acts 16:16 And it came to pass, as we went to prayer, a certain damsel possessed with a spirit of divination met us, which brought her masters much gain by soothsaying:
> 16:17 The same followed Paul and us, and cried, saying, These men are the servants of the most high God, which shew unto us the way of salvation.

It is ironic that the evil spirit that was channeled by the girl was compelled to speak the truth when it encountered the Holy Spirit in Paul.

If you intentionally dabble in drugs, the occult, Satanism, witchcraft, black magic, casting spells, or if you attempt to contact the dead, you open yourself to demonic influence. These occult practices involve seeking paranormal guidance or power from a source other than God. Those who want to explore witchcraft, black magic and Satanism can get help from a loosely structured organization of people, with representatives at every major university and metropolitan area. They can offer contact with different spirits that have specific powers, that act as lures that appeal to different people and personalities. Many who accept do not realize that they are falling under the devil's sway.

If you expose yourself to this temptation, you will experience mysterious happenings that have no scientific explanation. People tell of seeing hidden spirit beings that manifest themselves. There are numerous reports that spirits are able to harness some form of energy. They inspire fear and can establish control over their subjects.

We know from the story of the demoniac and the Gadarene swine that evil spirits hate to be disembodied. They seek people who are open to falling under their control, and inject themselves into them on a spiritual level. These can also be people with physical illnesses whose spiritual defenses are weakened. Once an evil spirit gains access to someone, it can induce further physical or mental illness.

Others who are easy targets are women (and their partner men) who rationalize having repeat abortions. They can give way to demonic suggestion, because they have already committed themselves to the spirit of death. You can fall sway if you deliberately sin, especially in the areas of pornography and sexual perversion. Also, an act of sexual intercourse with someone who is demonized will allow spirits to pass from one person to another. And spiritualists who act as gateways to the spirit world often have children who become mediums also.

A very devious demonic influence is the idea of white witchcraft. Those who practice it console themselves that they are using it only for the good and wellbeing of others. However, once you open the door to the occult, you cannot control what comes in, white or black. All forms of witchcraft are wrong, and you should repent of it.

A society that was historically rooted in Judeo-Christian values, but which turns away from biblical morality, no longer has it as a collective defense against demonic inroads. It becomes so much easier for individuals to submit.

Jesus gave his immediate disciples a fourfold charge to ministry. It included deliverance, which is exorcism, the casting out of demons who are possessing people. In his instructions, he clearly delineates between sickness and demonization:

> Matthew 10:8 Heal the sick, cleanse the lepers, raise the dead, cast out devils: freely ye have received, freely give.

In the case of the slave girl in Acts who predicted the future by the spirit of divination, Paul followed Christ's charge and ministered deliverance:

> Acts 16:18 And this did she many days. But Paul, being grieved, turned and said to the spirit, I command thee in the name of Jesus Christ to come out of her. And he came out the same hour.

In the ancient church, and in the Eastern Orthodox Church of my day, when a priest baptizes someone, he ministers a mild form of exorcism, with words like: "May Almighty God deliver you from powers of darkness, and lead you in the light and obedience of Christ." Beware that if you go through a public ceremony to *reverse* your baptism, or if you do so privately, you are renouncing God's protection from demonic oppression.

If you know someone who is subject to an evil spirit, please seek the aid of any believer in Christ who has experience in delivering people from evil spirits. During the tribulation, such a minister could be one of the 144,000 Jewish evangelists (Zechariah 8:20-23 K18) whom God has sealed and sent throughout the world. Or it could be any believer, either man or woman.

When an experienced believer tries to minister deliverance to someone, the evil spirit will usually seek to hide. But its presence is revealed by irrational behavior on the part of the victim. For example, the person may start abusing others verbally in a different tone of voice, then immediately change their manner and apologize. They will fling insults at the minister, accusing him or her of ignorance of the spirit realm, and that they have no idea what they are doing.

The believer should challenge the person, by the name of Jesus, to renounce their occult power. There is no need to shout. The evil spirit is aware of the authority and faith of the believer. The believer should also call out the evil spirit to go out of the person, by the power of Jesus. Use words like: "I come in the name of the Lord Jesus Christ, and command every spirit contrary to the Holy Spirit of God to leave."

It is advisable to deliver the person out of the demon's grip before praying for them to be filled with the Holy Spirit. Otherwise, a violent battle between the demon and the Spirit may take place inside them.

The evil spirit knows that the believer is bringing a circle of defense to the person by the power of Jesus. The person might become aware that the spirit is pacing up and down, like a tiger, seeking to break the circle. The spirit may undermine the believer's confidence, claiming that he or she has no right to use the name of Jesus. Respond to that with even greater authority! With words like, "How dare you speak like that; I stand in the righteousness of Jesus Christ, cleansed by his blood, and in his name I command you to leave."

The key to victory over demonic influence is the shield of faith in Christ.

K33

The four evil angels gather armies that slay another third of men

9:12 One woe is past; and, behold, there come two woes
more hereafter.
9:13 And the sixth angel sounded, and I heard a voice from
the four horns of the golden altar which is before God,
9:14 Saying to the sixth angel which had the trumpet, Loose
the four angels which are bound in the great river
Euphrates.
9:15 And the four angels were loosed, which were prepared
for an hour, and a day, and a month, and a year, for to slay
the third part of men.
9:16 And the number of the army of the horsemen were two
hundred thousand thousand: and I heard the number of
them.
9:17 And thus I saw the horses in the vision, and them that
sat on them, having breastplates of fire, and of jacinth, and
brimstone: and the heads of the horses were as the heads of
lions; and out of their mouths issued fire and smoke and
brimstone.
9:18 By these three was the third part of men killed, by the
fire, and by the smoke, and by the brimstone, which issued
out of their mouths.
9:19 For their power is in their mouth, and in their tails: for
their tails were like unto serpents, and had heads, and with
them they do hurt.
9:20 And the rest of the men which were not killed by these
plagues yet repented not of the works of their hands, that
they should not worship devils, and idols of gold, and silver,
and brass, and stone, and of wood: which neither can see,
nor hear, nor walk:
9:21 Neither repented they of their murders, nor of their
sorceries, nor of their fornication, nor of their thefts.

The first four trumpet judgments affected a third of many creatures and resources: the third part of trees (8:7 K29), of the sea (8:8 K29), of all ships (8:9 K29), of the rivers (8:10-11 K30), of the light of the sun, moon, and stars (8:12 K31).

The fifth trumpet tormented men with demons, but left them alive (9:1-5 K32). It was the first woe (9:12).

This sixth trumpet (9:13) is also so extreme that it is counted as the second woe (11:14 K36). As the trumpet sounds, a voice is heard from the golden altar in heaven. God uses the altar, a place symbolizing sacrifice, as the backdrop of this announcement. He now judges rebellious mankind by permitting four evil angels to carry out the scheme that they have been planning with Satan (9:14-15). The choice of heavenly altar as backdrop indicates that God is continuing to answer the prayers of the martyred believers (6:10 K26).

The four evil agents, although agents of Satan, will be used by God to convey judgment on the rebels of the tribulation, whether they oppose the beast or follow him. They are territorial spirits. Their focus up till now has been the Euphrates river basin (9:14), covering areas of Iraq, Iran, Turkey, Syria, Saudi Arabia, and Kuwait.

Territorial spirits are thought to be powerful demons who operate in certain geographic locations over periods of centuries or millennia. They make it their work to block people from hearing the gospel of repentance, forgiveness, and salvation in Christ, and from responding favorably. For example, in the Old Testament an angel told Daniel about a spiritual being called a "prince of Persia", focused on the territory of modern day Iran:

> Daniel 10:13 But the prince of the kingdom of Persia withstood me one and twenty days: but, lo, Michael, one of the chief princes, came to help me; and I remained there with the kings of Persia.

At this time during the great tribulation, the four angels provoke the greatest military campaign the world has ever known. Weapons are provided for 200 million men.

There has never been such a large army composed entirely of professional soldiers. However, it is imaginable to have such a colossal number if one thinks of a huge amount of volunteers issued weapons, who act as auxiliaries for a professional army that forms the core of the force.

The dreamlike imagery that John uses to articulate his vision (9:17-19) could well be describing weapon systems twenty or more centuries beyond his time.

Verse 9:15 tells us about the timing of this action. In the original Greek text, the definite article *the* is used only once, before the word *hour*, but not before the words day, month, or year. Most interpreters therefore say it occurs at the appointed year, month, day, and hour. In this case, the gathered army continues to fight and inflict the named number of casualties until the second coming of Christ (which occurs in 19:11 K38). If the verse actually means an hour *plus* a day, a month, and a year (of 360 days), the time scale given for this action is just over 391 days total. That is a realistic measure of the time required for a full mobilization and invasion campaign in the militaristic world of the beast.

The vast army likely joins the existing professional forces of the beast. They spread across areas of the globe that are resisting. In the ensuing battles, a third of all people die (9:15,18). The casualties would include civilians and opposing soldiers. We see a world at war, with armies of the beast, armies with their warlords opposed to him, civilians on both sides, and scattered among them martyrs who have turned in repentance to Christ.

God allows a third of people to die by the hands of the massed armies. Out of the world's population at the beginning of the great tribulation, at least 50% are now dead. Never since the time of Noah's flood has such a substantial proportion of the earth's population come under God's wrath. But unlike in Noah's day, many of his enemies are still alive. He continues to give them opportunity to turn away from the beast and other leaders, and come to him. Little time remains until Jesus returns. The window of opportunity is closing. God's offer to save you is still open:

> Romans 5:8 But God commendeth his love toward us, in that, while we were yet sinners, Christ died for us.

By targeting a *third* in all these cases, God is mocking the number of the beast, 666. He wrenches away the third portion lacking in that number, to emphasize how powerless the beast is in asserting absolute kingship over the world. When Jesus does come, he will add the third back to 666, and will rule as the true righteous king. He will rule for the perfect period of fulfillment, 1,000 years.

Tragically, the vast number of men and women who still survive do not repent of their murders, their wicked sorceries, their fornication, or their thefts. They continue to worship Satan, the beast, and their proxies (9:20-21).

K34

Satan kills the two witnesses

> 11:3‡[K19] And I will give power unto my two witnesses, and
> they shall prophesy a thousand two hundred and threescore
> days, clothed in sackcloth.
> 11:7 And when they shall have finished their testimony, the
> beast that ascendeth out of the bottomless pit shall make
> war against them, and shall overcome them, and kill them.
> 11:8 And their dead bodies shall lie in the street of the great
> city, which spiritually is called Sodom and Egypt, where also
> our Lord was crucified.
> 11:9 And they of the people and kindreds and tongues and
> nations shall see their dead bodies three days and an half,
> and shall not suffer their dead bodies to be put in graves.
> 11:10 And they that dwell upon the earth shall rejoice over
> them, and make merry, and shall send gifts one to another;
> because these two prophets tormented them that dwelt on
> the earth.

In section K19, we saw the two witnesses from God who began a prophetic ministry even before the beast overthrew the woman of Babylon. They have continued their work for their own three-and-a-half-year term (11:3), stretching from the tribulation into much of the great tribulation. They have come to the city where Jesus was crucified (11:8). This city must therefore be Jerusalem, though with the travail brought to it by the beast and the false prophet, it is labeled here in spiritual terms as Sodom and Egypt, two places of great wickedness in the Old Testament. They have come as witnesses pointing to Jesus, and to share in the suffering he underwent in Jerusalem during his first coming. I have already recounted how the witnesses demonstrate miracles from God – speaking fire to consume forces sent against them, stopping the rain, bloodying the waters. They have the power of Elijah and Moses, and might even be them in person, returned to earth.

The beast's government is continuously embarrassed by their spite. They are an obstacle to wickedness, unbelief, and satanic power. Because of them, countless people have forsaken the beast and turned to Christ. They are enemies number 1A and 1B.

The two witnesses continue their work, even now that the beast's forces have expanded exponentially, with 200 million armed followers spreading out from the region of the Euphrates (9:16 K33). They are fearless, despite the fact that a third of all people remaining are being killed in the latest wars (9:18 K33).

In the middle of the world-wide war, the beast and his government make more extreme efforts to take them out, perhaps as a propagandistic diversion from the failures of the war. But the beast's forces, with all their manpower and weaponry, are unable to kill them. The world dictator can only get the job done by enlisting the direct demonic aid of Satan, his spiritual mentor. Satan has supernatural power as the angel (9:11 K32) and beast of the bottomless pit, who freed the devils who were imprisoned there (9:2 K32), and then ascended with them back to earth (11:7).

As part of his plan, God allows Satan to overcome the witnesses and kill them both (11:7). In this way they join many of God's prophets who came before them. But the power of Christ will shine forth through their weakness. The apostle Paul, another great prophet of God, speaks of this:

> 2 Corinthians 12:9 And he [the Lord] said unto me, My grace is sufficient for thee: for my strength is made perfect in weakness. Most gladly therefore will I rather glory in my infirmities, that the power of Christ may rest upon me. 12:10 Therefore I take pleasure in infirmities, in reproaches, in necessities, in persecutions, in distresses for Christ's sake: for when I am weak, then am I strong.

The two witnesses have been so despised by the authorities for the past three and a half years that they do not allow them the honor of burial. Instead, they let their dead bodies just lie there in the street (11:8). I imagine that the media puts on a spectacle for three and a half days, with constant propaganda video of their bodies broadcast 24-7 from Jerusalem, vilifying their ministry and cursing the almighty God in heaven whom they represented. Great throngs of people come to gawk at those whom they much feared in life. Countless others rejoice, most likely online, in the many languages of the world (11:9). They hold feasts, and celebrate with gifts (11:10). The promise of the beast's beneficial dominion over the world seems close to fulfillment after all.

It is possible to silence the words of truth by death, but it is impossible to put truth to death.

How is God's strength is made perfect? The perfection of his power reaches culmination when weakness seems to be overcome by worldly opposition. It takes spiritual eyes to see that the true victor over the world is the crucified Christ. His is a power that Satan, the beast, and all who have emulated them through the ages, can never understand.

K35

God resurrects the two witnesses

> 11:11 And after three days and an half the Spirit of life from
> God entered into them, and they stood upon their feet; and
> great fear fell upon them which saw them.
> 11:12 And they heard a great voice from heaven saying unto
> them, Come up hither. And they ascended up to heaven in a
> cloud; and their enemies beheld them.
> 11:13 And the same hour was there a great earthquake, and
> the tenth part of the city fell, and in the earthquake were
> slain of men seven thousand: and the remnant were
> affrighted, and gave glory to the God of heaven.

If this event occurs in the decades near to my time, it might go something like this:

The internet live stream from Jerusalem, watched by billions, suddenly shows something dramatic happening. The viewers see the two dead bodies start to move, the witnesses come to life, and they stand on their feet! (11:11) Everyone watching is transfixed. Even the engineers controlling the feed are wondering if this is part of the propaganda narrative. After half a minute word is screamed from the management control line to shut down the live stream. A quick cut, followed by ten seconds of dead time, then a switch to recorded public bulletins. The authorities keep watching the feed, and join an emergency web conference. After five minutes of announcements that extol the virtues of the government, a news anchor comes on to explain the event, with a suitable cover story. This story was already prepared as a contingency by Information Ministry analysts that specialize in counter-biblical propaganda.

However, a large crowd is on hand in Jerusalem celebrating the demise of the two witnesses three and a half days ago. They see exactly what is happening. They know that the two witnesses have been raised from the dead. It could only be the almighty God of heaven, the beast's sworn enemy, who has done this miracle.

These people start flooding social media with the incredible news. Even though the live stream has been suspended, the news is getting messaged and re-messaged across the net. The government big data system debits the social credit scores of millions of people, for future disciplinary action.

The crowds hear the voice of God from heaven that calls the witnesses (11:12). Then they see the two witnesses levitate from the ground, rise up far into the sky, and disappear into a cloud above Jerusalem.

The authorities struggle to shut down internet access out of Jerusalem. One of the interior ministry commanders issues shock orders to black-helmeted police battalions, who quickly arrive at the scene with confused instructions from different sources: to disperse the crowd, arrest everyone there, or to shoot them so that no witnesses are left. But the police are so awestruck that they are incapable of carrying out orders. The crowds begin to disperse on their own. After half an hour the minister of information issues the order to shut off social media worldwide by throwing the global internet kill switch.

Those who are familiar with Jesus Christ from the Bible can see an unmistakable parallel between the rising of the two witnesses into the sky and the ascension of Jesus after his first coming almost two thousand years ago. On the fortieth day after his resurrection, he gathered with a great crowd of his disciples. They then saw him rise up from the ground and disappear into a cloud:

> Acts 1:6 When they therefore were come together, they asked of him, saying, Lord, wilt thou at this time restore again the kingdom to Israel?
> 1:7 And he said unto them, It is not for you to know the times or the seasons, which the Father hath put in his own power.
> 1:8 But ye shall receive power, after that the Holy Ghost is come upon you: and ye shall be witnesses unto me both in Jerusalem, and in all Judaea, and in Samaria, and unto the uttermost part of the earth.
> 1:9 And when he had spoken these things, while they beheld, he was taken up; and a cloud received him out of their sight.
> 1:10 And while they looked stedfastly toward heaven as he went up, behold, two men stood by them in white apparel;
> 1:11 Which also said, Ye men of Galilee, why stand ye gazing up into heaven? this same Jesus, which is taken up from you

> into heaven, shall so come in like manner as ye have seen him go into heaven.

There is also a parallel between the timeline of events of Christ's first earthly ministry compared with the ministry of the two witnesses.

When Jesus came to earth at his first coming, he ministered for three years. Note that three years can be considered as *six* periods of six months. At the end of this time, he was crucified, and confirmed as dead during the next three days. Then he was resurrected. The three days are six periods of three days plus three nights. The number six measures both his ministry and his death. It is the number of incompleteness. It looks ahead to the return of Jesus at his second coming.

This is in contrast with the witnesses' ministry, which was for three *and one half* years. This exactly matches the ruling times of the woman of Babylon and the beast. After the witnesses are killed, their bodies are dead for three and a half days, then God resurrects them. The three and a half years are *seven* periods of six months. The three and a half days are also seven periods: four days and three nights. In all these the number seven is prominent. It is the number of perfection. It will lead us to the millennial kingdom and perfect rule of Christ.

God is in control of all the times.

Earlier, in the sixth seal, an earthquake occurred (6:12 K27). God sent that great earthquake in response to the martyrs' plea, as a prelude to his coming retribution. The seventh seal came afterward, with complete silence in heaven and a foreboding sense of the wrath of God (8:1 K28). After the silence there was another earthquake. Both tremors were at unspecified locations.

Here, within an hour of the witnesses' resurrection, another earthquake occurs (11:13). This time it is localized to Jerusalem.

Earthquakes happen with an approximate 80-year cycle in the holy city. Jerusalem sits in the Great Rift Valley – a tectonic plate boundary that runs for almost 5000 km from Syria down to Mozambique. There are 10 meters of unrelieved stress at the city's portion of the fault line. In the Old Testament, Zechariah 14:5 mentions an earthquake in Jerusalem that occurred in the days of King Uzziah of Judah. Scientists estimate it was 8.0 on the Richter Scale. Another in 1546 was 6.7. The most recent one was in 1927 and caused the Allenby Bridge to collapse.

This new earthquake is not a random occurrence, but a direct act of God. It puts his exclamation point on the resurrection of the two witnesses. We are told that 10 percent of the city is destroyed, and 7,000 people killed (11:13). If any internet connection to Jerusalem remains, it is cut off now.

Exceedingly great fear falls on those who are still alive in the city. They had seen the valiant actions of the two witnesses, and their impeccable holiness. They had heard their preaching that pointed to Christ. Now many are compelled to admit that Christ is truly the son of God. They give glory to the "God of heaven" (11:13). This is a title for God often used in the Old Testament to distinguish the true God from pagan deities. There are at least some in shaken Jerusalem who now understand that the beast and his mentor Satan are false gods.

The apostle Paul invites you to turn your allegiance to Christ also:

> Romans 10:9 That if thou shalt confess with thy mouth the Lord Jesus, and shalt believe in thine heart that God hath raised him from the dead, thou shalt be saved.

K36

Angels announce seven coming plagues of divine wrath

11:14 The second woe is past; and, behold, the third woe
cometh quickly.
11:15 And the seventh angel sounded; and there were great
voices in heaven, saying, The kingdoms of this world are
become the kingdoms of our Lord, and of his Christ; and he
shall reign for ever and ever.
11:16 And the four and twenty elders, which sat before God
on their seats, fell upon their faces, and worshipped God,
11:17 Saying, We give thee thanks, O Lord God Almighty,
which art, and wast, and art to come; because thou hast
taken to thee thy great power, and hast reigned.
11:18 And the nations were angry, and thy wrath is come,
and the time of the dead, that they should be judged, and
that thou shouldest give reward unto thy servants the
prophets, and to the saints, and them that fear thy name,
small and great; and shouldest destroy them which destroy
the earth.
11:19 And the temple of God was opened in heaven, and there
was seen in his temple the ark of his testament: and there
were lightnings, and voices, and thunderings, and an
earthquake, and great hail.
14:14 And I looked, and behold a white cloud, and upon the
cloud one sat like unto the Son of man, having on his head a
golden crown, and in his hand a sharp sickle.
14:15 And another angel came out of the temple, crying with
a loud voice to him that sat on the cloud, Thrust in thy sickle,
and reap: for the time is come for thee to reap; for the
harvest of the earth is ripe.
14:16 And he that sat on the cloud thrust in his sickle on the
earth; and the earth was reaped.
14:17 And another angel came out of the temple which is in
heaven, he also having a sharp sickle.
14:18 And another angel came out from the altar, which had
power over fire; and cried with a loud cry to him that had
the sharp sickle, saying, Thrust in thy sharp sickle, and
gather the clusters of the vine of the earth; for her grapes
are fully ripe.
15:1 And I saw another sign in heaven, great and marvellous,
seven angels having the seven last plagues; for in them is
filled up the wrath of God.

> 15:5 And after that I looked, and, behold, the temple of the tabernacle of the testimony in heaven was opened:
> 15:6 And the seven angels came out of the temple, having the seven plagues, clothed in pure and white linen, and having their breasts girded with golden girdles.
> 15:7 And one of the four beasts gave unto the seven angels seven golden vials full of the wrath of God, who liveth for ever and ever.
> 15:8 And the temple was filled with smoke from the glory of God, and from his power; and no man was able to enter into the temple, till the seven plagues of the seven angels were fulfilled.

At the fifth trumpet, men and women were tormented with demons, but were left alive. That was the first woe (9:3-6 K32). At the sixth trumpet, a third of all people were killed by the beast's expanded army of 200 million men. It was the second woe (9:16,18 K33).

After the murders of the two witnesses (11:7 K34) and their miraculous resurrection (11:11 K35), an angel sounds the seventh and last trumpet, signaling a third and final woe (11:14). Great voices from heaven announce that earthly rule will soon pass directly into the hands of God (11:15). The end of the age is rapidly approaching.

The scene has shifted to heaven. The raptured believers have seen what is happening in the tribulation. In response, the twenty-four elders (11:16), who represent the raptured church (4:4 K14), are worshipping God. They are pleading on behalf of the new believers who are suffering at the hands of the nations. They are asking God to intervene, to strike down those who are killing the followers of Christ, and to reward those who have turned to him. The elders request that God resurrect the dead martyrs and favorably judge them (11:18). We shall see this will indeed happen in 20:4 K43, following the plagues of the seven vials and the second coming of Christ.

Earlier in the great tribulation, those martyred up to that point also called out for retribution (6:10 K26). God answered with the judgments of the seven trumpets (K29-K33, K36), which covered a period of many months. This new plea from the raptured saints is on behalf of the increasing number of martyrs and the believers still alive on earth. God's response will be to send plagues, in the trials of seven vials.

But God's first reaction to their prayers and worship is to allow the raptured saints a view of the heavenly temple (11:19). This will be an entirely new experience for them. There was not even an earthly temple during most of the church age, it having been destroyed by the Romans in 70 CE.

This is the heavenly version of the earthly temples that were in Jerusalem: the one destroyed by the Babylonians in 586 BCE; rebuilt by the exiles returned from Babylon; rebuilt again by King Herod but destroyed; and the temple of the tribulation which the false prophet has desecrated with the abomination that causes desolation. Here the heavenly temple is shown to be holding the original ark of the covenant, which was lost after destruction of the earthly temple in 70 CE. The ark contained the ten commandments, also lost, written by the finger of God on two tablets of stone. This heavenly temple will be replaced by Jesus himself in the eternal kingdom of the new heaven (21:22 K49).

The elders and raptured saints whom they represent are shown both the temple and the ark, to remind them of God's righteous judgment on those who violate his commandments. God's rule is about to be enforced. He must do so to uphold his holiness. The gravity of his coming action is emphasized by correspondingly serious omens that reverberate on earth at this moment: lightning and thunder, an earthquake, and great hail (11:19).

Brought into the picture is Jesus Christ, crowned in gold and sitting on a white cloud. We recognize him by his title *son of man* (14:14). Jesus has been waiting in heaven since he briefly came to earth in the rapture, when he took up the church saints before the tribulation. "Son of man" is the favorite title that he used during his ministry on earth. He used it to identify with the people that he came to save. In Matthew, he used the same title to tell us he would ultimately return at his second coming, at which time would be the judgment of the sheep and the goats:

> Matthew 25:31 When the Son of man shall come in his glory, and all the holy angels with him, then shall he sit upon the throne of his glory:
> 25:32 before him shall be gathered all nations: and he shall separate them one from another, as a shepherd divideth his sheep from the goats:

From his place in the cloud overseeing the earth, Christ is holding a sharp sickle. (Before the age of mechanization, the sickle was the tool of farmworkers to reap grain crops). He thrusts it down upon the earth (14:16), to initiate a reaping of men. In another place in Matthew, he described the sequence of this harvest judgment at the end of the age:

> Matthew 13:36 Then Jesus sent the multitude away, and went into the house: and his disciples came unto him, saying, Declare unto us the parable of the tares of the field.
> 13:37 He answered and said unto them, He that soweth the good seed is the Son of man;
> 13:38 The field is the world; the good seed are the children of the kingdom; but the tares are the children of the wicked one;
> 13:39 The enemy that sowed them is the devil; the harvest is the end of the world; and the reapers are the angels.
> 13:40 As therefore the tares are gathered and burned in the fire; so shall it be in the end of this world.
> 13:41 The Son of man shall send forth his angels, and they shall gather out of his kingdom all things that offend, and them which do iniquity;
> 13:42 And shall cast them into a furnace of fire: there shall be wailing and gnashing of teeth.
> 13:43 Then shall the righteous shine forth as the sun in the kingdom of their Father. Who hath ears to hear, let him hear.

The tares of the above Matthew passage are those who reject Christ. Matthew 13:42 says they will be cast into fire – these are the unbelievers (the goats of Matthew 25:32) still alive at the end of the tribulation who at its end will die for their sins (2:27 K42). After the millennium they will undergo fiery judgment (20:15, 21:8 K46). Matthew 13:43 says that the good seed, those who put their trust in Christ, will shine in God's kingdom – these are the tribulation believers (the sheep of Matthew 25:32) who at its end will be counted in the judgment of the righteous (20:4 K43), and ushered into the millennial kingdom.

We will later see that before the tares are cast into the fire, the way they will be reaped will be by bloodshed inflicted on a historic scale on the armies of the beast (19:15 K38, 14:20 K40). But that is still in the future. There must first occur the judgments of the seven vials, which are encompassed in the seventh trumpet. Seven more angels now come forward with seven vials, each containing a plague to be released (15:1,5-8). Together they will express the final totality of the wrath of God upon the rebels of the tribulation.

K37

The first five plagues:
God sends boils, blood on the sea and waters, heat, darkness

16:1 And I heard a great voice out of the temple saying to the
seven angels, Go your ways, and pour out the vials of the
wrath of God upon the earth.
16:2 And the first went, and poured out his vial upon the
earth; and there fell a noisome and grievous sore upon the
men which had the mark of the beast, and upon them which
worshipped his image.
16:3 And the second angel poured out his vial upon the sea;
and it became as the blood of a dead man: and every living
soul died in the sea.
16:4 And the third angel poured out his vial upon the rivers
and fountains of waters; and they became blood.
16:5 And I heard the angel of the waters say, Thou art
righteous, O Lord, which art, and wast, and shalt be, because
thou hast judged thus.
16:6 For they have shed the blood of saints and prophets,
and thou hast given them blood to drink; for they are
worthy.
16:7 And I heard another out of the altar say, Even so, Lord
God Almighty, true and righteous are thy judgments.
16:8 And the fourth angel poured out his vial upon the sun;
and power was given unto him to scorch men with fire.
16:9 And men were scorched with great heat, and
blasphemed the name of God, which hath power over these
plagues: and they repented not to give him glory.
16:10 And the fifth angel poured out his vial upon the seat of
the beast; and his kingdom was full of darkness; and they
gnawed their tongues for pain,
16:11 And blasphemed the God of heaven because of their
pains and their sores, and repented not of their deeds.

The seven angels pour out their seven vials in succession. Each results in a plague upon the entire earth. They do not exactly compare to the seven trumpet judgments, which affected only one-third of the earth. They also differ from the judgments of the seven seals or the seven trumpets, in that they occur in rapid fire. The timeframe here is likely compressed over a period of weeks, towards the close of the great tribulation.

The saints who are true believers in the Lord Jesus Christ are not mentioned in the first five vials. Presumably, they will not suffer the plagues that ensue.

The first plague (16:2) results in sores or boils inflicted on the skin of those who have the mark of the beast and worshipped his image (13:15-17 K24). The beast's followers survive, but they undergo great pain. This is like the sixth plague, the plague of boils, visited on ancient Egypt for enslaving the Jews (Exodus 9:8-12). In fact, the Greek word for sore or ulcer *helkos* used here is the same word used for boil in the Septuagint's translation of Exodus. That was the first Greek version of the Old Testament, translated by Jewish scholars before Christ was born.

The second plague is the vial poured upon the sea. It becomes like blood. Every living ocean creature is affected and dies (16:3).

The third plague is the vial poured upon the rivers. These fresh waters also become blood (16:4). Blood is the appropriate payback for the killings of the believers committed in the name of the beast. It is universal testimony to all men that God will soon come to avenge his martyred saints (16:5-7).

Time is rapidly running out for men and women, because their lives depend on sea and river creatures that they take for granted. But they will not repent.

The next angel therefore continues with the fourth plague. He pours a vial upon the sun. The result is that unbelievers are scorched with great heat, in a flash of global warming worldwide (16:8). They remain alive. But like the Pharaoh who ruled Egypt when God struck it with plagues, their response is to blaspheme and curse the Almighty (16:9). They refuse to submit to God, even though they recognize that the plagues come from him.

Needless to say, all these events are miracles that cannot be explained scientifically. The God who created the universe in six days can certainly suspend the physical laws that he put in place as the framework for his universe, and act upon it as he chooses.

The fifth plague is the vial poured upon the seat, or throne of the beast. It results in unnatural and prolonged darkness over the entire world (16:10-11). This is like the ninth plague upon Egypt, the plague of darkness (Exodus 10:21-29). There is great pain and torment among millions, though once again they remain alive. Still, they curse God and will not repent of their evil deeds. This is the last reference in Revelation of their failure to repent.

Left on its own, the sinful heart of man is desperately wicked (Jeremiah 17:9). God's holy word refutes the notion that evil men will quickly repent when faced with catastrophic demonstrations of judgment.

But God has the power to change a sinful heart. If you are reading this, it is not too late to ask him to change yours:

> 1 John 1:9 If we confess our sins, he is faithful and just to forgive us our sins, and to cleanse us from all unrighteousness.

K38

The second coming of Christ, and the sixth plague: the battle of Armageddon

16:12 And the sixth angel poured out his vial upon the great river Euphrates; and the water thereof was dried up, that the way of the kings of the east might be prepared.
16:13 And I saw three unclean spirits like frogs come out of the mouth of the dragon, and out of the mouth of the beast, and out of the mouth of the false prophet.
16:14 For they are the spirits of devils, working miracles, which go forth unto the kings of the earth and of the whole world, to gather them to the battle of that great day of God Almighty.
16:16 And he gathered them together into a place called in the Hebrew tongue Armageddon.
17:14 These shall make war with the Lamb, and the Lamb shall overcome them: for he is Lord of lords, and King of kings: and they that are with him are called, and chosen, and faithful.
16:15 Behold, I come as a thief. Blessed is he that watcheth, and keepeth his garments, lest he walk naked, and they see his shame.
19:11 And I saw heaven opened, and behold a white horse; and he that sat upon him was called Faithful and True, and in righteousness he doth judge and make war.
1:7 Behold, he cometh with clouds; and every eye shall see him, and they also which pierced him: and all kindreds of the earth shall wail because of him. Even so, Amen.
19:12 His eyes were as a flame of fire, and on his head were many crowns; and he had a name written, that no man knew, but he himself.
19:13 And he was clothed with a vesture dipped in blood: and his name is called The Word of God.
19:16 And he hath on his vesture and on his thigh a name written, KING OF KINGS, AND LORD OF LORDS.
19:14 And the armies which were in heaven followed him upon white horses, clothed in fine linen, white and clean.
19:19 And I saw the beast, and the kings of the earth, and their armies, gathered together to make war against him that sat on the horse, and against his army.
19:15‡[K42] And out of his mouth goeth a sharp sword, that with it he should smite the nations: *and he shall rule them*

> *with a rod of iron:* and he treadeth the winepress of the
> fierceness and wrath of Almighty God.
> 19:17 And I saw an angel standing in the sun; and he cried
> with a loud voice, saying to all the fowls that fly in the midst
> of heaven, Come and gather yourselves together unto the
> supper of the great God;
> 19:18 That ye may eat the flesh of kings, and the flesh of
> captains, and the flesh of mighty men, and the flesh of
> horses, and of them that sit on them, and the flesh of all
> men, both free and bond, both small and great.
> 14:19 And the angel thrust in his sickle into the earth, and
> gathered the vine of the earth, and cast it into the great
> winepress of the wrath of God.
> 19:21 And the remnant were slain with the sword of him that
> sat upon the horse, which sword proceeded out of his mouth:
> and all the fowls were filled with their flesh.

The sixth plague brings on the long awaited second coming of Christ, and the notorious battle of Armageddon.

Before the tribulation, Jesus briefly came from heaven to rapture the church saints (K13), then immediately went back. This time he has come to earth to stay. Unlike the rapture, at the second coming there will be no possible way to fool people into thinking that Jesus has not come.

The vision of Revelation keeps wrapping around itself to disclose this event. It appears or is hinted at in five different passages. I have collected those passages and attempted to place them in chronological order above.

Christ will descend from the clouds in such a miraculous way that all on earth will know of his coming. His immediate task will be to meet the forces of Satan and the beast in the battle of Armageddon. Where do those forces come from?

Once again, the Euphrates river region enters the end-time geography. Earlier, in the sixth trumpet of section K33, the four territorial spirits of the Euphrates (9:14 K33) launched the gathering of the greatest army in history, consisting of 200 million professionals and auxiliaries. The dictatorship of the beast has been struggling with rebellions against the world government (13:7-8 K23). In the worldwide wars that have been fought since then, a third of all people have lost their lives. All those wars are about to come to an abrupt end.

At this time, the sixth vial is poured upon the Euphrates, causing its waters to dry up completely (16:12). Three unclean spirits like frogs come out of the mouths of the dragon Satan, the beast, and the false prophet (16:13). They demonically inspire the army, or at least an elite reserve of it, to move westward. (Even a two million man elite force that is well equipped should be enough to overwhelm the strongest possible opposition in the tiny land of Israel). The generals of this force are kings of the east, who are apparently allies of the beast. The elite force is joined by more detachments, led by various kings of the earth (16:14). The massive army concentrates its final attack on God's holy land of Israel. According to the prophet Zechariah, they take Jerusalem:

> Zechariah 14:1 Behold, the day of the Lord cometh, and thy spoil shall be divided in the midst of thee.
> 14:2 For I will gather all nations against Jerusalem to battle; and the city shall be taken, and the houses rifled, and the women ravished; and half of the city shall go forth into captivity, and the residue of the people shall not be cut off from the city.

Satan's intention is to obliterate the history of the city of God, and to make it his city.

The central body of the force then finds itself at a place north of Jerusalem named as Armageddon (16:16).

This is the only verse in the Bible that the word Armageddon appears. The word is a Greek transliteration of the Hebrew *har* (mountain of) *megiddo*. Megiddo was a fortification made by King Ahab, ruler of the northern ten tribes of Israel from 874–853 BCE. It dominated the Jezreel valley. The name itself is prophetic, for Megiddo means "place of crowds." The valley is only 380 square kilometers in size. The army from the east undoubtedly spreads far beyond it.

The prefix *har*, or mountain, suggests the ridge called Mount Carmel that rises above Ahab's original Megiddo fortress.[13] At Mount Carmel,

---

[13] *Megiddo, The Place of Battles*, https://biblearchaeology.org/research/conquest-of-canaan/3084-megiddo-the-place-of-battles, accessed June 11, 2022.

Ahab sponsored the worship of the false god Baal. This led Elijah, the prophet of the Almighty, to call for a contest to determine who truly deserved the title of God (1 Kings 18:21). Elijah and the 400 prophets of Baal both made altars for their sacrifices. Following the total failure of Baal's followers, and the ignition of water by fire from heaven, Elijah commanded that the prophets of Baal be seized and executed (1 Kings 18:40). The Lord's dramatic victory was a miniature precursor of the final battle of Armageddon.

The vast army has arrived for a showdown. They believe it will result in a history-changing victory for the beast, whom they worship and revere. But their opponent is not like any of the other armies of the world. It is an army from heaven, led by the Lamb, who is the lord of lords and king of kings, Jesus Christ the son of God (17:14). He announces: "behold, I come as a thief" (16:15). This is his long awaited, and much prayed for, second coming.

The second coming of Jesus Christ should not come as a surprise to any of you living in the tribulation, as long as you are seeking truth from God's word the Bible, and have turned away from revering the beast. It has now been seven years since he and the woman of Babylon came to power, and three and a half years since he has been supreme ruler on his own. But the beast and his followers live in their own bubble. For them, the return of Jesus is shocking and indeed comes like a thief.

In the Bible, several passages describe what happens at the second coming of Christ.

In the Old Testament:

> Psalm 50:3 Our God shall come, and shall not keep silence: a fire shall devour before him, and it shall be very tempestuous round about him.
> 50:4 He shall call to the heavens from above, and to the earth, that he may judge his people.

In the gospel of Matthew, in words spoken directly by Jesus:

> Matthew 24:30 And then shall appear the sign of the Son of man in heaven: and then shall all the tribes of the earth mourn, and they shall see the Son of man coming in the clouds of heaven with power and great glory.

> 24:27 For as the lightning cometh out of the east, and shineth even unto the west; so shall also the coming of the Son of man be.

In the New Testament letter from Jude, the brother of Jesus:

> Jude 14 And Enoch also, the seventh from Adam, prophesied of these, saying, Behold, the Lord cometh with ten thousands of his saints,
> 15 To execute judgment upon all, and to convince all that are ungodly among them of all their ungodly deeds which they have ungodly committed, and of all their hard speeches which ungodly sinners have spoken against him.

And the continuation from Zechariah above:

> Zechariah 14:3 Then shall the Lord go forth, and fight against those nations, as when he fought in the day of battle.

All these passages agree with Christ's descent from heaven described above in 19:11, 1:7, and 19:12-13. Together they say that:

- He comes on the clouds, which drive a tempest of tropical force wind.
- His eyes are flames of fire, a fire that devours before him.
- He comes with a trumpet, the sound of a great blast.
- He calls out with the voice of God, to those living and those dead.
- He comes as the cosmic king, wearing many crowns.
- His uniform is dipped in blood, come in righteousness to execute war and pass judgment. His enemies can only wail and moan.
- All the world sees him: his enemies, and those whom they have pierced with sword, spear, bomb or bullet.
- He comes to gather his followers, and rescue them from every corner of the earth.

Christ the conquering king is riding a white horse. So also did the beast at the beginning of the tribulation. But that one came as the false messiah (6:2 K16). This time the horseman is not an impostor. He is the faithful and true one from God, come to destroy those who blasphemously tried to usurp his kingdom.

Jesus does not come alone. He is at the head of a great army from heaven. They follow him, also upon white horses. They are clothed in fine linen of sinless purity, white and clean (19:14).

Who makes up the armies that accompany Jesus? It is unclear from Revelation whether they are angels, or believers resurrected in the rapture now in their glorified bodies, or both.

We have a strong clue that they are the angels, from two other verses elsewhere in the Bible.

First, in Jude 14 above, the Greek word *hagias*, translated as "saints," is used for the army that Jesus leads. This apparently refers to the angels, because in the New Testament, *hagias* is used several times to refer specifically to holy angels: in Matthew 25:31, Mark 8:38, Luke 9:26, Acts 10:22, Revelation 14:10 (K42).

Second, in Revelation 20:4 (K43), the ones ushered into the millennial kingdom are those who became believers during the tribulation. This includes those who have died, and those still alive at the end of the tribulation. (In K43 we will discuss passages outside of Revelation that hint that Old Testament believers who put their trust in God's future messiah will also enter into the millennial kingdom, alongside the tribulation saints).

If the *hagias* who descend with Christ include the church saints, we would expect them to stay afterwards as dwellers on earth for the thousand years. They would be left to experience the sin that occurs at the end of the millennium, in the return of Satan and the rebellion of Gog and Magog (see 20:7-9 K45), and other lesser sins throughout the thousand years. This would be contrary to God's promise that once they were in heaven, they would never again see sin and death. But verse 20:4 K43 does not explicitly refer to the church saints. This suggests that they will remain in heaven during the millennium. They will make their appearance on the new earth in 19:7 K47.

The beast is the supreme earthly king over many kings. His forces take up battle formation. This will be the battle of the ages – the battle of kings (19:19) against the heavenly king of kings (19:16).

With his army of angels, Christ the lord of lords is come to smite the rebel nations of the world with the fierceness and wrath of God. In the ensuing battle, the beast's armies have no time to bring their forces into action. The army of heaven does not achieve victory by engaging them in battle order. Instead, the battle is over before it is even fought. Out of the mouth of the rider on the white horse comes a sword of astonishing power (19:15). With it, the armies of the beast meet their prompt and utter destruction (19:21).

This is not the first time that God defeats the greatest army of its time by the word of his power. In the time of Hezekiah, a king of Judah in the Old Testament, the invincible Assyrian army laid siege to Jerusalem. God answered Hezekiah's prayer for deliverance, not by means of weaponry, but by his word alone:

> 2 Kings 19:35 And it came to pass that night, that the angel of the Lord went out, and smote in the camp of the Assyrians an hundred fourscore and five thousand: and when they arose early in the morning, behold, they were all dead corpses.

At the close of the battle, an angel appears in John's vision (14:19). This is the angel of 14:17 K36 who has been waiting outside the heavenly temple with a sharp sickle. He beckons to the scavenger birds of the air to feast on the flesh of the army of the dead.

The angel's words can be compared to these words near the close of the prophecy of Ezekiel chapters 38 and 39:

> Ezekiel 39:17 And, thou son of man, thus saith the Lord God; Speak unto every feathered fowl, and to every beast of the field, Assemble yourselves, and come; gather yourselves on every side to my sacrifice that I do sacrifice for you, even a great sacrifice upon the mountains of Israel, that ye may eat flesh, and drink blood.
> 39:18 Ye shall eat the flesh of the mighty, and drink the blood of the princes of the earth, of rams, of lambs, and of goats, of bullocks, all of them fatlings of Bashan.
> 39:19 And ye shall eat fat till ye be full, and drink blood till ye be drunken, of my sacrifice which I have sacrificed for you.
> 39:20 Thus ye shall be filled at my table with horses and chariots, with mighty men, and with all men of war, saith the Lord God.

However, the prophecy of Ezekiel 38-39 is not referring to Armageddon, but to a different battle that will happen after my day which is not mentioned in Revelation. Ezekiel describes an army of six nations that invades the promised land and is then defeated on the mountains of Israel. That event likely happens after the rapture but before the seven-year tribulation. The battle of Ezekiel is not to be confused with the Revelation battle of Armageddon, where God is contending with the armies of the entire world. It takes the coming of Christ to bring the wars of the tribulation to their conclusion.

Having called upon the birds to be ready, the angel thrusts his sickle into the earth. With it he gathers the vines for the winepress of the wrath of God.

K39

The seventh plague: the physical destruction of Babylon

> 16:17 And the seventh angel poured out his vial into the air;
> and there came a great voice out of the temple of heaven,
> from the throne, saying, It is done.
> 16:18 And there were voices, and thunders, and lightnings;
> and there was a great earthquake, such as was not since men
> were upon the earth, so mighty an earthquake, and so great.
> 16:19 And the great city was divided into three parts, and the
> cities of the nations fell: and great Babylon came in
> remembrance before God, to give unto her the cup of the
> wine of the fierceness of his wrath.
> 16:20 And every island fled away, and the mountains were
> not found.
> 16:21 And there fell upon men a great hail out of heaven,
> every stone about the weight of a talent: and men
> blasphemed God because of the plague of the hail; for the
> plague thereof was exceeding great.

The seventh angel pours out the last vial into the air (16:17). Whereas the sixth plague was limited to the beast and his armies, this one befalls everyone alive. The result is the greatest earthquake that mankind has ever known (16:18).

The only event of similar destructive power was possibly at the beginning of the year-long worldwide flood of Noah's day. Some creation scientists hypothesize that the flood was triggered by monstrous tremors that liberated geysers of subterranean waters. The ensuing flood together with the earthquakes caused the separation of the earth's original landmass into continents, the rising of mountain ranges, and a complete rearrangement of the stratigraphy of the earth, all within the period of a year.

The earthquakes that occur after Armageddon are even more cataclysmic in their effect. Whole islands disappear, and mountain ranges are obliterated (16:20). Hailstones weighing 50 kilograms half a meter in diameter fall from the sky (16:21). Most men and women who are not killed send curses up to heaven.

For those of you who scoff that geography needs millions of years to change, ask yourself if time is your god. The God who created time can work his miracles within it.

In section K17 I stated that Jerusalem was one of two main cities of the tribulation. It was overrun by the armies of the beast just before the battle of Armageddon, in the sixth vial (Zechariah 14:1 K38). That was not a direct action by the Lord, but was commanded by the beast, the tool of Satan.

The other city of the tribulation is referred to by the name Babylon, which brings to bear many biblical allusions. In K17 we saw indications that it was the capital of Europe at the beginning of the tribulation, and became the government headquarters for the woman of Babylon's joint rule with the beast. It could possibly be Rome, Istanbul (Constantinople), Brussels, or some other European city.

Babylon was overthrown at the time of the second seal by the beast and the ten kings allied with him. That was the beginning of the great tribulation (17:16 K21). They set fire to it, and its buildings mostly burned to the ground (18:9 K22). It then became the habitation of devils (18:2 K21). Those were not direct actions by God, but were instigated by Satan. God allowed these things to happen to Babylon because she made all nations drink of her obsessions: promiscuity, fornication, and adultery (14:8 K21).

Even in this hotbed of hedonism, some who had their homes in Babylon had repented of their sinful lifestyle and accepted Jesus to be the Lord of their lives going forward. God, who knows all his children, warned them to flee: "Come out of her, my people, that ye be not partakers of her sins, and that ye receive not of her plagues" (18:4-5 K21). This is reminiscent of when God sent the angels to rescue Lot from Sodom, before raining down burning sulfur upon that city, in judgment for its sexual excess (Genesis 19).

At this time after Armageddon, the earthquakes destroy all the major cities of the world. As this is happening, the formerly great Babylon comes to special remembrance before God. He gives unto her the final "cup of the wine of the fierceness of his wrath." The quakes split what remains of the city into three disconnected parts (16:19). Babylon, once the glory of the earth, is physically destroyed. Those who did not heed God's warning to flee, but instead clung to the city, are no more.

Why not place this physical destruction of Babylon immediately after the firing of the city in section K22? It is because the sequence of the seals, trumpets, and vials drives the chronology of Revelation. Since this physical destruction of Babylon waits to happen in the seventh seal, the proper placing of this event is at the very end of the tribulation. This time the destruction is due to the direct action of God. He waits three and a half years after the burning of the city to do it.

K40

The final defeat of the beast and his armies

> 19:20 And the beast was taken, and with him the false
> prophet that wrought miracles before him, with which he
> deceived them that had received the mark of the beast, and
> them that worshipped his image. These both were cast alive
> into a lake of fire burning with brimstone.
> 14:20 And the winepress was trodden without the city, and
> blood came out of the winepress, even unto the horse
> bridles, by the space of a thousand and six hundred furlongs.

The battle of Armageddon is suddenly over. The greatest army ever assembled has been struck down. Babylon and other great godless cities of the tribulation have been physically destroyed by earthquakes.

Afterwards, the beast and his deputy the false prophet apparently try to the flee the scene of battle to some place of safety. But their escape is foiled. They are captured by the Christ's heavenly army. It takes the power of angels to subdue the rebel leaders. Though they are mortal men, they are empowered by Satan. They embody the spirit of empire that has been working in human history in opposition to God ever since the tower of Babel (K02).

These two arch conspirators, the military and religious leaders of the great tribulation, now meet their final end. They are the first two defiant enemies of God to be cast into the eternal lake of fire burning with brimstone (19:20). This is the destiny of "perdition" that almighty God planned for them at the beginning of time (17:8 K02).

Their destiny is observed with bitterness by their followers, who have the mark of the beast upon them. Without their champions, they know that inevitable judgment awaits them.

Satan has been attempting to rewrite fate, but here at the end of the tribulation he has been outmatched by God's son. Satan himself and the rest of unbelievers will follow into the lake of fire at a later time, at the end of the thousand-year millennial kingdom (20:10 K45).

The cream of the beast's army is shattered. The dead cover the ground, like the blood of grapes from a winepress of geographic dimensions. The killed are spread across 1600 furlongs (14:20) or 320 km in all directions from Armageddon. They cover the land of Israel and beyond. It is the last resting place of the greatest massed army in history. Their blood spatters as high as the bridles of horses. This is the work of the angel who drew his sharp sickle at the close of Armageddon (14:19 K38).

The seven seals, seven trumpets, and seven vials are done. The final plague is sealed with blood. It marks God's judgment on the final age of man gone wrong.

K41

An angel offers the message of the everlasting gospel one last time

> 14:6 And I saw another angel fly in the midst of heaven, having the everlasting gospel to preach unto them that dwell on the earth, and to every nation, and kindred, and tongue, and people,
> 14:7‡[K42] Saying with a loud voice, Fear God, and give glory to him; for the hour of his judgment is come: and worship him that made heaven, and earth, and the sea, and the fountains of waters.

The elite vanguard of the beast has met their death. Jesus has returned to earth in his second coming. Some followers of the beast around the world are still alive after Armageddon and the physical destruction of whole cities. They have all experienced at first hand the unmatched power and majesty of Christ.

But after the seven plagues of judgment, a very hopeful thing happens.

An angel flies in the heavens over the whole earth to tell those still alive that the hour of judgment is about to take place (14:7). It will happen very soon, in 14:9-11 of the next section K42. But the angel holds out one last hope, by reminding them of the everlasting gospel (14:6).

I have chosen to place these verses, 14:6-7, here in K41. The verse that follows, 14:8, is the announcement that Babylon is fallen, which happened many sections ago in K21, at the end of the first three and a half years. But the verses after that, 14:9-11, definitely concern the punishment by death of the rebels still alive at the end of the second three and a half years, which happens next in K42. This verse placement, and the loving kindness of God, are good indicators that the announcement of the gospel occurs here, soon after the second coming of Christ and Armageddon.

This is the one and only time that the word *gospel* is found in Revelation.

During the tribulation, everyone in the world has undoubtedly heard the gospel. It came by way of the 144,000 Jewish evangelists whom God sealed and sent throughout the world (7:3-4, Zechariah 8:20-23 K18). It also came from the testimony of the two witnesses which the propaganda ministry of the beast broadcast to every corner of the earth, thinking they could discredit them (11:3-6 K19, 11:7-10 K34, 11:11-13 K35). The angel in some miraculous way now brings the gospel message again, giving the people of the tribulation one last opportunity to turn from death to life.

Perhaps some of you are not familiar with the Bible, and you are reading my book because the end times is a compelling topic. This is your opportunity to hear this gospel, as you contemplate the future trials of the tribulation. It is not usually recommended to read the last chapter of a book before you read the rest. But with the Bible, God's holy book, he permits you to start in Revelation. You can start from any point in scripture to find the riches that are yours, the gospel message of the Bible.

What is the gospel?

The Greek word for gospel in the New Testament is *euangelion*, meaning "good news." In the Old Testament the Hebrew word is *besora*. The root word is much the same in Arabic, and many Middle Eastern people have names along these lines: Bashar, Bshara, etc. The word in these languages was originally connected to messengers bringing word of victory in battle.

The good news is this: Jesus, God's son, is victorious over sin and death. He gives forgiveness and freedom to all of you who ask it with a sincere heart. He then becomes your advocate before the Father in heaven. When he died a criminal's death on the cross, he paid the price for your sins, and made you spotless in God's eyes. You are thus allowed to enter into the Father's eternal and sinless presence. That is the greatest conceivable news you could ever dream of. We the receivers of this good news then become God's messengers to declare it to others.

Our Lord Jesus Christ, the son of God, spoke of the gospel frequently. His most famous saying about it is John 3:16:

> John 3:16 For God so loved the world, that he gave his only begotten Son, that whosoever believeth in him should not perish, but have everlasting life.

To believe the gospel is to accept that:

- God is holy.
- You are a sinner – unable and unwilling to live according to God's standards of righteousness.
- By your actions you have brought great shame to God who gave you your life.
- Christ died and rose from the dead to pay the cost of your sin, and redeem you from slavery to sin and death.
- This great salvation is given, not because of anything you have done, to receive it you only need to live by faith in Christ.
- Your relationship with Jesus and obedience to him will bring you everlasting and ever-increasing joy, no matter the trials in your life.

Christ offers you this free gift of eternal life today. He died for you.

The great loser in the gospel is Satan, the arch-enemy of God and his son. Also losers are the vast majority of people who are deceived by Satan and refuse this free gift of salvation. Their end will be to join him in the eternal lake of fire, away from God's presence forever.

Here are more verses from the Bible that show the riches of the gospel:

> Romans 3:10 As it is written, There is none righteous, no, not one:
> 3:11 There is none that understandeth, there is none that seeketh after God.

> John 6:28 Then said they unto him, What shall we do, that we might work the works of God?
> 6:29 Jesus answered and said unto them, This is the work of God, that ye believe on him whom he hath sent.

> 2 Corinthians 6:2b behold, now is the accepted time; behold, now is the day of salvation.

> Matthew 24:14 And this gospel of the kingdom shall be preached in all the world for a witness unto all nations; and then shall the end come.

> Matthew 7:14 Because strait is the gate, and narrow is the way, which leadeth unto life, and few there be that find it.

> Hebrews 2:14 Forasmuch then as the children are partakers of flesh and blood, he also himself likewise took part of the same; that through death he might destroy him that had the power of death, that is, the devil;
> 2:15 And deliver them who through fear of death were all their lifetime subject to bondage.

The preaching of the gospel is the preaching of "the unsearchable riches of Christ" (Ephesians 3:8).

The gospel verse Revelation 14:6 has as its sister verse John 14:6:

> John 14:6 Jesus saith unto him, I am the way, the truth, and the life: no man cometh unto the Father, but by me.

In that verse Jesus tells us that there is only one way that you and I can come before the throne of the Father in heaven, and be forgiven for our transgressions against him. That is by the one who is "the way, the truth, and the life" – Jesus Christ the son of God.

There are some who say that faith in Christ is the path to salvation only during the church age, which lasts from the day of Pentecost (when the Holy Spirit descended upon the apostles), up to the time of the tribulation. They say that during the tribulation, and also during the Old Testament period, people are saved by doing good works, or by following God's commandments. This view is not correct. The gospel is an *everlasting* one (14:6). Those of the Old Testament period who will be welcomed into God's eternal fellowship, are those who put their faith and trust in God's promise to send a Messiah. Only he could save them, despite their sins. And those of you alive during the tribulation, even at the very end of it, will have the opportunity to walk away from your rebellious record against the Almighty God. You can embrace the savior that he will send again: Christ at his second coming.

Those of you who still insist that there are multiple paths to heaven, or who believe there are none and that heaven does not even exist, should be thankful there is this one way. It is guaranteed by the holiest man who ever lived, the God-man. Please accept this way with your whole heart. Those who do not will have a different destiny, one of everlasting destruction:

> 2 Thessalonians 1:7b when the Lord Jesus shall be revealed from heaven with his mighty angels,
> 1:8 In flaming fire taking vengeance on them that know not God, and that obey not the gospel of our Lord Jesus Christ:
> 1:9 Who shall be punished with everlasting destruction from the presence of the Lord, and from the glory of his power.

Here at the end of the tribulation, our God, who has recently poured out the greatest punishments in human history upon his enemies, sends his angel flying in the heavens to offer his love to them one last time – he will still forgive them, if they repent and turn back to Jesus. That will be the sign that they have hearts that have changed to truly fear God, and willingly give him glory and worship.

It is surprising that the angel opens the door to God's loving kindness to those who least deserve it. Just as Jesus offered salvation to the two thieves hanging on crosses next to him, God offers salvation to those condemned to die. One of the thieves scoffed, but the other's heart was changed. Jesus told him, "Today you will be with me in paradise" (Luke 23:43). So will it be at the end of the tribulation. Some will accept Christ's offer with a contrite heart that has been changed by God. He will take them to himself. They will be the few last ones who will be saved from hell.

K42

The live unbelievers do not survive the end of the great tribulation

14:7‡[K41] *Saying with a loud voice,* Fear God, and give glory to
him; for the hour of his judgment is come: and worship him
that made heaven, and earth, and the sea, and the fountains
of waters.
2:27 And he shall rule them with a rod of iron; as the vessels
of a potter shall they be broken to shivers: even as I received
of my Father.
12:5‡[K05] *And she brought forth* a man *child,* who was to rule
all nations with a rod of iron: *and her child was caught up
unto God, and to his throne.*
19:15‡[K38] *And out of his mouth goeth a sharp sword, that with
it he should smite the nations:* and he shall rule them with a
rod of iron: *and he treadeth the winepress of the fierceness
and wrath of Almighty God.*
14:9 And the third angel followed them, saying with a loud
voice, If any man worship the beast and his image, and
receive his mark in his forehead, or in his hand,
14:10 The same shall drink of the wine of the wrath of God,
which is poured out without mixture into the cup of his
indignation; and he shall be tormented with fire and
brimstone in the presence of the holy angels, and in the
presence of the Lamb:
14:11 And the smoke of their torment ascendeth up for ever
and ever: and they have no rest day nor night, who worship
the beast and his image, and whosoever receiveth the mark
of his name.
20:1 And I saw an angel come down from heaven, having the
key of the bottomless pit and a great chain in his hand.
20:2 And he laid hold on the dragon, that old serpent, which
is the Devil, and Satan, and bound him a thousand years,
20:3‡[K45] And cast him into the bottomless pit, and shut him
up, and set a seal upon him, that he should deceive the
nations no more, *till the thousand years should be fulfilled:
and after that he must be loosed a little season.*

Tragically, many at the end of the tribulation will cling to false hopes, or are filled with pure spite, and will refuse the offer of the everlasting gospel. They must now die for their crimes of aiding and abetting Satan against the holy God of heaven.

There will be no more chances for the rebels to accept the gospel.

Another angel now compels those who despised the good news to submit to the God who stands behind it. They will have no choice but to bow down to him in worship (14:7). But they do so with curses under their breath. They know they are condemned because they chose to worship the image of the beast. They willingly received the mark of the beast, signifying his ownership over them (14:9).

The standards of God cannot be set aside. He does not freely give his love to those who continually spurn his son. He died on the cross as a substitute for those who take refuge in him, but not for those who reject him.

They who repudiated the testimony of the Bible, of God's angels and evangelists, must drink the wine of his wrath. This is the cup of his indignation, poured unmixed (14:10), that is, untempered, by his mercy and grace.

At three times during his vision of Revelation, John sees ahead of the event at hand to one who will rule the nations with a rod of iron: in the prophecy to the church of Thyatira (2:27, see K09), in the vision of the incarnation and ascension of Jesus (12:5, see K05), and in the battle of Armageddon (19:15, see K38).

Most interpreters take the expression "rule all nations with a rod of iron" as representing the form of government during Christ's upcoming thousand-year kingdom: an unyielding, absolute government under which people of all nations are required to conform to the righteous standards of God.

But I shall take a different view. Christ uses the rod, not in the act of ongoing *rule*, but to make a one-time *ruling* that cleanses the world of all who reject him. This echoes two prophecies from the Old Testament:

> Psalm 2:7 I will declare the decree: the LORD hath said unto me, Thou art my Son; this day have I begotten thee.

> 2:8 Ask of me, and I shall give thee the heathen for thine inheritance, and the uttermost parts of the earth for thy possession.
> 2:9 Thou shalt break them with a rod of iron; thou shalt dash them in pieces like a potter's vessel.

> Isaiah 11:4 But with righteousness shall he judge the poor, and reprove with equity for the meek of the earth: and he shall smite the earth with the rod of his mouth, and with the breath of his lips shall he slay the wicked.

This action at the end of the tribulation paves the way for his millennial kingdom. In section K44, we shall see that most who live through that kingdom will do right willingly, with no need for force. But now, before the inauguration of the millennium, and with the rod as his visible instrument of judgment, Christ issues the ruling that is binding on people of all the nations who continue their allegiance to the antichrist.

They are now put to death. "As the vessels of a potter shall they be broken to shivers" (2:27). This must be done to uphold God's holy standards. This will purify the earth from unrepentant sin, and will make way for the thousand-year kingdom of righteousness.

Their physical death is partial fulfillment of two different sayings of Jesus – his parables of the tares of the field, and his prophecy of the sheep and the goats:

> Matthew 13:36 Then Jesus sent the multitude away, and went into the house: and his disciples came unto him, saying, Declare unto us the parable of the tares of the field.
> 13:37 He answered and said unto them, He that soweth the good seed is the Son of man;
> 13:38 The field is the world; the good seed are the children of the kingdom; but the tares are the children of the wicked one;
> 13:39 The enemy that sowed them is the devil; the harvest is the end of the world; and the reapers are the angels.
> 13:40 As therefore the tares are gathered and burned in the fire; so shall it be in the end of this world.
> 13:41 The Son of man shall send forth his angels, and they shall gather out of his kingdom all things that offend, and them which do iniquity;
> 13:42 And shall cast them into a furnace of fire: there shall be wailing and gnashing of teeth.

> Matthew 25:31 When the Son of man shall come in his glory, and all the holy angels with him, then shall he sit upon the throne of his glory:
> 25:32 before him shall be gathered all nations: and he shall separate them one from another, as a shepherd divideth his sheep from the goats:
> 25:33 he shall set the sheep on his right hand, but the goats on the left.
> 25:41 Then shall he say also unto them on the left hand, Depart from me, ye cursed, into everlasting fire, prepared for the devil and his angels:
> Matthew 25:42 I was an hungred, and ye gave me no meat: I was thirsty, and ye gave me no drink:
> 25:43 I was a stranger, and ye took me not in: naked, and ye clothed me not: sick, and in prison, and ye visited me not.
> 25:44 Then shall they also answer him, saying, Lord, when saw we thee an hungred, or athirst, or a stranger, or naked, or sick, or in prison, and did not minister unto thee?
> 25:45 Then shall he answer them, saying, Verily I say unto you, Inasmuch as ye did it not to one of the least of these, ye did it not to me.
> 25:46 And these shall go away into everlasting punishment: but the righteous into life eternal.

In both passages, Jesus tells of everlasting fire, the place of eternal and spiritual death (Matthew 13:40, 25:41). We will see the unbelievers get thrown into this lake of fire in 20:15 and 21:8 (both in K46), after the millennium is complete and before the new heaven and the new earth arrive to take its place. Here in K42, they must first experience physical death. That is why the fulfillment is only partial at this point.

John then anticipates the rest of the fulfillment: the future fire of hell (14:10), which will be everlasting (14:11).

Next, John's vision shifts focus to the remaining rebels: the multitude of devils.

The once perfect angel, Satan, who near the beginning of creation decided he should reign supreme in place of the one who created him, now receives his due. He is the old serpent, who deceived Adam and brought all mankind into a condition of sin and death. He is the dragon who inspired the beast, the false prophet, the woman of Babylon, and all the kings who led the wars of the tribulation.

God sends a special angel to render sentence on Satan (20:1-3). The angel is given the power needed to overcome him. This is likely the great archangel Michael, who after the rapture led the other angels against Satan and the devils to permanently expel them from heaven (12:7 K15).

The angel has a great chain in his hand. With it he binds Satan with force that he cannot overcome.

The angel also has the key to the bottomless pit. This pit was the prison of some of the wicked angels or demons, whom God allowed Satan to temporarily release to torment unbelievers for five months in the judgment of the fifth trumpet (9:1 K32).

The angel casts Satan into the pit and locks it. He puts a seal upon the entrance that will alert all creation of any attempt at escape. Presumably, the rest of the devils share the fate of their leader.

The bottomless pit becomes Satan's place of imprisonment. The sentence imposed is confinement for one thousand years. That is about one sixth of the age of the universe, after God formed the angels and all other creatures. Satan will not be able to deceive men and women during this time.

The souls of his followers lament bitterly as they see his defeat.

However, this is not final for Satan. Though he is bound, God has not sent him to join the beast and the false prophet, whom he has already cast into the lake of fire (19:20 K40). Instead, the imprisonment gives Satan one final chance at rehabilitation. While he is bound in the pit, he will surely be aware of the glories of the millennium. Afterwards, God will release him, and will give Satan one last opportunity to redeem himself.

K43

The still-living believers and resurrected tribulation martyrs ushered into the millennial kingdom after judgment of the righteous

14:1 And I looked, and, lo, a Lamb stood on the mount Sion,
and with him an hundred forty and four thousand, having his
Father's name written in their foreheads.
14:2 And I heard a voice from heaven, as the voice of many
waters, and as the voice of a great thunder: and I heard the
voice of harpers harping with their harps:
14:3 And they sung as it were a new song before the throne,
and before the four beasts, and the elders: and no man could
learn that song but the hundred and forty and four thousand,
which were redeemed from the earth.
14:5 And in their mouth was found no guile: for they are
without fault before the throne of God.
15:2 And I saw as it were a sea of glass mingled with fire:
and them that had gotten the victory over the beast, and
over his image, and over his mark, and over the number of
his name, stand on the sea of glass, having the harps of God.
15:3 And they sing the song of Moses the servant of God, and
the song of the Lamb, saying, Great and marvellous are thy
works, Lord God Almighty; just and true are thy ways, thou
King of saints.
15:4 Who shall not fear thee, O Lord, and glorify thy name?
for thou only art holy: for all nations shall come and worship
before thee; for thy judgments are made manifest.
20:4‡[K24] And I saw thrones, and they sat upon them, and
judgment was given unto them: and I saw the souls of them
that were beheaded for the witness of Jesus, and for the
word of God, and which had not worshipped the beast,
neither his image, neither had received his mark upon their
foreheads, or in their hands; and they lived and reigned with
Christ a thousand years.
20:5‡[K46] *But the rest of the dead lived not again until the
thousand years were finished.* This is the first resurrection.

Only God's people are left alive. The millennial kingdom is at hand.

Just prior to this, the trumpet prophesied by Jesus shall sound:

> Matthew 24:31 And he shall send his angels with a great sound of a trumpet, and they shall gather together his elect from the four winds, from one end of heaven to the other.

Those words of Jesus promised the resurrection of the tribulation martyrs and their ascent into heaven.

We have already met the disembodied souls of these martyrs who had been killed during the tribulation. Many were beheaded (20:4). They were crying out to God for justice, in their distress for those whom they left behind (6:10 K26). We also recall that during the tribulation, the raptured church saints also were pleading that God would resurrect the dead martyrs, and favorably judge them (11:16,18 K36).

God now answers these cries, and fulfills Jesus' promise. He raises all the martyrs from the dead. They live again (20:4). Their souls are reunited with perfect, deathless, glorified bodies, similar to what happened to church saints at the rapture. The resurrection of the martyrs is "the first resurrection" (20:5), and occurs here before the millennium. That is in contrast to the unbelievers, who will be resurrected last, after the millennium. (See Appendix E for a list of these and other resurrections in the Bible).

The resurrected martyrs come before the throne of God in judgment (20:4). They are surrounded by a sea of glass mingled with fire (15:2). The glass reflects the glory of God. The fire purges all impurity before him. Jesus the Lamb stands with them (14:1). He will be their advocate before the Father. They are the sheep of Jesus' parable of the sheep and the goats:

> Matthew 25:32 before him shall be gathered all nations: and he shall separate them one from another, as a shepherd divideth his sheep from the goats:
> 25:33 he shall set the sheep on his right hand, but the goats on the left.

Each person comes one by one before the throne of God.

> Romans 14:10b for we shall all stand before the judgment seat of Christ.
> 14:11 For it is written, As I live, saith the Lord, every knee shall bow to me, and every tongue shall confess to God.

> 14:12 then every one of us shall give account of himself to God.

The above verses from Romans apply to all the throne judgments of God. Each individual who ever lived will come before him in a judgment. Earlier, at the rapture, there was a throne judgment of the church believers (K13). There will be more believers judged after the millennium (20:11-12 K46). At the core of each person's account is that they have trusted their life and eternal destiny to their savior Jesus Christ:

> Galatians 2:20 I am crucified with Christ: nevertheless I live; yet not I, but Christ liveth in me: and the life which I now live in the flesh I live by the faith of the Son of God, who loved me, and gave himself for me.

On the other hand, those who died throughout all ages and did not put their trust in God's son, will not live again until the coming thousand years are over (20:5). They will then appear at the great white throne judgment (20:11-12 K46). The account they give will be different. So will be God's verdict.

God's response to the martyrs' cry, and to their advocates among the raptured church saints, is exceedingly glorious. He grants the martyrs eternal life, with the special privilege of entering into the millennial kingdom in their glorified bodies:

> Matthew 25:34 Then shall the King say unto them on his right hand, Come, ye blessed of my Father, inherit the kingdom prepared for you from the foundation of the world:
> 25:46 And these shall go away into everlasting punishment: but the righteous into life eternal.

After this judgment event, we now proceed to the ushering of God's chosen – the "good seed" of the parable of the tares (Matthew 13:37-38 K42) – into the millennial kingdom:

> Matthew 13:43 Then shall the righteous shine forth as the sun in the kingdom of their Father. Who hath ears to hear, let him hear.

Three different groups of people will be invited.

The first are the tribulation martyrs in their glorified bodies. They are given thrones, so that they can reign with Christ as his adjutants for the thousand-year period. If they are going to rule with him, they will need to be alive in the same sense that he is, namely, having a glorified body.

The second are the 144,000 Jewish evangelists (Zechariah 8:20-23 K18) who were sealed for God's service with his name on their foreheads (14:1). Their lives were specially preserved from death (7:3-4 K18). They lived like true men of God in fearless holiness (14:5). They are praising God with a song of redemption (14:3). The 144,000 stand triumphantly with the Lamb at the beginning of his millennial reign (14:1), and enter the kingdom in their natural bodies.

The third are those new believers still alive, both Jew and gentile, who did not willingly receive the mark of the beast (15:2). They earn entry into the millennium because they did not worship the beast (20:4 K24). After many trials they responded with gratitude to the gospel. This group would include those saved at the last minute when the angel flew over the whole earth proclaiming the everlasting gospel (14:6 K41). All these living converts are worthy to join in the song of redemption, like the Jews sang after God parted the Red Sea and delivered them from Pharaoh's army into the promised land (15:3). This large group also enters into the millennial kingdom with their natural bodies. Among them will be the gentile nations that will worship God in Jerusalem, as prophesied by Isaiah:

> Isaiah 2:2 And it shall come to pass in the last days, that the mountain of the Lord's house shall be established in the top of the mountains, and shall be exalted above the hills; and all nations shall flow unto it.
> 2:3 And many people shall go and say, Come ye, and let us go up to the mountain of the Lord, to the house of the God of Jacob; and he will teach us of his ways, and we will walk in his paths: for out of Zion shall go forth the law, and the word of the Lord from Jerusalem.

There is a fourth group that the Bible hints will be resurrected and enter into the thousand-year kingdom. These are the Old Testament believers: all those who lived before the incarnation of Christ, and whose faith was in God's future plan of salvation. Most of them are Jewish. A passage from Daniel suggests this:

> Daniel 12:1 And at that time shall Michael stand up, the great prince which standeth for the children of thy people: and there shall be a time of trouble, such as never was since there was a nation even to that same time: and at that time thy people shall be delivered, every one that shall be found written in the book.
> 12:2 And many of them that sleep in the dust of the earth shall awake, some to everlasting life, and some to shame and everlasting contempt.
> 12:3 they that be wise shall shine as the brightness of the firmament; and they that turn many to righteousness as the stars for ever and ever.

Daniel 12:1 is a picture of the tribulation end times event when the archangel Michael stands up for God's people. This ties in with his binding of Satan for a thousand years (20:1-3 K42).

Daniel 12:2 speaks of two sets of people who will be resurrected. Those who will awake to everlasting contempt will do so in the resurrection of the unbelievers at the close of the millennium (20:5 K46). Those who awake to everlasting life are an unspecified group of believers. I join many interpreters in believing this set is likely raised from the dead here at the outset of the millennium, and is equal to the fourth group that we are considering.

The following passage from Ezekiel helps identify this fourth group of believers with more focus:

> Ezekiel 37:9 Then said he unto me, Prophesy unto the wind, prophesy, son of man, and say to the wind, Thus saith the Lord God; Come from the four winds, O breath, and breathe upon these slain, that they may live.
> 37:10 So I prophesied as he commanded me, and the breath came into them, and they lived, and stood up upon their feet, an exceeding great army.
> 37:11 Then he said unto me, Son of man, these bones are the whole house of Israel: behold, they say, Our bones are dried, and our hope is lost: we are cut off for our parts.
> 37:12 Therefore prophesy and say unto them, Thus saith the Lord God; Behold, O my people, I will open your graves, and

> cause you to come up out of your graves, and bring you into the land of Israel.
> 37:13 And ye shall know that I am the Lord, when I have opened your graves, O my people, and brought you up out of your graves,
> 37:14 And shall put my spirit in you, and ye shall live, and I shall place you in your own land: then shall ye know that I the Lord have spoken it, and performed it, saith the Lord.

We see from Ezekiel 37:11 that the "house of Israel" is the fourth group. They are being resurrected to return to their own land (Ezekiel 37:12), which is Israel.

Isaiah 11 also speaks of this:

> Isaiah 11:11 And it shall come to pass in that day, that the Lord shall set his hand again the second time to recover the remnant of his people, which shall be left, from Assyria, and from Egypt, and from Pathros, and from Cush, and from Elam, and from Shinar, and from Hamath, and from the islands of the sea.
> 11:12 And he shall set up an ensign for the nations, and shall assemble the outcasts of Israel, and gather together the dispersed of Judah from the four corners of the earth.
> 11:16 And there shall be an highway for the remnant of his people, which shall be left, from Assyria; like as it was to Israel in the day that he came up out of the land of Egypt.

Daniel, Ezekiel, and Isaiah all imply the believing Old Testament Jews, long dead, will be ushered into the millennium in their resurrected and glorified bodies. They will also be subordinates of Christ, and will reign alongside him. They are different from the church saints who were resurrected in the rapture, and whose immediate destination was heaven. The Old Testament believers also come before the throne of God in judgment. Their testimony is that they trusted their eternal destiny to the Messiah whom God had promised. The prophet Isaiah was one of many who invited the ancient Israelites to faith in the future *mashiakh*:

> Isaiah 53:3 He is despised and rejected of men; a man of sorrows, and acquainted with grief: and we hid as it were our faces from him; he was despised, and we esteemed him not.

> 53:4 Surely he hath borne our griefs, and carried our sorrows: yet we did esteem him stricken, smitten of God, and afflicted.
> 53:5 But he was wounded for our transgressions, he was bruised for our iniquities: the chastisement of our peace was upon him; and with his stripes we are healed.
> 53:6 All we like sheep have gone astray; we have turned every one to his own way; and the Lord hath laid on him the iniquity of us all.
> 53:7 He was oppressed, and he was afflicted, yet he opened not his mouth: he is brought as a lamb to the slaughter, and as a sheep before her shearers is dumb, so he openeth not his mouth.
> 53:8 He was taken from prison and from judgment: and who shall declare his generation? for he was cut off out of the land of the living: for the transgression of my people was he stricken.
> 53:9 And he made his grave with the wicked, and with the rich in his death; because he had done no violence, neither was any deceit in his mouth.
> 53:10 Yet it pleased the Lord to bruise him; he hath put him to grief: when thou shalt make his soul an offering for sin, he shall see his seed, he shall prolong his days, and the pleasure of the Lord shall prosper in his hand.

Not all Jews who lived before Christ are saved, however. Those who prided themselves on their circumcision, their relative goodness, or the level of personal perfection that they have achieved, are not counted worthy. They in actuality rejected the coming Messiah as their savior, in favor of the sufficiency of their own works. But the apostle Paul explains that God's mark of circumcision for the Jews was meant to point to a deeper spiritual reality, which they refused to apprehend:

> Romans 2:28 For he is not a Jew, which is one outwardly; neither is that circumcision, which is outward in the flesh:
> 2:29 But he is a Jew, which is one inwardly; and circumcision is that of the heart, in the spirit, and not in the letter; whose praise is not of men, but of God.

God will wait on dealing with Old Testament Israelites who put their own works above his. Sadly, they will not partake of the blessings of the millennium or of eternal life. He will address them, along with the rest of rebel humanity, at the great white throne judgment. Another passage from Ezekiel confirms such will be the end-time judgment on Israel:

> Ezekiel 20:34 And I will bring you out from the people, and will gather you out of the countries wherein ye are scattered, with a mighty hand, and with a stretched out arm, and with fury poured out.
> 20:35 And I will bring you into the wilderness of the people, and there will I plead with you face to face.
> 20:36 Like as I pleaded with your fathers in the wilderness of the land of Egypt, so will I plead with you, saith the Lord God.
> 20:37 And I will cause you to pass under the rod, and I will bring you into the bond of the covenant:
> 20:38 And I will purge out from among you the rebels, and them that transgress against me: I will bring them forth out of the country where they sojourn, and they shall not enter into the land of Israel: and ye shall know that I am the Lord.

The survivors and resurrected martyrs of the tribulation, along with the resurrected believers of the Old Testament, now enter into the glorious thousand-year kingdom of God's son, the Lord Jesus Christ.

K44

The millennial kingdom

> 20:6‡[K46] Blessed and holy is he that hath part in the first resurrection: on such the second death hath no power, but they shall be priests of God and of Christ, and shall reign with him a thousand years.

The book of Revelation spans all of cosmic time, but it is foremost a letter to the tribulation. Fifteen of its twenty-two chapters (5 through 19) concern just that seven-year period at the end of our present age.

The most contentious area for Bible interpreters is when John gets a glimpse of the future millennial kingdom, which occurs after the tribulation and Christ's second coming. He will rule as king of the whole world for a thousand years from his throne in Jerusalem.

The thousand-year duration is specifically mentioned only in chapter 20, but there it is repeated six times in six consecutive verses: 20:2 through 20:7. We have already encountered the beginning of the millennium in the K42 account of the binding of Satan (20:2-3), and in the resurrection of the tribulation martyrs in K43 where they are promised to rule with Christ for that time (20:4-5). At the end of the millennium in K45, Satan will be released from the bottomless pit (20:7).

The verse under consideration here is 20:6, which properly speaking covers the thousand-year period.

Many commentators are so overwhelmed with the one-time events of Revelation, unmatched in their severity, that they refuse to take much of John's apocalyptic prophecy literally. They proceed from that basis to say that this is the only place in the Bible that a thousand-year period is mentioned, and since there is no scripture outside of Revelation that spells it out, that this period of time is merely a symbol of eternity. Most go on to say that Revelation 20 parallels the earlier chapters and is not prophecy, but only constitutes another recapitulation of the book's apocalyptic vision.

This type of interpretation is called amillennialism, because it holds that there will not really be a separate one-thousand-year kingdom. (Hence the prefix *a*-). Instead, the millennium is another way that John's vision is hinting at the perfect kingdom of God, which will eventually come in the age of eternity. Working from this position as a baseline, they feel free to interpret chapters 5 through 19 regarding the tribulation in figurative terms as well.

Amillennialists who hold this perspective do not deal with an important question: what is God's purpose in providing all the inner detail of the numerous specific events in the earlier chapters? What more would God have to write in his Word to make it clear it should be taken literally? (The same could be asked of the accounts of six-day creation in Genesis 1-2, and Noah's worldwide flood in Genesis 6-9).

A non-literal approach dispenses depth of understanding to conform to human logic. But the literal approach wherever possible is a faith builder. Believers look forward to the working out of God's sovereign plan, as we walk our lives with Jesus. We may be in human error in getting the literal interpretation exactly correct, but it is worth the attempt. In the process of grappling with scripture, you will grow nearer in your relationship with Jesus Christ.

Those of you reading this in the tribulation already know the literal truth of Revelation. If somehow you have the luxury of time amidst your great adversity, please let others know where my book can be improved in the interpretation of the prophecies. That will help many others to persevere despite the trials.

So far in John's vision, we have been given some information about the millennial kingdom.

We know that it will be one thousand years in duration. This contrasts with Satan's counterfeit kingdom of the beast, which lasted only seven years.

We know that only people who have truly put their faith in Jesus Christ as Lord and Savior are ushered into the kingdom.

One group will be the survivors of the tribulation. They will be in their natural bodies. They are still subject to a future death and resurrection.

The other group will be men and women with glorified bodies, courtesy of the "first resurrection" (20:6) that happened after Christ's return and the battle of Armageddon. It is impossible for them to die again, because they are not under the power of the "second death" (20:6) which will be brought upon unbelievers who will be cast into hell at the end of the millennium (20:15, 21:8 K46). The ones entering the kingdom will include the martyrs of the tribulation, along with the believers of the Old Testament. They will have a special role in the millennium as priests of God and of Christ (20:6). They will rule with Christ (20:4-5 K43), and be administrators of the kingdom. They will serve as pastors around the world, and evangelists to those born during the millennium. Those in Jerusalem will minister as priests in the millennial temple, which I will talk about below.

There was only one time in history where people in their natural bodies mingled with someone in a glorified body – during the forty days when the resurrected Christ was with his disciples, before his ascension into heaven (Luke 24:13-52, John 20:14-21:22, Acts 1:3-8). In the millennial kingdom, there will be a large number of people in natural bodies, and another large number in glorified bodies. They will have the most amazing interaction and fellowship.

We have to turn to other books of the Bible written before Revelation to learn more about the millennial kingdom.

The prophet Isaiah looked ahead to a future kingdom of God in many verses of his Old Testament prophecy. Two of them, Isaiah 65:17 and 66:22, speak specifically of the new heaven, the new earth, and the new Jerusalem. These new places will replace the ones that we are familiar with when God transitions the universe to the perfect eternal state. I will discuss them in section K47 (21:1,10). But most of the end-time verses in Isaiah describe the thousand years that occurs prior to that. They take place on the earth desolated by the tribulation and now renewed, but not yet remade. Here are the two key verses that point to this time:

> Isaiah 65:20 There shall be no more thence an infant of days, nor an old man that hath not filled his days: for the child shall die an hundred years old; but the sinner being an hundred years old shall be accursed.

> 65:23 They shall not labour in vain, nor bring forth for trouble; for they are the seed of the blessed of the Lord, and their offspring with them.

Isaiah 65:20 clearly describes the mortality of some residents of a future idyllic kingdom. Those in their natural bodies will live an extra-long life, but nevertheless some will die. This points to the millennial kingdom, and not the eternal state, because in that final age all of God's children have glorified bodies and will live forever. The extended lifetimes will be reminiscent of those who lived before Noah's flood, the longest being Methuselah, who died at age 969 (Genesis 5:27). Perhaps the presence of immortals in their glorified bodies will be the greatest contributor toward increased lifespans. Another factor is the absence of Satan, and no more of his schemes that bring illness and death to people.

Isaiah 65:23 above talks of child-bearing. Ever since the fall of man into sin, every mother has shared the anguish that God promised to Eve:

> Genesis 3:16a Unto the woman he said, I will greatly multiply thy sorrow and thy conception; in sorrow thou shalt bring forth children.

But in the future kingdom, child bearing and child raising will be easy, compared with what all generations since Eve have known. Mothers shall "not bring forth in trouble" (Isaiah 65:23), and will give birth to children who will be blessed far more than what we experience in our time. This cannot be referring to the eternal state, because Jesus told us there would not be marriage in eternity (Luke 20:34-36). Presumably human beings living in the eternal age will not have children, because they will not be married, and all of them will have glorified bodies that can never die again. Therefore Isaiah 65:23 must refer to children who will be born during the thousand years.

The above two verses thus serve as a gateway to many others in Isaiah, and in other Old Testament prophets, that speak of the millennium.

What will the millennial kingdom be like?

The thousand-year golden age is a preview of heaven on earth in the eternal age. In the church age from which I am writing, the kingdom of God is his invisible spiritual reign in the hearts of believers. It expresses itself to the fallen world when his followers act as salt and light to those around them. The millennial kingdom is much more. It will be the visible rule of God's divine son, the lamb, come to live on earth:

> Isaiah 16:1 Send ye the lamb to the ruler of the land from Sela to the wilderness, unto the mount of the daughter of Zion.

Christ the Messiah will reign from Jerusalem, also known as Mount Zion:

> Isaiah 2:2 And it shall come to pass in the last days, that the mountain of the Lord's house shall be established in the top of the mountains, and shall be exalted above the hills; and all nations shall flow unto it.
> 24:23b the Lord of hosts shall reign in mount Zion, and in Jerusalem, and before his ancients gloriously.

He will rule over the entire world:

> Psalm 2:6 Yet have I set my king upon my holy hill of Zion.
> 2:7 I will declare the decree: the Lord hath said unto me, Thou art my Son; this day have I begotten thee.
> 2:8 Ask of me, and I shall give thee the heathen for thine inheritance, and the uttermost parts of the earth for thy possession.

He will rule in peace and tranquility. His government will be completely just for all. It will be absolute in power and authority, and sinful actions will be punished:

> Isaiah 11:2 And the spirit of the Lord shall rest upon him, the spirit of wisdom and understanding, the spirit of counsel and might, the spirit of knowledge and of the fear of the Lord;
> 11:3 And shall make him of quick understanding in the fear of the Lord: and he shall not judge after the sight of his eyes, neither reprove after the hearing of his ears:
> 11:4 But with righteousness shall he judge the poor, and reprove with equity for the meek of the earth: and he shall smite the earth: with the rod of his mouth, and with the breath of his lips shall he slay the wicked.
> 11:5 And righteousness shall be the girdle of his loins, and faithfulness the girdle of his reins.
> 16:5 And in mercy shall the throne be established: and he shall sit upon it in truth in the tabernacle of David, judging, and seeking judgment, and hasting righteousness.

War will be no more anywhere in the world, for the first time in human memory:

> Isaiah 2:4 And he shall judge among the nations, and shall rebuke many people: and they shall beat their swords into plowshares, and their spears into pruninghooks: nation shall not lift up sword against nation, neither shall they learn war any more.

Jews and gentiles will live in peace. The children of Israel will be given a special favored place as God's chosen people. Gentiles will also receive spiritual blessing, and will give honor to the Jewish followers of *Yeshua haMashiach* :

> Isaiah 14:1 For the Lord will have mercy on Jacob, and will yet choose Israel, and set them in their own land: and the strangers shall be joined with them, and they shall cleave to the house of Jacob.
> 49:22 Thus saith the Lord God, Behold, I will lift up mine hand to the Gentiles, and set up my standard to the people: and they shall bring thy sons in their arms, and thy daughters shall be carried upon their shoulders.
> 60:14 The sons also of them that afflicted thee shall come bending unto thee; and all they that despised thee shall bow themselves down at the soles of thy feet; and they shall call thee; The city of the Lord, The Zion of the Holy One of Israel.
> 60:15 Whereas thou has been forsaken and hated, so that no man went through thee, I will make thee an eternal excellency, a joy of many generations.
> 60:16 Thou shalt also suck the milk of the Gentiles, and shalt suck the breast of kings: and thou shalt know that I the Lord am thy Saviour and thy Redeemer, the mighty One of Jacob.

There will be great prosperity. To describe it, Isaiah used the most superlative words comprehensible in his agricultural and rural context of the eighth century BCE:

> Isaiah 30:23 Then shall he give the rain of thy seed, that thou shalt sow the ground withal; and bread of the increase of the earth, and it shall be fat and plenteous: in that day shall thy cattle feed in large pastures.
> 30:24 The oxen likewise and the young asses that ear the ground shall eat clean provender, which hath been winnowed with the shovel and with the fan.

> 35:1 The wilderness and the solitary place shall be glad for
> them; and the desert shall rejoice, and blossom as the rose.
> 35:2 It shall blossom abundantly, and rejoice even with joy
> and singing: the glory of Lebanon shall be given unto it, the
> excellency of Carmel and Sharon, they shall see the glory of
> the Lord, and the excellency of our God.
> 65:21 And they shall build houses, and inhabit them; and
> they shall plant vineyards, and eat the fruit of them.
> 65:22 They shall not build, and another inhabit; they shall
> not plant, and another eat: for as the days of a tree are the
> days of my people, and mine elect shall long enjoy the work
> of their hands.

The animals of the earth will return to the state of complete harmony and *shalom* that they had in the garden of Eden, before Satan tempted Adam and the whole human race into sin:

> Isaiah 11:6 The wolf also shall dwell with the lamb, and the
> leopard shall lie down with the kid; and the calf and the
> young lion and the fatling together; and a little child shall
> lead them.
> 11:7 And the cow and the bear shall feed; their young ones
> shall lie down together: and the lion shall eat straw like the
> ox.
> 11:8 And the sucking child shall play on the hole of the asp,
> and the weaned child shall put his hand on the cockatrice'
> den.
> 11:9a They shall not hurt nor destroy in all my holy
> mountain.

The spiritual life in the millennium will be of greater magnitude and broader in scope than ever before:

> Isaiah 11:9b for the earth shall be full of the knowledge of
> the Lord, as the waters cover the sea.
> 11:10 And in that day there shall be a root of Jesse, which
> shall stand for an ensign of the people; to it shall the
> Gentiles seek: and his rest shall be glorious.
> 2:3 And many people shall go and say, Come ye, and let us go
> up to the mountain of the Lord, to the house of the God of
> Jacob; and he will teach us of his ways, and we will walk in
> his paths: for out of Zion shall go forth the law, and the word
> of the Lord from Jerusalem.

There will be many more people intensively living their lives by the Holy Spirit, and dedicated to Christ, than at any time in history:

> Isaiah 32:15 Until the spirit be poured upon us from on high, and the wilderness be a fruitful field, and the fruitful field be counted for a forest.
> 32:16 Then judgment shall dwell in the wilderness, and righteousness remain in the fruitful field.
> 32:17 And the work of righteousness shall be peace; and the effect of righteousness quietness and assurance for ever.
> 32:18 And my people shall dwell in a peaceable habitation, and in sure dwellings, and in quiet resting places.
> 44:3 For I will pour water upon him that is thirsty, and floods upon the dry ground: I will pour my spirit upon thy seed, and my blessing upon thine offspring:
> 44:4 And they shall spring up as among the grass, as willows by the water courses.
> 44:5 One shall say, I am the Lord's; and another shall call himself by the name of Jacob; and another shall subscribe with his hand unto the Lord, and surname himself by the name of Israel.

A controversial aspect of the millennial kingdom is whether or not there will be a temple in Jerusalem, and sacrifices made there. Verses 11:1-2 in K18 pictures such a temple during the tribulation, when it was trampled underfoot by unbelieving gentiles. Isaiah also alludes to a future temple, perhaps the same one. But it is now exalted by the gentiles. This places its activity during the millennial kingdom:

> Isaiah 66:20 And they shall bring all your brethren for an offering unto the Lord out of all nations upon horses, and in chariots, and in litters, and upon mules, and upon swift beasts, to my holy mountain Jerusalem, saith the Lord, as the children of Israel bring an offering in a clean vessel into the house of the Lord.

Ezekiel chapters 40 through 46 describes in great detail this magnificent future temple. It will serve the people of the world as the center for rituals and offerings to God. Presumably the priests of the temple will be the resurrected saints in their glorified bodies who entered into the thousand-year kingdom (20:6). The glory of the Lord will fill this temple, as it did when King Solomon dedicated the first temple:

> Ezekiel 43:4 And the glory of the Lord came into the house by the way of the gate whose prospect is toward the east.

> 43:5 So the spirit took me up, and brought me into the inner court; and, behold, the glory of the Lord filled the house.

Ezekiel mentions a health-giving river that flows from the temple. Zechariah also mentions this river:

> Ezekiel 47:1 Afterward he brought me again unto the door of the house; and, behold, waters issued out from under the threshold of the house eastward: for the forefront of the house stood toward the east, and the waters came down from under from the right side of the house, at the south side of the altar.
> 47:12 And by the river upon the bank thereof, on this side and on that side, shall grow all trees for meat, whose leaf shall not fade, neither shall the fruit thereof be consumed: it shall bring forth new fruit according to his months, because their waters they issued out of the sanctuary: and the fruit thereof shall be for meat, and the leaf thereof for medicine.

> Zechariah 14:8 And it shall be in that day, that living waters shall go out from Jerusalem; half of them toward the former sea, and half of them toward the hinder sea: in summer and in winter shall it be.

The priests of the people will make daily sacrifices:

> Ezekiel 46:13 Thou shalt daily prepare a burnt offering unto the Lord of a lamb of the first year without blemish: thou shalt prepare it every morning.

However, with the idea of future sacrifices we must remember the truth that Christ's shed blood on the cross was sufficient, once and for all future time, to pay for our sins. This is made clear in the New Testament book of Hebrews:

> Hebrews 10:11 And every priest standeth daily ministering and offering oftentimes the same sacrifices, which can never take away sins:
> 10:12 But this man, after he had offered one sacrifice for sins for ever, sat down on the right hand of God.
> 9:28 So Christ was once offered to bear the sins of many; and unto them that look for him shall he appear the second time without sin unto salvation.

Some interpreters suggest that Ezekiel and Hebrews can both be taken literally, by taking the millennial sacrifices as a memorial of Christ's sacrifice on Calvary, much as Old Testament sacrifices looked forward to fulfillment in his death. People living in the millennium in their natural bodies will still sin and still die. The temple with its memorial sacrifices is there to remind them of their need for repentance. It also reminds them of Christ's sacrifice that is offered them to redeem from sin.

In conclusion, let me share with you Psalm 72, which is a picture of the righteous reign of Christ in the millennial kingdom:

> Psalm 72:1 Give the king thy judgments, O God, and thy righteousness unto the king's son.
> 72:2 He shall judge thy people with righteousness, and thy poor with judgment.
> 72:3 The mountains shall bring peace to the people, and the little hills, by righteousness.
> 72:4 He shall judge the poor of the people, he shall save the children of the needy, and shall break in pieces the oppressor.
> 72:5 They shall fear thee as long as the sun and moon endure, throughout all generations.
> 72:6 He shall come down like rain upon the mown grass: as showers that water the earth.
> 72:7 In his days shall the righteous flourish; and abundance of peace so long as the moon endureth.
> 72:8 He shall have dominion also from sea to sea, and from the river unto the ends of the earth.
> 72:9 They that dwell in the wilderness shall bow before him; and his enemies shall lick the dust.
> 72:10 The kings of Tarshish and of the isles shall bring presents: the kings of Sheba and Seba shall offer gifts.
> 72:11 Yea, all kings shall fall down before him: all nations shall serve him.
> 72:12 For he shall deliver the needy when he crieth; the poor also, and him that hath no helper.
> 72:13 He shall spare the poor and needy, and shall save the souls of the needy.
> 72:14 He shall redeem their soul from deceit and violence: and precious shall their blood be in his sight.
> 72:15 And he shall live, and to him shall be given of the gold of Sheba: prayer also shall be made for him continually; and daily shall he be praised.
> 72:16 There shall be an handful of corn in the earth upon the top of the mountains; the fruit thereof shall shake like

Lebanon: and they of the city shall flourish like grass of the
earth.
72:17 His name shall endure for ever: his name shall be
continued as long as the sun: and men shall be blessed in
him: all nations shall call him blessed.
72:18 Blessed be the Lord God, the God of Israel, who only
doeth wondrous things.
72:19 And blessed be his glorious name for ever: and let the
whole earth be filled with his glory; Amen, and Amen.
72:20 The prayers of David the son of Jesse are ended.

K45

Rebellion at the end of the millennium

> 20:3‡[K42] *And cast him into the bottomless pit, and shut him up, and set a seal upon him, that he should deceive the nations no more,* till the thousand years should be fulfilled: and after that he must be loosed a little season.
> 20:7 And when the thousand years are expired, Satan shall be loosed out of his prison,
> 20:8 And shall go out to deceive the nations which are in the four quarters of the earth, Gog and Magog, to gather them together to battle: the number of whom is as the sand of the sea.
> 20:9 And they went up on the breadth of the earth, and compassed the camp of the saints about, and the beloved city: and fire came down from God out of heaven, and devoured them.
> 20:10 And the devil that deceived them was cast into the lake of fire and brimstone, where the beast and the false prophet are, and shall be tormented day and night for ever and ever.

Satan's sentence of one thousand years is over. The bottomless pit is unlocked and the seal is removed. He is released from his imprisonment (20:3,7). However, he is not at all chastened or reformed. He returns to earth immediately to recruit new followers for another battle (20:8). He will be like Napoleon who escaped in 1815 back to France from imprisonment on the isle of Elbe, and rallied his followers to one last battle that turned out to be Waterloo.

Who will be attracted to Satan's cause, out of all those living in this most ideal time in history? It would not be any who survived the tribulation and saw the beginning of the millennium. Those are people converted from their sinful past, and fully devoted to Christ.

However, as the millennium continues, children will be born to the survivors of the tribulation. Many new generations shall experience the blessing of Christ's kingdom. They face the question of whether they will trust their eternal lives to Christ. Some will outwardly conform, yet not actually be born again and be saved. Over time they massively outnumber the first inhabitants of the kingdom. They did not suffer the trials that happened before Christ's second coming, so they refuse to understand how good they have it. Not one can make any concrete complaint of injustice or favoritism. Nevertheless, many succumb to their sinful nature and imagine they can obtain something better than the rule of Christ, the son of God. Some of them will die prematurely, before the end of the millennium, because of their thanklessness:

> Isaiah 65:20 There shall be no more thence an infant of days, nor an old man that hath not filled his days: for the child shall die an hundred years old; but the sinner being an hundred years old shall be accursed.

But the secret rebels who remain alive till the appearance of Satan will be tempted by his promises.

There is a parallel between the time before Noah's flood and this time at the end of the millennium. One was at the end of the first age of human history, the other at the end of the last. Both began with people devoted to God and blessed exceedingly by him: in the paradise of the garden of Eden, and in Christ's visible millennial kingdom. Both ended in the rebellion of large numbers of their descendants. Even under the most favorable circumstances, in the most perfect environment imaginable, many people will choose not to follow the God who blesses them, but choose sin because it appeals to them. Apart from the grace of God and new life in Christ, they remain at heart only evil and opposed to God's commandments.

We are told that the rebels who join Satan are from the four quarters of the earth, meaning, from many different nations. Collectively they are described as "Gog and Magog" (20:8).

The names Gog and Magog appear without context in John's vision. Magog is mentioned in Genesis 10:2 as one of the sons of Japheth, and grandson of Noah. In the prophecy of Ezekiel 38-39, Gog is the chief prince of the nation descended from Magog. He is also prince of Meshach and Tubal (Ezekiel 38:2), nations that are apparently also descended from grandsons of Noah who bore those names. Allied with Gog are more descendants of Noah: Gomer and Togarmah, and the nations of Persia, Ethiopia, and Libya.

Together they invade Israel from the north (Ezekiel 38:15). The invasion is described in prophetic detail in Ezekiel 38-39. The event, which involves God's supernatural intervention, would therefore likely occur during the short intermediate period after the rapture and before the tribulation begins.

The Jewish politician and historian Josephus, who wrote *Antiquities of the Jews* in 93 CE, uses the Greek word *Scythia* in place of the Hebrew Magog. The Christian theologian Jerome (died 420) does the same. Among the writers of that time, Scythians was a collective word, denoting all unknown, barbarous tribes to the northeast of the Roman empire.

Perhaps the rebels born during the millennium trade fanciful stories of that failed invasion, and are inspired to insurrection by imagining what could have happened. If only their uprising would be more vicious, with even greater force and surprise, then they could once and for all defeat what they see as the overbearing correctness of Christ, his people, and all the resurrected saints around them. Satan again uses Gog and Magog as his earthly brand to deceive mankind. In their lack of experience with temptation, these children of the millennium are ripe to fall for Satan's schemes. God allows his deceptions as a test to make it evident who will follow Satan, Gog, and Magog, another false Trinity, into wickedness. This is the final assault against the truth.

However, those in harmony with God will not be deceived.

In his vision, John sees that Satan has formed this mass of grumblers and complainers against Christ, born across fifty millennial generations, into yet another formidable army. It seems that to the end, Satan favors war. They are gathered for battle. Their number is as the sand of the sea, and they surround the camp of believers in Jerusalem, the beloved city (20:9).

But fire comes down from heaven and devours them. This reminds us of how God destroyed Dathan, Abiram, and the sons of Korah. They were also grumblers and complainers, who after the parting of the Red Sea, rebelled and wanted the Israelites to return to Egypt (Numbers 16:35).

Satan now meets his final destiny by being cast into the eternal lake of fire, never again to tempt God's people (20:10). His dream of taking God's place of preeminence in the universe is conclusively shattered. He joins the beast and the false prophet, who have already been in the lake for a thousand years (19:20 K40). The devils who are devoted to Satan undoubtedly share his fate. Their preference may be to be annihilated and destroyed with no trace. Instead, their punishment is much worse – they will be tormented day and night forever and ever.

K46

Resurrections after the millennium, then judgment at the great white throne

20:5‡[K43] But the rest of the dead lived not again until the thousand years were finished. *This is the first resurrection.*
20:6‡[K44] *Blessed and holy is he that hath part in the first resurrection:* on such the second death *hath no power, but they shall be priests of God and of Christ, and shall reign with him a thousand years.*
20:13 And the sea gave up the dead which were in it; and death and hell delivered up the dead which were in them: and they were judged every man according to their works.
20:11 And I saw a great white throne, and him that sat on it, from whose face the earth and the heaven fled away; and there was found no place for them.
2:26 And he that overcometh, and keepeth my works unto the end, to him will I give power over the nations.
2:28 And I will give him the morning star.
20:12 And I saw the dead, small and great, stand before God; and the books were opened: and another book was opened, which is the book of life: and the dead were judged out of those things which were written in the books, according to their works.
20:15 And whosoever was not found written in the book of life was cast into the lake of fire.
21:8 But the fearful, and unbelieving, and the abominable, and murderers, and whoremongers, and sorcerers, and idolaters, and all liars, shall have their part in the lake which burneth with fire and brimstone: which is the second death.
20:14 And death and hell were cast into the lake of fire. This is the second death.

We have already seen two judgments of the resurrected. One was at the end of the tribulation – of the tribulation martyrs and Old Testament followers of the Messiah. That was the "first resurrection" of 20:5 K43. The other was earlier, of the church believers who were raptured (K13). (See Appendix F *Judgments before the throne of God*).

The thousand years are over. The last and final judgment is at hand. Now a fantastic assembly is gathered. It includes all the unbelievers who ever lived. They did not seek God. They rejected his offer of salvation. The unbelievers alive at the end of the millennium undoubtedly arrive at God's throne by being physically caught up to heaven, similar to what happened to the believers who were alive at the rapture (K13). Those souls who died and have been waiting in the intermediate location of *hades* (inaccurately translated as "hell" in the King James of 20:13), receive resurrected physical bodies and live again (20:5). They also appear before the throne.

Another group that must come to the throne are the believers who lived during the millennium. Revelation does not speak to their fate, but it must be assumed that they follow in the track of the church saints who were raptured (K13). The ones alive have their natural bodies transformed into glorified ones. Those who have died are resurrected. Together, they are the just who are taken up to heaven along with the unbelievers:

> Acts 24:15b there shall be a resurrection of the dead, both of the just and unjust.

The earth has been vacated of all human beings, both living and dead. It is no longer the abode of mankind. At this moment, "the earth and the heaven fled away; and there was found no place for them" (20:11). This is describing the total annihilation of God's physical creation, including the earth and the universe. Time as we know it stops. (After the judgment is over, in 21:1 K47 he will replace all things with a perfect new heaven and new earth). This titanic event of cosmic dissolution was prophesied by Peter:

> 2 Peter 3:10 But the day of the Lord will come as a thief in the night; in the which the heavens shall pass away with a great noise, and the elements shall melt with fervent heat, the earth also and the works that are therein shall be burned up.

And by Jesus:

> Matthew 24:35 Heaven and earth shall pass away, but my words shall not pass away.

With no heaven and no earth, a great white throne appears beyond space, beyond all dimensions (20:11), with Christ sitting on it. Jesus prophesied of this in the book of Matthew:

> Matthew 25:31 When the Son of man shall come in his glory, and all the holy angels with him, then shall he sit upon the throne of his glory.

Next, every unbeliever, and the believers living or died from the millennium, gives an account before the throne. The holy angels are witnesses. Christ, the son of God, judges each according to his or her works (20:13).

God already has the events of our lives recorded in his books (20:12). He now asks each person to give their own testimony:

> Romans 14:10b For we shall all stand before the judgment seat of Christ.
> 14:11 For it is written, As I live, saith the Lord, every knee shall bow to me, and every tongue shall confess to God.
> 14:12 So then every one of us shall give account of himself to God.

What account can you give of yourself before God? If you publicly rejected Jesus Christ and supported the persecution of God's people to your dying breath, the religion or ideology that you followed has no power to save your soul from everlasting hell. If you are not such a persecutor, you might speak of friends who think you were a good person. In either case, you are really saying that you don't need to trust your life to a savior to act on your behalf, and that you deserve heaven because God should be satisfied with your life.

Yes, you will indeed be judged according to your works. But they fall short of the glory of God (Romans 3:23).

Underneath the good works that you may claim are others that you wish to forget. Every one of us have disobeyed God's law many times. He gave us a summary of them in his ten commandments. In simple terms that a child can understand, they are:

1. Put God first.
2. Do not dedicate yourself to substitutes for God.
3. Respect God's name.

4. Respect God's day of rest.
5. Respect your parents.
6. Do not commit murder, even in your imagination.
7. Do not have sexual relations outside of marriage between a man and a woman, or even desire it.
8. Do not steal.
9. Do not lie.
10. Do not covet what is not yours.

In the first half of the tribulation, the woman of Babylon actively advocated for the exact opposite of all these commandments. Hers are anti-commandments. She rewarded people for converting others to her cause (17:2, 18:13, 18:23, all in K20). In the great tribulation, the beast and the false prophet did as well, though their emphases were different (13:4,7-8,10 in K23 and 13:12,14 K24).

Verse 21:8 shows us how God regards those who stand before his throne on the basis of their own righteousness. They are the fearful, the unbelieving, the abominable, murderers, whoremongers, sorcerers, idolaters, and liars.

Thankfully, the followers of Jesus will not be judged by the standard of their own works, but by their faith in the one who did the greatest work of all time:

> John 6:28 Then said they unto him, What shall we do, that we might work the works of God?
> 6:29 Jesus answered and said unto them, This is the work of God, that ye believe on him whom he hath sent.

The work of Christ was to sacrifice his blameless life on the cross, thus paying for the sins of all those who give their faith and their lives to him:

> John 15:13 Greater love hath no man than this, that a man lay down his life for his friends.

The church saints who were raptured, the tribulation martyrs, and Old Testament believers have given testimonies of faith at the earlier judgments (K13 and 20:4 K43). They are all among the heavenly observers of the great white throne scene. In their walk with the Holy

Spirit, they opposed the temptations of Satan. They are now granted power to participate in the judgment of the unbelievers from many nations. They join with Christ in trying, condemning, and consigning his enemies to punishment (2:26), as fulfillment of the promise Jesus made early in the vision to the church of Thyatira (K09). They do so under the light of God's "morning star" (2:28), which in the Roman times of John's vision was a symbol of kingly authority and sovereignty. The millennial believers who just arrived and gave their accounts of faith will also participate in overseeing the judgment of the unbelievers.

The morning star Venus often appears in the night sky just before the dawning of a new day. Jesus conducts the white throne judgment to completely cleanse the universe from evil, prior to the dawn of a new heaven and a new earth. Jesus will then replace Venus as the new morning star, one that heralds all eternity (22:16 K50).

The unbelievers who spurn Christ may assert their own views of right and wrong. Or perhaps they claim the goodness of an alternate worldview, religion or ideology. In any case, they cling to a worthless idol, and forfeit the grace that could have been theirs (Jonah 2:8). The God of the universe who rules beyond the dimension of time has known from its beginning that they are not written into his book of life (20:12). They are now judged to be the goats of Jesus' parable, which we also saw in section K43:

> Matthew 25:32 before him [the Son of man] shall be gathered all nations: and he shall separate them one from another, as a shepherd divideth his sheep from the goats.

Among the throng of unbelievers are the Old Testament Jews who claim they have acceptably followed God's law. But at the judgment of their brothers and sisters at the end of the tribulation, God did not allow their testimony and skipped over them. As a result, they did not see the blessings of the millennial kingdom. Neither will they enter into the final promised land of the new earth (K43):

> Ezekiel 20:38 And I will purge out from among you the rebels, and them that transgress against me: I will bring them forth out of the country where they sojourn, and they shall not enter into the land of Israel: and ye shall know that I am the Lord.

The verdict handed down to all the wicked from the great white throne is shame, damnation, and everlasting contempt:

> Daniel 12:2 And many of them that sleep in the dust of the earth shall awake, some to everlasting life, and some to shame and everlasting contempt.

> John 5:28 Marvel not at this: for the hour is coming, in the which all that are in the graves shall hear his voice,
> 5:29 And shall come forth; they that have done good, unto the resurrection of life; and they that have done evil, unto the resurrection of damnation.

The punishment meted out is the second death (21:8). It means to suffer eternal exclusion from the presence of the Lord:

> 2 Thessalonians 1:7b when the Lord Jesus shall be revealed from heaven with his mighty angels,
> 1:8 In flaming fire taking vengeance on them that know not God, and that obey not the gospel of our Lord Jesus Christ:
> 1:9 Who shall be punished with everlasting destruction from the presence of the Lord, and from the glory of his power.

The destiny of eternal punishment for unbelievers is not because God wished it, but because they would not come to him for the grace which he freely offered.

The sentence is carried out immediately. The wicked have already been given resurrection bodies suited for never-ending punishment. They are now cast into the eternal lake of fire (20:15). This is the fire of hell, which will be everlasting, as promised by the angel in 14:10-11 K42. Jesus also promised it two thousand years ago:

> Matthew 13:41 The Son of man shall send forth his angels, and they shall gather out of his kingdom all things that offend, and them which do iniquity;
> 13:42 And shall cast them into a furnace of fire: there shall be wailing and gnashing of teeth.

There they join Satan, the beast, and the false prophet. Some of them knowingly supported the beast during the tribulation. Others unwittingly gave allegiance to Satan when they lived before the tribulation. In the lake of fire, the place of perdition, they will continue in existence forever. They thus share the fate of Satan – they will "behold the beast that was, and is not, and yet is" (17:8 K02). So is fulfilled the portion of John's vision that occurred at the beginning of the timeline of Revelation.

The fact of hell is a torment to contemplate. But it makes the love of God all the more wonderful for those who embrace his salvation.

The days of evil are done. Death and hell are cast into the lake of fire (20:14). They will never again be encountered in the coming new creation. An eternity of perfect goodness with God awaits.

K47

The new heaven, the new earth, and the new Jerusalem

21:1 And I saw a new heaven and a new earth: for the first
heaven and the first earth were passed away; and there was
no more sea.
21:9 And there came unto me one of the seven angels which
had the seven vials full of the seven last plagues, and talked
with me, saying, Come hither, I will shew thee the bride, the
Lamb's wife.
21:10 And he carried me away in the spirit to a great and
high mountain, and shewed me that great city, the holy
Jerusalem, descending out of heaven from God.
21:2 And I John saw the holy city, new Jerusalem, coming
down from God out of heaven, prepared as a bride adorned
for her husband.
21:11 Having the glory of God: and her light was like unto a
stone most precious, even like a jasper stone, clear as
crystal;
21:12 And had a wall great and high, and had twelve gates,
and at the gates twelve angels, and names written thereon,
which are the names of the twelve tribes of the children of
Israel:
21:13 On the east three gates; on the north three gates; on
the south three gates; and on the west three gates.
21:14 And the wall of the city had twelve foundations, and in
them the names of the twelve apostles of the Lamb.
21:15 And he that talked with me had a golden reed to
measure the city, and the gates thereof, and the wall thereof.
21:16 And the city lieth foursquare, and the length is as large
as the breadth: and he measured the city with the reed,
twelve thousand furlongs. The length and the breadth and
the height of it are equal.
21:17 And he measured the wall thereof, an hundred and
forty and four cubits, according to the measure of a man,
that is, of the angel.
21:18 And the building of the wall of it was of jasper: and the
city was pure gold, like unto clear glass.
21:19 And the foundations of the wall of the city were
garnished with all manner of precious stones. The first
foundation was jasper; the second, sapphire; the third, a
chalcedony; the fourth, an emerald;

> 21:20 The fifth, sardonyx; the sixth, sardius; the seventh, chrysolite; the eighth, beryl; the ninth, a topaz; the tenth, a chrysoprasus; the eleventh, a jacinth; the twelfth, an amethyst.
> 21:21 And the twelve gates were twelve pearls; every several gate was of one pearl: and the street of the city was pure gold, as it were transparent glass.
> 21:3 And I heard a great voice out of heaven saying, Behold, the tabernacle of God is with men, and he will dwell with them, and they shall be his people, and God himself shall be with them, and be their God.
> 3:12 Him that overcometh will I make a pillar in the Temple of my God, and he shall go no more out: and I will write upon him the name of my God, and the name of the city of my God, which is new Jerusalem, which cometh down out of heaven from my God: and I will write upon him my new name.

On the day God created our universe, there were no onlookers on hand.

There are, however, onlookers as he unveils a new heaven and a new earth. After the annihilation of the cosmos (20:11 K46), and after all the wicked are cast into the lake of fire (20:15, 21:8 K46), only the resurrected born-again believers in their glorified bodies remain, along with the angels. They are somewhere outside of space and time. They are forever free from evil. God has granted them eternal liberty. They are the audience for God's awesome re-creation, an entirely new order suited for eternity. According to Genesis 1, God created our universe in six days. He can certainly re-create a perfect one in the manner that he chooses.

Other passages of the Bible look ahead to this new creation. For example, after Peter foresaw the fold up of our cosmos in 2 Peter 3:10 (K46), a few verses later he says:

> 2 Peter 3:13 Nevertheless we, according to his promise, look for new heavens and a new earth, wherein dwelleth righteousness.

There are also two verses in Isaiah that speak of the new heaven and the new earth, God's vehicles for eternity after the millennium:

> Isaiah 65:17 For, behold, I create new heavens and a new earth: and the former shall not be remembered, nor come into mind.
> 66:22 For as the new heavens and the new earth, which I will make, shall remain before me, saith the Lord, so shall your seed and your name remain.

We are told that in the new creation, "there was no more sea" (21:1). This could mean that there are no bodies of water on the new earth, which is unlikely since there will be a river of life (22:2 K49). But the word "sea" reminds us of the opening verses of the Bible:

> Genesis 1:1 In the beginning God created the heaven and the earth.
> 1:2 And the earth was without form, and void; and darkness was upon the face of the deep. And the Spirit of God moved upon the face of the waters.

The Hebrew word for "deep" here is *tehom*, meaning the deep sea, the primeval ocean, the waters below, the abyss or the grave. This sea in this context is thus the uncreated state, the chaos that preceded God's ordering of creation. From this I believe 21:1 is telling us there will be no more chaos in heaven or on earth.

Later in this section, we will discuss the new Jerusalem descending from heaven to earth to become the capital city of the new creation. In section K49 we will get a glimpse of what the new earth is like, and the river of everlasting life that will continuously flow to it from the new Jerusalem (22:1-2 K49).

We have much less experience of heaven to serve as launching point for what the new heaven could be. Once again, the Bible provides some clues. Let me build on them for a theological understanding of the new heaven.

The main one is from Paul, who mentions he knew someone (probably himself) who was briefly caught up to the third heaven:

> 2 Corinthians 12:2 I knew a man in Christ above fourteen years ago, (whether in the body, I cannot tell; or whether out of the body, I cannot tell: God knoweth;) such an one caught up to the third heaven.

We can figure out fairly easily what the three different heavens are, from the Bible.[14] The *first heaven*, or the firmament, consists of the clouds and the atmosphere. It is for the "fowls of the heaven" (Genesis 2:19; 7:3,23; Psalm 8:8, etc.). The biblical expressions "doors of heaven" or "windows of heaven" are speaking of the first heaven, as in "the windows of heaven were opened. And the rain was on the earth forty days and forty nights" (Genesis 7:11-12). We can gaze through the atmosphere of the first heaven to see the stars and planets beyond it:

> Genesis 1:14a And God said, Let there be lights in the firmament of the heaven to divide the day from the night.

The *second heaven*, also called "the heavens" in Scripture, are the sun, moon, solar system, milky way, and galaxies to the utter ends of outer space (Jeremiah 8:2; Matthew 24:29). The distances involved are staggering. Scientists tell us that light would take billions of years to travel from the farthest quasars. What is more amazing is that God created the heavens in six days just over 6,000 years ago. Substantial evidence supports such a young universe, even billions of light years in size.[15] No wonder the Bible states in Psalm 19:1: "The heavens declare the glory of God; and the firmament sheweth his handywork."

The *third heaven* transcends the dimensions that we know. It is where God and the holy angels dwell. It is also where the resurrected believers will go after the rapture. It is called "the heaven of heavens" (Deuteronomy 10:14, 1 Kings 8:27). This is the dwelling-place of God to which Paul was taken, and whose wonders he was permitted to behold (2 Corinthians 12:2). Paul also calls it "paradise" (2 Corinthians 12:4).

Here in the book of Revelation, God promises to replace these first three original heavens with the new heaven (21:1). But God gives us tantalizingly little information about the new heaven. Apparently, he leaves it to our faith to imagine what life will be like.

---

[14] *How many heavens are there and what is the third heaven Paul speaks of in 2 Corinthians 12*, http://letusreason.org/Biblexp130.htm, accessed July 29,2022, no author.

[15] D. Russell Humphreys, *Evidence for a Young World*, https://www.icr.org/article/evidence-for-young-world/, June 1, 2005, accessed July 30, 2022.

If you think about it, God will break down the separation between the second and third heavens. Right now, we are creatures tainted by sin, slowly aging, and dying in our natural bodies. We do not have access to the third heaven the way the angels do. We cannot see God. But in the new heaven, we shall see God face-to-face (22:4 K49). There seems to be nothing in future to stop us from traveling between earth and heaven, the way angels are used to doing, by following the path the new Jerusalem took when it descended from the new heaven to the new earth (21:10,2). And there will be no sin to prevent us from having direct access to the presence of God. This is how the distinction between the second and third heavens will be dissolved.

Therefore, we are justified for looking at the second heaven that we know as a launching point for understanding what the new heaven will be like.

Let us consider the words of Paul, where he compares the liberty of the resurrected believers to the liberty that will be granted to the new heaven itself when it is re-created:

> Romans 8:19 For the earnest expectation of the creature [creation] waiteth for the manifestation of the sons of God.
> 8:20 For the creature was made subject to vanity, not willingly, but by reason of him who hath subjected the same in hope,
> 8:21 Because the creature itself also shall be delivered from the bondage of corruption into the glorious liberty of the children of God.

What could God's word mean here? How can this new universe itself "be delivered from the bondage of corruption into the glorious liberty of the children of God"?

Intelligent design proponents have formulated the *anthropic principle*, which states that some higher power has providentially engineered the universe to suit the specific needs of human beings. There are many scientific examples of different aspects of the universe that could not have come about and integrated together by chance. For example: the unique properties of water, the life-giving composition of earth's atmosphere, the protectiveness of earth's reflectivity and magnetic field, the optimal orbit of earth in the solar system, our solar system's favorable location in the spiral arms of the galaxy, the ideal color and temperature of our sun, etc., etc. These and many more are indicators of special design and foresight to make life possible for the pinnacle of God's creation, the human race. Also, our existence in this universe depends on numerous cosmological constants and parameters whose numerical values must fall within a very narrow range. If even a single variable were off, even slightly, we would not exist.

Creation scientists also refer to the anthropic principle to defend Genesis as a literal creation account, with the Almighty God as the creator. In his love, God distinguished man and woman from all other creatures by creating them in his image (Genesis 1:26, see also Appendix A).

Unfortunately, most scientists of my day are not creationists. Instead, they are scoffers who refuse to look at the evidence for God and for a young universe. Many of them are popularizing another view as to how an advanced life form like ours can be present. It is called the *multiverse*. They imagine it to be an infinity of universes, each having different values for the cosmological constants. This infinity of universes somehow originated not by a prime mover, but by a still-unknown quantum mechanism. The particular universe that we live in is the one with the optimum set of properties that accommodates advanced life forms. All the others have no life, and no beings are present within them to be conscious of that fact. In this way, we can be here, and owe no favoritism to the whim of a hypothetical higher power.

It is interesting that these scientists dwell on a continuum of constants that vary between their imagined universes, but they do not call into question the equations of the physical laws which refer to those constants. For instance, the second law of thermodynamics, which describes how all things eventually run down and decay, would be operational in all the instances of the multiverse. Here we have a key to the foolishness of men and women who don't want to recognize God's original working:

> Romans 1:20 For the invisible things of him from the creation of the world are clearly seen, being understood by the things that are made, even his eternal power and Godhead; so that they are without excuse:

> 1:21 Because that, when they knew God, they glorified him not as God, neither were thankful; but became vain in their imaginations, and their foolish heart was darkened.
> 1:22 Professing themselves to be wise, they became fools.

Returning to Romans 8:21, it says that the new heaven and new earth will have no "bondage of corruption." That tells us that God's new creation will not have elements of decay. That is because his new heaven does not need to be subject to the same cosmological constants that govern us now, or even to the same physical law equations. The second law of thermodynamics will no longer govern. God chooses to re-create outside of any multiverse that would presume to restrict him within a limited physical law framework, vast though its options may be. The new heaven and new earth will be perfect for our glorified bodies. I personally believe that in God's new creation, the limiting speed of light will also be lifted, which will allow easy communication and transport across the new heaven.

After the creation of the new heaven and new earth, in John's vision he sees a new Jerusalem descend from heaven to earth (21:10,2). It is described as a bride adorned for her husband (21:9,2). This bride is not a person, but a place. It will be the new home, or tabernacle (21:3) for God, who is also identified as the Alpha and Omega (21:6). That is a title that Jesus Christ used for himself (1:8 K00), the first and last letters of the Greek alphabet, signifying that he is the beginning and end of all things. In the next section 19:7-9 K48, this place will welcome another bride: the church saints of the rapture.

The new Jerusalem is the eternal city that Abraham looked forward to:

> Hebrews 11:9 By faith he [Abraham] sojourned in the land of promise, as in a strange country, dwelling in tabernacles with Isaac and Jacob, the heirs with him of the same promise:
> 11:10 For he looked for a city which hath foundations, whose builder and maker is God.

How does the new Jerusalem come about? It is a perfect re-creation of the Jerusalem that we know, God's holy city, the place where the Old Testament Jews offered sacrifices to atone for their sins before God. That is where Jesus offered himself as the perfect and final sacrifice.

During his first coming, he told his disciples that he would soon leave them and go to his death. But he encouraged them not to be troubled:

> John 14:1 Let not your heart be troubled: ye believe in God, believe also in me.
> 14:2 In my Father's house are many mansions: if it were not so, I would have told you. I go to prepare a place for you.
> 14:3 And if I go and prepare a place for you, I will come again, and receive you unto myself; that where I am, there ye may be also.

The place that Jesus went to prepare after his ascension is the new Jerusalem. This work was one of his main activities for the two thousand years prior to his coming to earth for the millennial kingdom. Apparently, during all that time, the new Jerusalem was separate from heaven and earth, so as not to be annihilated when they are (20:11 K46). After God creates the new heaven, he moves the new Jerusalem there. It then magnificently descends to the new earth (21:10,2), and is unveiled to God's people and God's angels.

John's vision of the new Jerusalem goes into some detail in describing the walls and gates for the central city of God's new universe.

The great cities of old were distinguished by their characteristic walls, gates, and temples. Walls marked off their area of jurisdiction from the surrounding countryside. Gates were entry points for commerce. Both were also used for defense. Temples brought their inhabitants together to honor the deities or ideologies that unified them. In the cities of our time, walls have been replaced by invisible boundary lines protected by monitoring systems and modern weaponry. City gates have been replaced by highways, railways, and airports. Instead of temples, many cities have large stadiums of assembly for patriotic or religious occasions.

We always think of our cities as being two dimensional, since they are situated on the surface of the earth. They are usually alongside a body of water to aid in trade. In the past two hundred years, skyscrapers have given them a bit of a third dimension. But according to 21:16, the new Jerusalem will be fully three dimensional, a cube of 12,000 furlongs in length, breadth and height, or about 2,400 kilometers to a side. You can imagine it as the length of Japan, also with the same width, accommodating a similar population density – and amazingly as a skyscraper of the same height.

Ancient cities went dark at night, our modern ones have many lights, but the new Jerusalem shimmers 24x7 with ongoing bright light like jasper stone (21:11). In John's vision we have no indications of how the interior of the cube city is arranged, or how gravity will work. I can conceptualize the city as consisting internally of concentric spherical layers, with the cube embedded within a mostly hollow outer sphere, also of many levels. The larger sphere would be the new earth. There could be many extended domed and lighted spaces to serve as countryside, and many smaller satellite cities as dwelling places. The new earth would be situated within the new heaven, and will be the home planet for the numerous planets, stars and galaxies that stretch into the beyond. This would be an awesome imagining of Christ's eternal cosmos.

There are a series of twelves in John's vision of the new Jerusalem. That number appears frequently in the Bible to quantify things, and also signal that they are perfect and complete in God's sight. The wall of the new Jerusalem is twelve times twelve cubits high (21:17). It has twelve foundations. In them are the names of the twelve New Testament apostles (21:14), and they are garnished with twelve different precious stones (21:19-20). The gates have twelve angels posted at them (21:12). They are made of twelve gargantuan pearls (21:21). Written on the gates are the names of the twelve Old Testament tribes of Israel (21:12).

The city measures twelve thousand furlongs on each side (21:16). It is made, partially at least, of pure gold that appears like a clear smooth sea made of glass (21:18). The same is true of its streets (21:21). The transparency of the city transmits the glory of God, in a spectrum of brilliant colors. It is a city of unsurpassed beauty.

The onlookers are now transported from their vantage point outside of space and time to the new creation. They are the resurrected born-again believers who are welcomed to the city of God. He will live among them. They will be his people, and he will be their God (21:3).

The onlookers include the church saints who were caught up to the original heaven at the rapture (K13). In their life on earth, they were faithful in their testimony and sure in their salvation. As a reward, the new Jerusalem was promised them early in John's vision. In his letter to the church of Philadelphia (K11), Christ gave the church saints the promise: they will overcome, and someday will be pillars of the temple of God (3:12). I have added that promise verse, addressed to all the New Testament believers, to the end of this section.

The words "pillar" and "temple" of 3:12 are both symbolic. God did not provide a temple for the church during their New Testament age, instead, Jesus Christ was their temple:

> John 2:18 Then answered the Jews and said unto him, What sign shewest thou unto us, seeing that thou doest these things?
> 2:19 Jesus answered and said unto them, Destroy this temple, and in three days I will raise it up.
> 2:20 Then said the Jews, Forty and six years was this temple in building, and wilt thou rear it up in three days?
> 2:21 But he spake of the temple of his body.
> 2:22 When therefore he was risen from the dead, his disciples remembered that he had said this unto them; and they believed the scripture, and the word which Jesus had said.

We shall see in 21:22 K49 that in the new Jerusalem, there also will be no temple. Instead, Christ will be the temple once again, and the church saints will be its pillars (3:12). That figure of speech is God's assurance that they will be with him through all eternity. He will write upon them his new name: the name of God and the name of new Jerusalem. Included in the promise is that they "shall go no more out," meaning they will no longer be exposed to the trials and temptations of this present life. Instead, the church saints will have their permanent residence in the presence of God.

And so is fulfilled the words of the book of Hebrews, addressed to all pilgrims who ever lived this life on earth in a journey towards the heavenly city:

> Hebrews 12:22 But ye are come unto mount Sion, and unto the city of the living God, the heavenly Jerusalem, and to an innumerable company of angels,

> 12:23 To the general assembly and church of the firstborn,
> which are written in heaven, and to God the Judge of all, and
> to the spirits of just men made perfect,
> 12:24a And to Jesus the mediator of the new covenant.

The new Jerusalem will be the favorite place of the new earth. It will be the home for all the saints who ever lived throughout all the ages. It will be the new sending city for God's people to go back and forth between the new earth and the new heaven.

The unveiling of the new heaven, new earth, and new Jerusalem sets the stage for the marriage feast celebrating Christ and his bride the church of God.

K48

The marriage supper between Christ and all his church, rejoiced over by believers of other ages

> 19:5 And a voice came out of the throne, saying, Praise our
> God, all ye his servants, and ye that fear him, both small and
> great.
> 19:6 And I heard as it were the voice of a great multitude,
> and as the voice of many waters, and as the voice of mighty
> thunderings, saying, Alleluia: for the Lord God omnipotent
> reigneth.
> 19:7 Let us be glad and rejoice, and give honour to him: for
> the marriage of the Lamb is come, and his wife hath made
> herself ready.
> 19:8 And to her was granted that she should be arrayed in
> fine linen, clean and white: for the fine linen is the
> righteousness of saints.
> 19:9 And he saith unto me, Write, Blessed are they which are
> called unto the marriage supper of the Lamb. And he saith
> unto me, These are the true sayings of God.
> 19:10 And I fell at his feet to worship him. And he said unto
> me, See thou do it not: I am thy fellowservant, and of thy
> brethren that have the testimony of Jesus: worship God: for
> the testimony of Jesus is the spirit of prophecy.

There is a major event in John's vision, recorded back in Revelation 19, which is best placed at this point of the chronology. It is the marriage supper of the Lamb and his bride. Multitudes upon multitudes join in celebrating.

The Lamb of God of course is Jesus Christ:

> John 1:29 The next day John [the Baptist] seeth Jesus coming unto him, and saith, Behold the Lamb of God, which taketh away the sin of the world.

There is a large assembly of well-wishers at this wedding feast (19:6-7). The angels are likely present. It probably also includes a large number of men and women belonging to God. We can deduce this from a few verses prior, in 19:1 K22, where there was an assembly during the great tribulation that included the still-to-be-resurrected tribulation martyrs and the raptured church saints. They thanked God for his judgment upon the end times rebellion of Babylon. By the proximity of these verses, referring to events more than a thousand years apart, we see that this new assembly of well-wishers at the wedding feast undoubtedly also has multitudes of men and women in it. The multitudes reappear within the cross-linking spiral of John's vision. But this time the composition of the multitudes is different.

The unveiling of the new heaven and the new earth in the previous section was performed in front of all the believers who ever lived. They represent six ages of human history. Each age began with a mighty work of God. Those miracles are largely ignored in secular history books.

The first age included the believers who lived before Noah's flood. They were in the generations immediately following Adam and Eve. They listened to the story of God creating heaven, the earth, and paradise, and the fall of the human race into sin. Those who believed looked forward to the fulfillment of God's promise: that a future seed of the woman would crush Satan, and that he would overcome the sin that enslaved them (Genesis 3:15).

The second age brought forth a preciously small number of believers, of different nations, who lived after Noah's flood. Unfortunately, until God's missionaries went out to the gentile nations during the New Testament age, the peoples of the world did not have easy access to God's word. But almost all of them had on record some account of the flood that had consumed nearly all of mankind. Some across the world clung to the story. They remembered how, by God's mercy, Noah and his family were preserved to become their earliest ancestors. They put their trust in the God who sent the flood to save them from future calamity and death.[16]

The third age includes the Jewish believers of the Old Testament period. They knew of their forbears' deliverance from Egypt, God's miraculous parting of the Red Sea, and how he gave the ten commandments from Mount Sinai, enveloped in fire and smoke. While all the other nations drifted away from the true God, and took to worshipping deities of their imagination, God sent prophets to Israel

[16] Charles Martin, *Flood Legends*, Master Books, 2009.

who spoke his word to them. It is interesting that the books of the Old Testament took almost exactly one thousand years to be written, by a large number of authors chosen by God. The first was Moses starting about 1440 BCE, the last was Malachi around 440 BCE. Scattered throughout the Old Testament are many prophecies of the coming Messiah, who would be God's son.

In a way, the faith of the believers of the first three ages was greater than those of the ages after them. That is because their faith was based on God's promise of a future deliverer, and not in someone who had already been seen by witnesses. Their numbers were also far fewer, compared with the population of the world since it was created. Most were the Jewish believers, descendants of Abraham. They lived in the two thousand years before the deliverer *Yeshua HaMashiakh* was born. In section K43, I cited the prophecies of Ezekiel 37:11, Ezekiel 37:12, and Isaiah 11:12, which imply that these believers of the first three ages will be resurrected into the millennial kingdom with deathless bodies. This will be the reward for their future-facing faith. They will reign alongside Christ over the thousand-year world. Also present will be believers from the fifth and sixth ages, in both glorified and natural bodies. The thousand years will be an almost perfect recapitulation of God's Old Testament kingdoms of Israel.

I write this book from the fourth age, which is the New Testament era of church believers. In John's lifetime, the first of them walked with Jesus, watched him die without sin on the cross, and saw him resurrected and ascend into heaven. But after those first disciples, generations more have put their faith in Jesus by faith alone, and not also by sight. They gathered in many different church congregations, and worshipped God in many languages and differing manners. Their faith was based on the witness of the New Testament, and the changed lives of other believers. These church saints make up a vast number from all nations, far greater in number than the believers from after the flood or the Old Testament saints.

The fifth age involves the believers of the tribulation. They heard the story of the miraculous rapture that had taken away the church believers from their midst. They repented from following the woman of Babylon, the beast, and all their confederates. Instead, they put their trust in the promised second coming of Jesus. As a consequence, many died at the hands of their enemies, but were resurrected by God. Both the believers who survived the tribulation, and the martyrs who were resurrected, then entered into Christ's millennial kingdom.

The sixth and final age includes the believers born during the millennium. They had opportunities to personally interact with Jesus, the king of kings, ruling the world from Jerusalem. They mixed with believers of earlier ages, now in glorified bodies, who were granted the privileged of being resurrected just before the millennium. The millennial children of God who put their faith in Christ were not tempted when Satan returned for one final rebellion.

Out of all these believers, who is the wife of Christ (19:7) at the marriage supper? If the onlookers are angels only, then his wife is the body of believers across all the ages. But since the well-wishers of 19:6-7 seem to also include men and women, a stronger case can be made that the wife is the church of the New Testament age.

The symbolism of God's marriage to his people has variations between the Old and New Testaments. Frequently in the Old, for instance in the book of Hosea, Israel is described as the unfaithful wife of Jehovah, to be restored to her position as a faithful wife in the future millennial reign:

> Hosea 1:2b And the LORD said to Hosea, Go, take unto thee a wife of whoredoms and children of whoredoms: for the land hath committed great whoredom, departing from the LORD.
> 1:10 Yet the number of the children of Israel shall be as the sand of the sea, which cannot be measured nor numbered; and it shall come to pass, that in the place where it was said unto them, Ye are not my people, there it shall be said unto them, Ye are the sons of the living God.
> 1:11 Then shall the children of Judah and the children of Israel be gathered together, and appoint themselves one head, and they shall come up out of the land: for great shall be the day of Jezreel.

By contrast, in the New Testament the church is pictured as a virgin waiting for the coming of her bridegroom:

> 2 Corinthians 11:2 For I am jealous over you with godly jealousy: for I have espoused you to one husband, that I may present you as a chaste virgin to Christ.

In Ephesians, Paul makes a comparison between the church as the wife of Christ and the holy marriage relationship between a man and a woman:

> Ephesians 5:23 For the husband is the head of the wife, even as Christ is the head of the church: and he is the saviour of the body.
> 5:24 Therefore as the church is subject unto Christ, so let the wives be to their own husbands in every thing.
> 5:25 Husbands, love your wives, even as Christ also loved the church, and gave himself for it;
> 5:26 That he might sanctify and cleanse it with the washing of water by the word,
> 5:27 That he might present it to himself a glorious church, not having spot, or wrinkle, or any such thing; but that it should be holy and without blemish.

The best interpretation therefore is that Jesus celebrates his marriage to the church as his wife. His guests are the various saints of all other ages, along with the angels. The only time in the chronology when all are together is after the unveiling of the new heaven and earth.

Why is the church singled out from the other believers with the privilege of being the wife of Christ? Revelation is silent on the topic of how the other groups of believers are honored. They might not be the wife of Christ, but God undoubtedly will give them an exalted status. John, who is the recipient of the vision and the author of the book, has a great personal interest in the church. He, after all, is one of the twelve apostles who obeyed Christ's call to start the church among all the nations. This call came from the parting words of Jesus before he ascended into heaven, his "great commission" for them and all their future followers to bring the church to the ends of the earth:

> Matthew 28:19 Go ye therefore, and teach all nations, baptizing them in the name of the Father, and of the Son, and of the Holy Ghost:
> 28:20 Teaching them to observe all things whatsoever I have commanded you: and, lo, I am with you always, even unto the end of the world. Amen.

It is in keeping with John's interest in the church that God would bring him the vision of its ultimate destiny – the marriage supper of the Lamb.

Why does the marriage celebration happen now, and not earlier when the church was raptured into heaven? And where does the celebration occur? I believe that God delays it until he gathers all the possible observers. The passage does not give the location, but it would make sense that God arranges it as part of the inauguration of the new Jerusalem.

According to old marriage custom, the marriage celebration is actually the final step in the marriage process. In much of the ancient world there were three steps toward consummation of marriage, drawn out over a period of time: (1) A marriage contract was agreed by the parents of the couple before they came of age, a dowry was paid, and the couple was then regarded as legally married. (2) After the bride comes of age, the bridegroom goes with his friends to the bride's house and escorts her to his home. (3) The marriage supper takes place, with guests in attendance.

This process is beautifully illustrated in the marriage of Christ to his church: (1) He adds each believer whom he saves to his wedding contract with his bride the church. They are now legally married, in a binding relationship that cannot be broken. (2) At the rapture he briefly appears on earth, his bride's home, and escorts her to his home in heaven. (3) After the interlude of the tribulation, and after Jesus goes to earth to preside over the millennial kingdom, the wedding feast occurs.

The new Jerusalem, freshly unveiled, is the perfect place for the marriage supper of the Lamb and his church.

The bride is described as dressed "in fine linen, clean and white." This represents the righteousness of the believers (19:8). In the original Greek the word righteousness here is the plural form *dikaiomata*. The plural indicates not their justification by faith in Christ (which would be the case if the singular was used), but the many righteous deeds they have done in gratitude for their salvation. Those deeds are the outcome of *sanctification* (see Ephesians 5:26 above), a word that describes disciples growing in their walk with Christ, reorienting their lives to obey his commands, and becoming more and more like him.

Those who are invited to the marriage supper are exceedingly blessed (19:9).

The angel speaking these words refuses John's worship and redirects him to worship God instead. He then tells him that "the testimony of Jesus is the spirit of prophecy" (19:10). This means that prophecy inspired by God is designed to unfold the character and splendor of our Lord and Savior Jesus Christ. An appreciation of prophecy is part of our sanctification. In the present age, the Holy Spirit not only sanctifies the life of believers, but also shows them things to come as they relate to Christ. Jesus is not only the major character of the Bible, but also the central theme of biblical prophecy. In the New Testament Gospels, he was revealed in rejection, humiliation, suffering, and death. In the book of Revelation, he returns in triumph, glory, sovereignty, and majesty. How blessed are Christians who grow in their relationship with Jesus, through a better understanding of the prophecies of the end times.

Eternal life with God now unfolds in all its glory to his children of all ages. It can finally proceed after the marriage supper of the Lamb, celebrating his union to his bride and pride, the church. They are the most numerous group of believers of the different ages, from all nations. They trusted the words of the Bible that recorded the eyewitness testimony of those who saw and heard the living Christ. While the millennial kingdom was an almost perfect recapitulation of the Old Testament, eternity will be an absolutely perfect recapitulation of the New.

K49

Eternal Life

21:22 And I saw no temple therein: for the Lord God
Almighty and the Lamb are the temple of it.
21:23 And the city had no need of the sun, neither of the
moon, to shine in it: for the glory of God did lighten it, and
the Lamb is the light thereof.
21:24 And the nations of them which are saved shall walk in
the light of it: and the kings of the earth do bring their glory
and honour into it.
21:25 And the gates of it shall not be shut at all by day: for
there shall be no night there.
21:26 And they shall bring the glory and honour of the
nations into it.
21:27 And there shall in no wise enter into it any thing that
defileth, neither whatsoever worketh abomination, or
maketh a lie: but they which are written in the Lamb's book
of life.
22:1 And he shewed me a pure river of water of life, clear as
crystal, proceeding out of the throne of God and of the Lamb.
22:2 In the midst of the street of it, and on either side of the
river, was there the tree of life, which bare twelve manner of
fruits, and yielded her fruit every month: and the leaves of
the tree were for the healing of the nations.
22:3 And there shall be no more curse: but the throne of God
and of the Lamb shall be in it; and his servants shall serve
him:
22:4 And they shall see his face; and his name shall be in
their foreheads.
22:5 And there shall be no night there; and they need no
candle, neither light of the sun; for the Lord God giveth them
light: and they shall reign for ever and ever.
21:4 And God shall wipe away all tears from their eyes; and
there shall be no more death, neither sorrow, nor crying,
neither shall there be any more pain: for the former things
are passed away.
21:5 And he that sat upon the throne said, Behold, I make all
things new. And he said unto me, Write: for these words are
true and faithful.
21:6 And he said unto me, It is done. I am Alpha and Omega,
the beginning and the end. I will give unto him that is athirst
of the fountain of the water of life freely.

> 21:7 He that overcometh shall inherit all things; and I will be his God, and he shall be my son.

The millennial kingdom was a preview of the eternal age. The qualities of Christ's thousand year reign now stretch into the perfection of eternity. He continues as king of kings and lord of lords. The scene of his rule over the earth shifts to the new heaven and the new earth.

The book of Revelation highlights a number of amazing things about eternal life.

There will be no central temple in the new Jerusalem, capital city of the universe. The Lord Almighty himself and his son the Lamb of God will be the temple (21:22). This is in contrast to the temples that were in the old Jerusalem: the Old Testament temples built by Solomon, by the Jews after their captivity in Babylon, and King Herod's temple; or the millennial temple prophesied in Ezekiel 40-46. Those were meant for the worship of God. No longer is the structure necessary. The word for temple here is the Greek *naos*, which was also used for the Holy of Holies. That was the interior chamber of the old Jerusalem temples, God's dwelling place, where only the high priest was allowed to enter once a year (Hebrews 9:7). God himself will be the new *naos*. You his saints will be in the immediate presence of the Lord. You will have no need for a temple priest to be your mediator. The shadows of things to come are replaced with the reality of eternity.

There will be no sun or moon as outdoor sources of light for the new Jerusalem (21:23, 22:5). This reminds us of the first six days of creation, when God created light on the first day, but it was not until the fourth day that he created the Sun, Moon and the stars:

> Genesis 1:3 And God said, Let there be light: and there was light.
> 1:5 And God called the light Day, and the darkness he called Night. And the evening and the morning were the first day.
> 1:16 And God made two great lights; the greater light to rule the day, and the lesser light to rule the night: he made the stars also.
> 1:19 And the evening and the morning were the fourth day.

In the eternal age, Christ will be the light:

> John 8:12 Then spake Jesus again unto them, saying, I am the light of the world: he that followeth me shall not walk in darkness, but shall have the light of life.

He will be the light not just in a spiritual way, but literally as well in some wonderful way that we will discover.

There will be no night in the new Jerusalem (21:25), no need for city gates to be shut, no enemies to guard against. Your glorified body will not grow tired. You will not need night to sleep in.

There will be a throne for God and for his son the Lamb (22:3). A river of living water will constantly flow from the throne, through the middle of the city (22:1, 21:6). Christ is the source of that living water:

> John 4:10 Jesus answered and said unto her [the woman at the well of Samaria], If thou knewest the gift of God, and who it is that saith to thee, Give me to drink; thou wouldest have asked of him, and he would have given thee living water.

His water will be the fountain of life for the entire universe, again not just spiritually, but literally as well.

The tree of life of the original garden of Eden (Genesis 2:9) will make its reappearance (22:2). In John's vision, the tree will straddle the river of life. It will bear twelve kinds of fruit every month. The leaves of this tree are for "the healing (Greek: *therapeian*) of the nations." We know there is no sickness or death in eternity, therefore it is better to understand that the tree of life is the source of health to all in the re-created universe.

The new heaven and new earth will be more marvelous than the garden of Eden, the first paradise (Genesis 2). That was the place that God first intended for the human race, a place where they were (in the theological Latin expression) *posse peccare posse non peccare*: able to sin and able not to sin. But when Adam and Eve and the human race rebelled against God, they became *non posse non peccare*: not able not to sin. In response, God cast them out of Eden, and the earth became subject to his curse upon sin.

To all who read this: God calls you to come back to him. If you turn to Christ in repentance for your sins, God will forgive you. He will regenerate you. He will help you become *posse non peccare*: able not to sin.

After this life, the state of your heart in eternity will be much better than all that came before. You will know everlasting innocence. There will never be sin, or temptation to sin, nothing that defiles, no abomination, no lie. The inhabitants of the universe will forever be only those written into God's book of life (21:27). His people will become like the angels, fully committed to him for all eternity. You will become *non posse pecarre*: not able to sin. We will deeply enjoy following God forever. Never again will there be a curse, no need for punishment, for sin will be no more (22:3).

We shall see God and be with him. We will be sons and daughters of his family (21:7). We will be his children saved from many nations (21:24). We own his name (22:4). We inherit all things (21:7), thus joining in the inheritance that the Father gave to Christ his son (Hebrews 1:2).

There will be no more death, tears, sorrow, no more crying or pain (21:4).

Christ makes all things new (21:5). They will never tarnish, fade, or decay. They will have eternal splendor.

This is how Revelation describes for us the new Jerusalem. But God leaves much to our imagination regarding life in the new heaven and the new earth, in the universe beyond the capital city. As discussed in section K47, the new earth surrounds the new Jerusalem. Our earth is familiar to us, so it is a basis for imagining what the new earth will be like. And the eternal heaven will merge the functions of the second and third heavens that we have now. Presumably it will consist of new stars and galaxies that will seem familiar, yet be eternal.

We have not discovered any life beyond earth. Even scientists recognize by common-sense logic that we should have discovered life by now if it was out there.[17] The universe outside our world consists of lifeless matter and energy, atoms and molecules. But the Bible strongly hints that life will flourish in the new heaven (see the discussion of Romans 8:19,21 in K47). I am convinced that we, the children of God, will be that life. The cosmos becomes the domain of the children of God.

The best book that I have read about the new heaven and the new earth is by Randy Alcorn, simply titled *Heaven.*[18] He dispenses with the idea that heaven is a place where disembodied spirits float in the clouds, and listen to harp music for eternity. Or that life in heaven is primarily a church service that never ends. He makes the case that heaven is a real, physical place where bodily resurrected people live and engage in various meaningful creative activities. It will not be a foreign place for you, but you will recognize it as home. There will be continuity between what humanity was called to do for a short time on this earth, and what we'll be able to do in the new creation. You will not lose your own identity. Everything good in your earthly life will be even better. Heaven will be fun. Worshiping God will happen through an eternity of exercising dominion over a renewed creation.

The fantastic aspects of the earth and heavens that we are familiar with will be magnified. I am convinced that this will expand to include the universe. God did not create millions of lifeless stars and planets just to have them replaced by another very limited version.

The glorified bodies that we shall receive will be ageless. Though our bodies will be new and perfect, it will still be you and me who live within them:

> Job 19:25 For I know that my redeemer liveth, and that he shall stand at the latter day upon the earth:
> 19:26 And though after my skin worms destroy this body, yet in my flesh shall I see God:
> 19:27a Whom I shall see for myself, and mine eyes shall behold, and not another.

---

[17] This is according to Fermi's Paradox, named for Italian-American nuclear physicist Enrico Fermi who remarked to colleagues in 1950 about extra terrestrial life: "Where is everybody?" Jonathan O'Callaghan, *What is the Fermi Paradox?*, https://www.livescience.com/fermi-paradox, December 05, 2021, accessed August 10, 2022.

[18] Randy Alcorn, *Heaven*, Tyndale Momentum, 2004.

Jesus Christ, the Alpha and Omega, declares “it is done” (21:6). This is the end to his work. The new Jerusalem, the new earth, the new heaven ... God, the Lamb, and we his family – will be a story of splendor that awaits.

K50

Concluding revelations and exhortations

22:6 And he said unto me, These sayings are faithful and
true: and the Lord God of the holy prophets sent his angel to
shew unto his servants the things which must shortly be
done.
22:7 Behold, I come quickly: blessed is he that keepeth the
sayings of the prophecy of this book.
22:8 And I John saw these things, and heard them. And when
I had heard and seen, I fell down to worship before the feet
of the angel which shewed me these things.
22:9 Then saith he unto me, See thou do it not: for I am thy
fellowservant, and of thy brethren the prophets, and of them
which keep the sayings of this book: worship God.
22:10 And he saith unto me, Seal not the sayings of the
prophecy of this book: for the time is at hand.
22:11 He that is unjust, let him be unjust still: and he which
is filthy, let him be filthy still: and he that is righteous, let
him be righteous still: and he that is holy, let him be holy
still.
22:12 And, behold, I come quickly; and my reward is with
me, to give every man according as his work shall be.
22:13 I am Alpha and Omega, the beginning and the end, the
first and the last.
22:14 Blessed are they that do his commandments, that they
may have right to the tree of life, and may enter in through
the gates into the city.
22:15 For without are dogs, and sorcerers, and
whoremongers, and murderers, and idolaters, and
whosoever loveth and maketh a lie.
22:16 I Jesus have sent mine angel to testify unto you these
things in the churches. I am the root and the offspring of
David, and the bright and morning star.
22:17 And the Spirit and the bride say, Come. And let him
that heareth say, Come. And let him that is athirst come. And
whosoever will, let him take the water of life freely.
22:18 For I testify unto every man that heareth the words of
the prophecy of this book, If any man shall add unto these
things, God shall add unto him the plagues that are written
in this book:
22:19 And if any man shall take away from the words of the
book of this prophecy, God shall take away his part out of

> the book of life, and out of the holy city, and from the things which are written in this book.
> 22:20 He which testifieth these things saith, Surely I come quickly. Amen. Even so, come, Lord Jesus.
> 22:21 The grace of our Lord Jesus Christ be with you all. Amen.

The timeline of human history is over. We have reached the concluding revelations and exhortations of Revelation.

John was so overwhelmed that he "fell down to worship before the feet of the angel which shewed me these things." But the angel redirects him: "see thou do it not ... worship God" (22:8-9). In a similar way, someone can become obsessed with ferreting out hidden meanings in the prophecies, and begin to boast of superior esoteric knowledge. But let us not forget that God reveals prophecy to draw us into a closer relationship with him.

The voice of the angel gives way to Christ, who speaks directly to us. Earlier, he dictated the letters to the seven churches. Then he and his angels showed John the series of visions: of the tribulation, the millennial kingdom, the great white throne judgment, and the new Jerusalem. Now he speaks in the first person: "I come quickly" (22:7,12,20), "I am Alpha and Omega, the beginning and the end, the first and the last" (22:13), "I, Jesus, have sent mine angel to testify unto you these things in the churches" (22:16). With these words of Christ, God shows he is pleased to speak to us through his son, the second person of the triune godhead, equal to the Father and the Holy Spirit, and at one with them.

Jesus encourages us who are alive today that he will return, and soon. "Behold, I come quickly" (22:7). "The time is at hand" (22:10). Though John recorded his words almost two thousand years ago, they remain true. We have learned that his first return will be in the rapture, which happens before the tribulation (K13). The Bible does not point us to an exact year or day of its happening. There will be no miraculous fore-warning. But it will be soon – Christ's return is imminent. "I am the root and the offspring of David, and the bright and morning star" (22:16). His coming will be the dawn of a new day for all those who have died and now lie asleep in the Lord. This promise of Christ's return in the rapture is the one dearest to John's heart, even more so than his second coming at the end of the tribulation (19:11, 1:7 K38), the millennium (20:6 K44), or eternal life (21:6 K49).

Jesus also says "my reward is with me, to give every man according as his work shall be" (22:12). This promise will come true at the rapture for the church saints. Their reward will be heaven. At his second coming, it will come true in an opposite way for the tribulation rebels still alive. They will be put to death. It will also come true for the survivors of the seven years who put their faith in him. They will receive glorified bodies and be ushered into the millennial kingdom.

"Blessed are they that do his commandments, that they may have right to the tree of life, and may enter in through the gates into the city" (22:14). Jesus calls on you to join this blessed company, to be one of his disciples. You can do it starting today, for "now is the day of salvation" (2 Corinthians 6:2). That means you can accept his water of life, learn his commandments, do them, and welcome the Holy Spirit of God to live in you. You will have internal joy, and peace with God amidst the troubles of this life, and in the paradise of the life to come.

The ultimate reward is that you will share eternity with God in his new and perfect universe. But be reminded that there is a burning lake of fire beyond the boundaries of the new heaven, waiting for those who refuse God's offer of salvation: "For without are dogs, and sorcerers, and whoremongers, and murderers, and idolaters, and whosoever loveth and maketh a lie" (22:15). There will be a gulf between heaven and hell that can never be crossed: "he that is unjust, let him be unjust still: and he which is filthy, let him be filthy still: and he that is righteous, let him be righteous still: and he that is holy, let him be holy still" (22:11).

"Seal not the sayings of the prophecy of this book" (22:10). Through the angel, God thus commands John to reduce to writing everything he saw and heard in his vision. It is amazing to think that after it was over, the numerous points of detail stayed imprinted on John's mind, and he was able to commit it to writing. He did this by the Holy Spirit working in him.

In the early centuries of the church, there was controversy whether Revelation was properly part of Holy Scripture. In the generations after John's death, almost every one of the church fathers (Papius around 125 CE, then Justin Martyr, Irenaeus, Hippolytus, Clement of Alexandria, Tertullian, Origen) accepted it as authoritative scripture on the grounds that the apostle John, the son of Zebedee, was the author. But in the late second century and into the third, after the memory of John had faded, there were some church leaders who thought it was written by some other John (as believed by Gaius, Dionysus of Alexandria, and Eusebius). Its written style as an apocalypse made it subject to greater scrutiny than the various gospel accounts, letters, and historical summaries written by the apostles and their associates. Some theologians (Gaius, Augustine) questioned whether the thousand-year kingdom (20:6 K44) should be taken literally. But eventually the church at large was convinced that the book in its entirety was the inspired and inerrant words of God, and accepted that Revelation is part of the canon of the New Testament.

It is appropriate to take Revelation's written words literally wherever possible, otherwise we may be in danger of adding to (22:18) or subtracting (22:19) from them. Much of the church of my time is doing that, to its peril. It is endangering the next generation, who is rapidly falling away from the church, and who are pursuing false ideologies that teach things contrary to God's holiness. God gives fair warning that they will suffer the trials described in Revelation, unless they repent of their rebellion or their lukewarmness.

Please notice that in the book of Revelation, the word church was at first very prominent in the letters to the seven churches of chapters 2 and 3 (K06 through K12). Then it was not mentioned a single time during the entire time of the tribulation and millennial kingdom. The church then came forth as the bride of Christ and wife of the Lamb in the marriage supper of the new Jerusalem (21:2 K47, 19:7 K48). Here in 22:16, as part of John's conclusion, we finally have the word church again. It is fitting that Revelation, which was given to the church, begins and ends with the church, the body of Christ (Ephesians 4:12).

Let us who belong to the church thank God that he has spoken these words to us through his servant John. Revelation is a such a unique book of special blessing. Jesus says "blessed is he that keepeth the sayings of the prophecy of this book" (22:7). He is encouraging us to treat the prophecy of Revelation as precious. It deserves to be studied. Through it, you will receive great comfort and assurance that God will see you through the trials that are coming. It certainly helped John, who was suffering in exile on the bleak island of Patmos. And to you who are reading my book during the years of the tribulation, please recognize that my words and thoughts of interpretation are but a pale reflection of God's glory given to us in John's vision. The Holy Spirit and the church beckon to you to claim the words as yours: "Let him that is athirst come. And whosoever will, let him take the water of life freely" (22:17).

If you believe the words of Revelation, the grace of the Lord will be with you (22:21).

Conclusion

If you have given your life to Jesus, and are reading this book before the tribulation, you can be exceedingly glad that Jesus will rapture you beforehand. He promises to deliver you from the wrath that is to come (1 Thessalonians 1:10, K13).

But churches should examine themselves and ask if they have stopped seeking the leading of the Holy Spirit. Those Christian gatherings who are satisfied with themselves may be guilty of not contesting for the lives of unbelievers. In the process, the church at large is unfortunately hastening the descent of the world around it into the godless end-time age.

God the Holy Spirit is so important to us. He sends saving grace that turns the hearts of individuals to Christ.

The Holy Spirit also delays the onset of godlessness, by bestowing common grace upon believers and unbelievers alike in nations throughout the world. This common grace allows for a basic set of biblical principles to be active, even within societies that are secularized. The Holy Spirit triggers the consciences of unbelievers to have some awareness of right and wrong.

We know from 2 Thessalonians 2:6-7 (K16) that the antichrist beast won't be revealed until the Holy Spirit withdraws from active intervention in the world. This includes his withdrawal of common grace. Consciences of people will no longer operate to steer them away from evil.

The Holy Spirit will also withdraw from the churches, or more likely, the churches shall withdraw from seeking him.

It is unclear from Thessalonians whether the Holy Spirit will withdraw gradually, in stages, or suddenly. But given the fact that the church age before the tribulation is the "lukewarm" age foreshadowed by the church of Laodicea (3:14-22 K12), the evidence of our time is that the Holy Spirit is withdrawing in stages.

What does it mean for churches to find and follow the fresh leading of the Holy Spirit? To find it, they should be open to prophetic voices both from within and without.

Christians whom God has given a prophetic spiritual gift, are not offering words that add to the holy scripture. The door for that was closed after the age of the twelve apostles of Christ, and the completion of the New Testament. But prophetic voices to this day apply the written word of God that we already have, to point the way through challenges facing the church and the world. God also uses prophetic voices to rebuke the church, goad it into difficult action, and issue warnings of consequences if the church does not work at following the way of Christ with a whole heart. Prophets also call out political and cultural leaders to seek the blessings of following God's ways, or else suffer the inevitable consequences of their sinful example.

A major area for churches to consider is whether they are preaching salvation from sin, without enumerating what new sins have crept into their midst and are flourishing. This is a more recent manifestation of cheap grace, again with no repentance and change attached to it.

If a church recommits to seeking the leading of the Holy Spirit, our study of the chronology of Revelation suggests that it should focus prayer on godless movements. Out of them candidates might arise, who in future will spawn the woman of Babylon and the beast. Churches should study the false gospels that these movements are promulgating. It is helpful to identify how they are recruiting future generations, including the young people in our own families. Then individual churches can intentionally stand up to these ideologies with a vigorous defense and apologetic, that shows the superiority and sufficiency of Christ. This will act as a magnet to attract people who are seeking Christ, and bring back those of the church who are being tempted by the ways of the world.

But churches who do not continuously seek God in the midst of current events will find themselves apathetic to them. It would not come as surprise that most people belonging to those churches are operating according to the principles of cheap grace. They may find themselves left behind after the rapture, to face the full fury of the tribulation.

If you are one of those left behind, and you have found my book, you should know that God has meant the book of Revelation to be sufficient for you to approach and endure the end times. It may be difficult to comprehend the meaning of the entire book. But you will recognize a declaration of hope. It is not too late to give your whole heart to Christ. In the midst of the world of wrath, you will have assurance of salvation.

If you are reading this during the tribulation, the prophetic interpretation of my book may prove to be inaccurate in some places. Our Father God in heaven will surprise us with certain actual events that will occur. When they do, the prophetic fulfillments will snap into focus. You will be convinced God is the Almighty who governs time and events.

Please come to God in faith, through the avenue that he has provided. Repent of your transgressions and self-sufficiency. Ask that the blood of his son Jesus Christ, shed on the cross for you, would cleanse you and make you free. If you do, God will gladly welcome you into his eternal kingdom!

Postscript

When the Lord burdened me to understand the book of Revelation by un-swirling John's vision to obtain the time sequence of events, I had no idea that the number of periods represented would be forty-nine, K01 through K49. For me, this is God's validation on this effort. This is because the number forty-nine is special in his sight. It is seven times seven.

Seven is a biblically perfect number representing spiritual perfection. After God created the universe in six days, he saw "that it was very good" (Genesis 1:31). He then made the seventh day of the week holy. Christ rose from the dead on Sunday, the seventh day. God instructed the Israelites of the Old Testament to observe seven holy feasts annually. We encounter seven churches in Revelation. Jesus also spoke seven times on the cross. There are seven blessings given in Revelation (1:3 K00, 14:13 K24, 16:15 K38, 20:6 K44 K46, 19:9 K48, 22:7 K50, 22:14 K50).

God blessed the related number forty-nine by making every fiftieth year for ancient Israel a year of jubilee:

> Leviticus 25:10 And you shall consecrate the fiftieth year, and proclaim liberty throughout the land to all its inhabitants. It shall be a jubilee for you, when each of you shall return to his property and each of you shall return to his clan.
> 25:11a That fiftieth year shall be a jubilee for you.

The numbers forty-nine and fifty point ahead to a greater spiritual truth. The year of jubilee was a time to proclaim liberty, both literally and figuratively. This reaches its greatest fulfillment in our Lord Jesus Christ. In Luke 4:18-19, he said:

> Luke 4:18 The Spirit of the Lord is upon me, because he hath anointed me to preach the gospel to the poor; he hath sent me to heal the brokenhearted, to preach deliverance to the captives, and recovering of sight to the blind, to set at liberty them that are bruised,
> 4:19 To preach the acceptable year of the Lord.

The forty-nine periods of time of Revelation call out for us to come before God. We should come with contrition in our hearts, and ask him to rescue us from our bondage to sin, and from times of tribulation. In his great mercy, he has arranged for his son Jesus to set us free. Our freedom will be the freedom of jubilee, freedom for eternity.

Appendix A: Why Satan hates Christ

The Bible starts the book of Genesis with the words "In the beginning God created the heaven and the earth" (Genesis 1:1). In the six days that followed he populated the world with his creatures. God tells us that plant life was created on the third day, on the fifth day the creatures of the sea and birds of the air, and on the sixth day the animals of the land.

Genesis implies that God also created the angels, the inhabitants of heaven, during the creation week. Revelation 5:11 suggests that angels were created in great numbers, perhaps more than 100 million: "I heard the voice of many angels round about the throne and the beasts and the elders: and the number of them was ten thousand times ten thousand, and thousands of thousands." The Bible gives the names of three of the angels: Michael, Gabriel, and Lucifer.

There is no indication that angels are capable of reproducing. For example, in the New Testament, when Jesus was asked whether there would be marriage between men and women in the life to come, he answered: "for in the resurrection they neither marry, nor are given in marriage, but are as the angels of God in heaven." (Matthew 22:30). We can strongly conclude that the number of angels was fixed for all time by God when he created them in the first week of creation. It is interesting to note that the number of human beings was initially far less than that of the angels, but now is far greater, due to the blessing that God bestowed on Adam and Eve: "be fruitful and multiply" (Genesis 1:28).

The angels, shortly after they were created, saw what took place when in Genesis 1:26, "God said, let us make man in our image, after our likeness: and let them have dominion over the fish of the sea, and over the fowl of the air, and over the cattle, and over all the earth, and over every creeping thing that creepeth upon the earth."

In the book of Job, the angels are referred to as sons of God when they presented themselves before him (Job 1:6). It also says they, the sons of God, rejoiced over him laying the foundations of the earth (Job 38:4,7).

But Lucifer, whom the Bible also calls Satan, did not rejoice when he heard that God said "let *us* make man in our image, after our likeness." From the word "us" he learned that God was not singular in his nature. The rest of the Bible gives numerous indications that God is a trinity, or God in three persons: God the Father, God the Son, and God the Holy Spirit. Out of all of God's creatures, the newly created humans Adam and Eve were most similar, not to the sons of God the angels, but to the *only begotten* and divine Son of God (John 3:16), the God-man Jesus Christ.

At this early stage in Satan's own existence, he and the other angels had surely come to know this Jesus, as they lived together in heaven with him.

There are two obscure Christian theologians from long ago, the Protestant Andreas Osiander (1498-1552) and the Catholic John Duns Scotus (1265-1308), who asked the question, would Jesus have become incarnated as a man on earth if Adam and Eve had not fallen into sin? John Calvin, who disputed Osiander's point of view, summarizes it: "he asserts that man was created in God's image because he was fashioned according to the pattern of the Messiah to come, that man might conform to him whom the Father had already determined to clothe with flesh."[19] The premise that Jesus was foreordained *before* the fall of Adam to come to earth as a man, is echoed in Revelation 13:8, which speaks of Jesus as "the Lamb slain from the foundation of the world."

I would like to extend the idea of Osiander and Duns Scotus. It is my contention that Jesus Christ, who is the eternal Son of God and second person of the Trinity, *already* existed as a perfect man, with an eternal spirit and a glorified body, *before* the creation. He was the template for Adam and Eve and all their descendants. This is supported in the New Testament by another 13:8 verse, namely Hebrews 13:8 - "Jesus Christ [is] the same yesterday, and to day, and for ever." The word "yesterday" looks from when Hebrews was written, back to the time that Jesus came to earth. It could just as well look all the way back to the creation.

---

[19] John Calvin, *Institutes of the Christian R-eligion*, Geneva, 1559, John T. McNeill ed., Ford Lewis Battles trans., The Westminster Press, Philadelphia, 1960, vol.1, p.470.

The word forever stands for the future of course, but could also covers the timeless time before creation.

Jesus as the *eternal* God-man explains four great mysteries of the Bible.

First, it explains the many appearances in the Old Testament of Christ as the Angel of God, or Angel of the Lord, having characteristics of both a man and an angelic spiritual being. He appeared in this way before he was born in Bethlehem to the virgin Mary, and temporarily gave up his glorified body to take on the natural flesh of fallen mankind.

Second, it explains the uniqueness of the earth. Some scientists and science fiction fans scoff at the idea that God singled out our planet and our race of creatures to send his son here in the form of a man. They would ask, would God also transform himself into other beings and go to their planets to save them?

The Bible testifies that indeed the focus of the triune God of the universe is upon earth. The earth is distinct from all the millions of planets scattered across the universe. It is our home. Scientists cannot explain how the earth randomly came to be such a privileged planet.[20] It is inexplicable that it seems to be the only world capable of supporting advanced life. Despite the search for other such planets, they cannot answer Fermi's paradox (see K49), namely why, if life outside earth exists, that creatures superior to us have not reached across the galaxies to contact us. Surely this would have happened by now, especially if the universe is billions of years old instead of just 6,000 as we would conclude from a literal reading of the Bible.

Third, it explains the uniqueness of humankind. Out of all the creatures of the universe, the focus of God is upon the human race, here on earth. We are specially created in the image of God:

> Genesis 1:26a And God said, Let us make man in our image, after our likeness.
> 1:27 So God created man in his own image, in the image of God created he him; male and female created he them.

---

[20] Guillermo Gonzalez, *The Privileged Planet: How Our Place in the Cosmos Is Designed for Discovery*, Regnery Publishing, 2003.

In this important biblical passage, God refers to himself as a plural entity, when he says "let *us* make man." This is the first pointer to the trinitarian nature of God in the Bible. He also says "let us make man in *our image*." Almost all interpreters explain this to mean that, in creating the human race, God bestowed on us certain elements of his character. Theologians call these elements the *communicable attributes* of God: the capacity for love, grace, mercy, goodness, relationship, rational thought and truthfulness; the sense of justice, and creativity. To God alone is reserved his *incommunicable attributes*: his omnipotence, omnipresence, omniscience, sovereignty, transcendence, immutability, and self-existence.

But God did not say, "let us make man *after our character*." He said, "*in our image*." If we accept Christ as the God-man even before all time, we are therefore created to resemble him not just in character, but in bodily form as well.

This sets our path on the destiny that God has ordained for us, as described at the end of Revelation. Those among us who believe in the triune God will inherit the entire universe – the new heaven and the new earth.

Fourth, Jesus as the eternal God-man explains the unrelenting hatred that arose in Satan's jealous heart, when he learned about Jesus and his connection to Adam, Eve, and their descendants to come. Satan, like the rest of the angels, was created without a body. Satan and his fallen angel followers were envious of Adam who was created in the image of Christ. They saw that Adam was given a spirit nature, created in rank over the animals. But what really provoked them was that, like the animals, Adam and Eve also were given physical bodies, and were meant to have children.

Adam was the created son of God, intended to live forever. Christ is the uncreated Son of God, existing eternally before creation occurred. When Adam fell into sin and was judged by God, his glorified body was cursed and became a corrupted body. We his descendants are all born with such a corrupted body. Adam died, and so do we all, because we are all sinners against God. To save us, and to give us new life, Jesus came to earth in the incarnation, in the form of a baby born of a virgin. He took on the corrupted body that all of us have. He descended to earth and lived among us.

When Christ died on the cross and was resurrected three days later, he received his glorified body again. Those who believe in Jesus, when they die, will also receive a perfect body, glorified by resurrection (John 11:25).

Satan, in those early days when he realized who Jesus was, saw him as the supreme obstacle in his goal to become equal to God. He determined to undermine the position of Jesus by attacking those created in his image. Therefore, he schemed, and soon appeared as a serpent to Eve when he saw the opportunity to tempt her over the tree of Good and Evil. If he could bring death to Adam and Eve, though they were created with glorified bodies, perhaps he could eventually do the same to Jesus. He was successful with Adam and Eve. As their descendants, you and I share in their fall. But Jesus will rescue those who trust in him.

Fifth, we now have a motive for the passages in Genesis which suggest that Satan and the devils somehow had sexual intercourse with women to produce a race of giants. Before Noah's flood, "there were giants [Hebrew: *Nephilim*] in the earth in those days; and also after that, when the sons of God came in unto the daughters of men, and they bare children to them, the same became mighty men which were of old, men of renown" (Genesis 6:4). After the flood destroyed all but Noah's family, it seems that the Nephilim gene pool remained, and men like the Nephilim arose in the land that God promised to the Jews. This was likely by Satan's design as well. Goliath, who was killed by David (1 Samuel 17), was a descendant of the race of Nephilim.

The line of the Nephilim eventually died out after warfare with generations of Israelites. This attempt of devils to reproduce was thwarted. There is no sign that afterwards Satan attempted this again in organized fashion. But the rise of the Nephilim can be traced back to the jealousy that Satan had for Christ the God-man.

Thousands of years later, Jesus surprised him by taking on Adam's fallen flesh and coming to this world. Satan saw in this an even greater opportunity, and worked through people as his agents to have Jesus put to death on the cross. But Jesus defeated Satan's plan by his resurrection. He rose in his glorified body, and made a path for believing men and women to do the same. Thus, they are granted a higher rank over the angels in God's ultimate plan for the universe (1 Corinthians 6:3 "Know ye not that we shall judge angels? How much more things that pertain to this life?").

Though Satan was frustrated at the cross, he continues to scheme and look for opportunities to defeat Jesus. His method is to attack human beings physically, by promoting disease, abortion, and war. He also attacks them spiritually, by promoting religions that have multitudes of gods (Hinduism, Animism), or have no use for the concept of God (Buddhism, Marxism-Globalism-Evolutionism), or violently enforce the belief that God is singular and there is no divine Son of God (Islam).

Satan will use any method possible to trick people to their doom. He fully intends for all people to die an eternal death, and in the process to wipe out God's image among them. If he can accomplish this goal, then he will once again turn and try to deal Jesus a death blow. The book of Revelation prophesies the future actions of Satan as he tries to accomplish his plan.

Appendix B: Varying counts of days for the tribulation in Revelation and Daniel

(The following is excerpted from https://www.gotquestions.org/tribulation-1260-1290-1335-days.html, accessed April 28, 2022, no author).

The books of Daniel and Revelation are often studied together, because their prophecies concerning the end times dovetail with each other nicely. Both books mention a certain number of days during the tribulation: Daniel mentions 1,290 days and 1,335 days; Revelation mentions 1,260 days, for a total "discrepancy" of 75 days (1,335 – 1,260 = 75).

> Daniel 12:11 And from the time that the daily sacrifice shall be taken away, and the abomination that maketh desolate set up, there shall be a thousand two hundred and ninety days.
> 12:12 Blessed is he that waiteth, and cometh to the thousand three hundred and five and thirty days.
>
> Revelation 13:4 And they worshipped the dragon which gave power unto the beast: and they worshipped the beast, saying, Who is like unto the beast? who is able to make war with him?
> 13:5 And there was given unto him a mouth speaking great things and blasphemies; and power was given unto him to continue forty and two months *[this equates to 1260 days at 30 days apiece]*

According to Daniel 9:27, the tribulation begins with the signing of a peace treaty between the antichrist and Israel, intended to be for one "seven," that is, a set of seven years. But the "seven" is divided into halves: midway through the seven years, the antichrist breaks the treaty and sets up in the temple a sacrilegious object (the "abomination that causes desolation"). The phrase "in the middle" indicates that the first half of the tribulation lasts for 3½ years (1,260 days, using a "prophetic year" of 360 days). Likewise, the second half of the tribulation lasts another 1,260 days (another 3½ years), for a total of seven years.

Revelation 13:5 specifically mentions forty-two months, which equates to 1,260 days. This corresponds exactly with Daniel's prophecy of the abomination of desolation.

The 1,260 days of the second half of the tribulation begins as the antichrist breaks the treaty, occupies the third Jewish temple, and sets up a profane and sacrilegious object of worship. This 1,260-day period ends when the antichrist is defeated at the battle of Armageddon upon Jesus' return to earth. At that time, the tribulation will be at an end.

Daniel 12:11 mentions 1,290 days, however, which is 30 days more than the second half of the tribulation. Different ideas have been put forward to explain what happens in those 30 extra days. One likely theory is that the land of Israel will be rebuilt in that month after the devastation it endured during the tribulation.

Then, according to Daniel 12:12, there will be an extra 45 days, on top of the extra 30 days, after which something else will happen. Daniel does not say explicitly what will happen, but he says those who remain until the end of that segment (1,335 days after the breaking of the treaty and 75 days after the end of the tribulation) will be "blessed." The blessing here is entry into the millennial kingdom. What will take place during those 45 days? Very likely, this is when the judgment of the gentile nations, described in Matthew 25:31-46, will take place. In this judgment, also called the judgment of the sheep and the goats, the gentiles are judged for their treatment of Israel during the tribulation. Did they aid Jesus' brothers and sisters (Matthew 25:40), or did they turn a blind eye to the Jews' troubles or, worse yet, aid in their persecution?

So, those who survive the tribulation and survive the sheep and goat judgment will enter the millennium. This is a blessing, indeed.

In summary, here is the timeline as we see it:

- Sometime after the rapture of the church, the antichrist enters a treaty with Israel. This begins the seven-year tribulation.
- At the midpoint of the tribulation (1,260 days later), the antichrist breaks the treaty, desecrates the temple, and begins to persecute the Jews.

- At the end of the tribulation (1,260 days after the desecration of the temple), Jesus Christ returns to earth and defeats the forces of the antichrist.
- During the next 30 days (leading up to 1,290 days after the desecration of the temple), Israel is rebuilt and the earth is restored.
- During the next 45 days (leading up to 1,335 days after the desecration of the temple), the Gentile nations are judged for their treatment of Israel.
- The millennium begins, and it will last for 1,000 years (Revelation 20:3,5-6).

Appendix C: Matthew 24 as a summary of Revelation

There is remarkable similarity between Revelation's account of end-time events, and the Olivet discourse given by Jesus Christ in Matthew 24. His words recorded in that gospel validate the overall outline of Revelation. They touch on seven of the forty-nine time periods of Revelation, mostly in the same order. They help us to see that the added detail of Revelation should be taken literally wherever possible.

In the Matthew passage, the disciples asked Jesus about his return and the end of the world:

> Matthew 24:3 And as he sat upon the mount of Olives, the disciples came unto him privately, saying, Tell us, when shall these things be? and what shall be the sign of thy coming, and of the end of the world?
> 24:4 And Jesus answered and said unto them, Take heed that no man deceive you.

He then summarizes the church age, which will cover the time starting with his ascension into heaven, up until the rapture. Troubles will always afflict the believers, which will get worse over time. But they need to persist in bringing the good news of salvation to all the nations:

> *(Before K13. The rapture and judgment of the church saints)*
> Matthew 24:5 For many shall come in my name, saying, I am Christ; and shall deceive many.
> 24:6 And ye shall hear of wars and rumours of wars: see that ye be not troubled: for all these things must come to pass, but the end is not yet.
> 24:7 For nation shall rise against nation, and kingdom against kingdom: and there shall be famines, and pestilences, and earthquakes, in divers places.
> 24:8 All these are the beginning of sorrows.
> 24:9 Then shall they deliver you up to be afflicted, and shall kill you: and ye shall be hated of all nations for my name's sake.
> 24:10 And then shall many be offended, and shall betray one another, and shall hate one another.
> 24:11 many false prophets shall rise, and shall deceive many.

> 24:12 because iniquity shall abound, the love of many shall wax cold.
> 24:13 he that shall endure unto the end, the same shall be saved.
> 24:14 And this gospel of the kingdom shall be preached in all the world for a witness unto all nations; and then shall the end come.

After the gospel has gone forth to the whole world, the tribulation will happen, which includes the great tribulation. False Christs will appear, and the abomination that causes desolation. These details of Matthew match identically with Revelation, where the false Christs are identified as the beast and the false prophet:

(K23. The supremacy of the beast)
(K24. The false prophet upholds the beast)

> Matthew 24:15 When ye therefore shall see the abomination of desolation, spoken of by Daniel the prophet, stand in the holy place, (whoso readeth, let him understand:)
> 24:16 Then let them which be in Judaea flee into the mountains:
> 24:17 Let him which is on the housetop not come down to take any thing out of his house:
> 24:18 Neither let him which is in the field return back to take his clothes.
> 24:19 And woe unto them that are with child, and to them that give suck in those days!
> 24:20 But pray ye that your flight be not in the winter, neither on the sabbath day:
> 24:21 For then shall be great tribulation, such as was not since the beginning of the world to this time, no, nor ever shall be.
> 24:22 And except those days should be shortened, there should no flesh be saved: but for the elect's sake those days shall be shortened.
> 24:23 Then if any man shall say unto you, Lo, here is Christ, or there; believe it not.
> 24:24 For there shall arise false Christs, and false prophets, and shall shew great signs and wonders; insomuch that, if it were possible, they shall deceive the very elect.
> 24:25 Behold, I have told you before.
> 24:26 Wherefore if they shall say unto you, Behold, he is in the desert; go not forth: behold, he is in the secret chambers; believe it not.

The remaining verses of Matthew 24 are not in perfect order chronologically, but do overlap with Revelation. Jesus tells us that the heavens shall be darkened. This matches the fourth trumpet event, which likely happens in the last year of the great tribulation:

(K31. God darkens the heavens)

> Matthew 24:29 Immediately after the tribulation of those days shall the sun be darkened, and the moon shall not give her light, and the stars shall fall from heaven, and the powers of the heavens shall be shaken.

Jesus' main point to the disciples is that he will indeed return in his second coming. We know from Revelation this will happen just prior to the battle of Armageddon. The supporters of the beast will mourn when they see Christ:

(K38. The second coming of Christ, and the sixth plague: the battle of Armageddon)

> Matthew 24:27 For as the lightning cometh out of the east, and shineth even unto the west; so shall also the coming of the Son of man be.
> 24:30 And then shall appear the sign of the Son of man in heaven: and then shall all the tribes of the earth mourn, and they shall see the Son of man coming in the clouds of heaven with power and great glory.

Jesus then describes eagles clustering around dead bodies. This corresponds to the defeat of the beast's armies in Armageddon:

(K40. The final defeat of the beast and his armies)

> Matthew 24:28 For wheresoever the carcase is, there will the eagles be gathered together.

After this, Jesus gathers his people, both the living and the dead. We can tell from the next verse that the event in question is not the rapture, but his second coming:

(K43. The still-living believers and resurrected tribulation martyrs ushered into the millennial kingdom after judgment of the righteous)

> Matthew 24:31 And he shall send his angels with a great sound of a trumpet, and they shall gather together his elect from the four winds, from one end of heaven to the other.

The non-church believers who are gathered will enter into the millennium kingdom.

But Jesus does not finish his discourse here. In the next verses he flashes back with a parable of the fig tree, a symbol of the nation of Israel. At his first coming, most Jews refused to recognize him as messiah. Jesus therefore cursed a fig tree that he came across for its unfruitfulness (Matthew 21:18-22). But he will lovingly reconstitute the fig tree Israel as a nation in the distant future (1948), as part of God's preparation for the end times:

> *(Before K13. The rapture and judgment of the church saints)*
> Matthew 24:32 Now learn a parable of the fig tree; When his branch is yet tender, and putteth forth leaves, ye know that summer is nigh:
> 24:33 So likewise ye, when ye shall see all these things, know that it is near, even at the doors.
> 24:34 Verily I say unto you, This generation shall not pass, till all these things be fulfilled.
> 24:35 Heaven and earth shall pass away, but my words shall not pass away.

The phrase "this generation" found in Matthew 24:34 refers not merely to those alive during the days of the apostles, but to the entire nation of the Jews – those present at Jesus' first coming, plus the children whom they generate in the future – until all his words be fulfilled.[21]

Jesus finally finishes Matthew 24 with the following long account. This time he is not speaking of his second and permanent coming at the end of the great tribulation. He shifts to his temporary coming, before the tribulation, to take all the church saints to heaven. This is the rapture. We can deduce this because he introduces this section with the words "but of that day," which is a break from his previous discussion.[22] He also describes how he will take some with him, and others will be left on

---

[21] *What does "this generation" mean in Matthew 24:34?* No author, undated, https://www.neverthirsty.org/bible-qa/qa-archives/question/what-does-this-generation-mean-in-matthew-24/, accessed April 19, 2023

[22] *Is Matthew 24 referring to the Rapture or the Second Coming?*, no author, June 18, 2020, https://versebyverseministry.org/bible-answers/is-matthew-24-referring-to-the-rapture-or-the-second-coming, accessed April 18, 2023.

earth. That will be true only of the rapture. This passage therefore fits in chronologically between the end of the church age in Matthew 24:14 "this gospel of the kingdom shall be preached in all the world for a witness unto all nations; and then shall the end come," and the great tribulation in Matthew 24:15 "ye therefore shall see the abomination of desolation":

> *(K13. The rapture and judgment of the church saints)*
> Matthew 24:36 But of that day and hour knoweth no man, no, not the angels of heaven, but my Father only.
> 24:37 But as the days of Noah were, so shall also the coming of the Son of man be.
> 24:38 For as in the days that were before the flood they were eating and drinking, marrying and giving in marriage, until the day that Noe entered into the ark,
> 24:39 And knew not until the flood came, and took them all away; so shall also the coming of the Son of man be.
> 24:40 Then shall two be in the field; the one shall be taken, and the other left.
> 24:41 Two women shall be grinding at the mill; the one shall be taken, and the other left.
> 24:42 Watch therefore: for ye know not what hour your Lord doth come.
> 24:43 But know this, that if the goodman of the house had known in what watch the thief would come, he would have watched, and would not have suffered his house to be broken up.
> 24:44 Therefore be ye also ready: for in such an hour as ye think not the Son of man cometh.
> 24:45 Who then is a faithful and wise servant, whom his lord hath made ruler over his household, to give them meat in due season?
> 24:46 Blessed is that servant, whom his lord when he cometh shall find so doing.
> 24:47 Verily I say unto you, That he shall make him ruler over all his goods.
> 24:48 But and if that evil servant shall say in his heart, My lord delayeth his coming;
> 24:49 And shall begin to smite his fellowservants, and to eat and drink with the drunken;
> 24:50 The lord of that servant shall come in a day when he looketh not for him, and in an hour that he is not aware of,
> 24:51 And shall cut him asunder, and appoint him his portion with the hypocrites: there shall be weeping and gnashing of teeth.

Thus, the words of Matthew 24:39: "And [they] knew not until the flood came, and took them all away; so shall also the coming of the Son of man be" – refers to the rapture, and not the second coming. Neither believers nor unbelievers will be able to forecast the exact time of the rapture. This is not true of Christ's second coming, which will occur exactly seven years after the beginning of the tribulation.

Those who are left on earth after the rapture will have "his portion with the hypocrites: there shall be weeping and gnashing of teeth" (Matthew 24:51). This will be fulfilled when they face the trials of the seven-year tribulation.

To conclude, those who say that Revelation is largely symbolic are forced to argue that all the above words of Jesus as recorded in Matthew are also metaphors, and that the literal similarity between Matthew and Revelation should not govern interpretation.

It is better to recognize that God's word reinforces itself. If God wanted to make it clear that he meant Revelation to be understood literally, what better way than to give a preview in Jesus' speech to his disciples, recorded by Matthew many decades before John's vision.

Appendix D: 1 Corinthians 15 as a summary of Revelation

In the previous appendix, we discussed Christ's brief timeline of the end times in Matthew 24. A second and even briefer summary was written by Paul in his first letter to the Corinthians. Please note that neither were written by John, but are independent of Revelation. They were also written many decades beforehand. They serve as two independent witnesses to Revelation.

The capsule summary in 1 Corinthians, though only six verses long, touches on thirty-two of the forty-nine time periods of Revelation, and does so in their chronological order.

Paul begins with the resurrection of Christ. This is a great starting place, for it was the foremost event of his own lifetime:

(K05. The incarnation and ascension of Jesus)

1 Corinthians 15:20 But now is Christ risen from the dead, and become the firstfruits of them that slept.
15:21 For since by man came death, by man came also the resurrection of the dead.
15:22 For as in Adam all die, even so in Christ shall all be made alive.
15:23a But every man in his own order: Christ the firstfruits.

The church saints shall be resurrected when Jesus returns to earth briefly at the rapture:

(K13. The rapture and judgment of the church saints)

1 Corinthians 15:23b afterward they that are Christ's at his coming.

After the rapture comes the tribulation:

(K15. Satan cast down to earth following the rapture, through K37. The first five plagues: God sends boils, blood on the sea and waters, heat, darkness)

1 Corinthians 15:24a Then cometh the end.

The second coming of Christ will bring on the end of the tribulation at the battle of Armageddon. He will defeat the beast and his followers. He will deliver their evil kingdom to judgment, and replace it with his own:

> *(K38. The second coming of Christ, and the sixth plague: the battle of Armageddon,*
> *through K42. The live unbelievers do not survive the end of the great tribulation)*
> 1 Corinthians 15:24b when he shall have delivered up the kingdom to God, even the Father; when he shall have put down all rule and all authority and power.

The millennial kingdom ensues. Christ will rule the earth:

> *(K43. The still-living believers and resurrected tribulation martyrs ushered into the millennial kingdom after judgment of the righteous)*
> *(K44. The millennial kingdom)*
> 1 Corinthians 15:25a For he must reign

At the end of the thousand years, Satan is loosed from the bottomless pit and will come back to earth to lead the final rebellion. However, he will be defeated and cast into the lake of fire. In this way Christ will complete the subjugation of his enemies:

> *(K45. Rebellion at the end of the millennium)*
> 1 Corinthians 15:25b till he hath put all enemies under his feet.

Finally, after the great white throne judgment, death itself will be cast into the lake of fire, and will be no more:

> *(K46. Resurrection of the unbelievers after the millennium, along with saints born and died in the millennium, then judgment of them at the great white throne)*
> 1 Corinthians 15:26 The last enemy that shall be destroyed is death.

Many interpreters of 1 Corinthians equate the "end" of 15:24a with the destruction of death in 15:26; Christ's coming in 15:23b with his assumption of all rule in 15:24b-25a; his "delivering up the kingdom to God" in 15:24b with putting all enemies under his feet in 15:25b. This kind of exposition neutralizes the prophetic timeline of the passage.

By doing this side-by-side comparison with the chronology of Revelation, we see that the verses of 1 Corinthians do not equate with one another, but proceed one after the other in time sequence. This tiny passage of just six verses substantiates the amazing detail given in the twenty-one chapters and forty-nine time periods of God's book of Revelation.

Appendix E: List of resurrections

There are eight true stories in the Bible of a man, woman, or child who had died, and then were miraculously raised up to live again:

- the widow's son in Zarephath (1 Kings 17:17–22)
- the Shunammite's son (2 Kings 4:18–37)
- the man thrown into Elisha's grave (2 Kings 13:20)
- Jairus' daughter (Mark 5:41)
- the young man at Nain (Luke 7:14)
- Lazarus (John 11:38–44)
- Tabitha/Dorcas (Acts 9:36–42)
- Eutychus (Acts 20:7–12)

In these events, many eyewitnesses knew the recently departed person intimately. They saw the person come back to life. The person then lived some more years in this world before dying a second time. At that final death, their natural body died again, and their everlasting soul went to dwell in the intermediate state. The rest of us who die once (Hebrews 9:27) will join them there.

Every soul who has been dead, either for a short or long time, awaits a permanent resurrection where he or she will receive a new body. This body will be eternal, and will never die again.

The first permanent resurrection was of Christ. He was the first from the dead to receive a glorified body (Matthew 28:1-7, Mark 16:1-11, Luke 24:1-12, John 20:1-18, see K05).

Many interpreters say that there will only be one more permanent resurrection, of everyone who ever lived, which will occur at the end of time. But the Bible makes a precedent for multiple resurrections. It records one more resurrection that has already happened. In it, many people have already been granted glorified bodies.

This second resurrection happened shortly after Christ's. The graves of many Old Testament saints, from generations ago, long dead, were opened. They came alive, with glorified bodies, and walked the streets of Jerusalem for a time (Matthew 27:50-51, see K13).

Based on this antecedent, a literal interpretation of Revelation and other books of the Bible points us to additional glorified resurrections.

The third resurrection event is the rapture of the church saints (1 Thessalonians 4:13-18, see K13). The rapture happens unexpectedly, with Jesus making his appearance in the clouds. All the dead souls who were ever baptized into the body of Christ, starting from the day of Pentecost (Acts 2), receive glorified bodies, and will rise into heaven.

The fourth will be of the two witnesses during the great tribulation (11:11-12 K35). It will occur after they are killed and are left lying in the streets of Jerusalem for three and a half days.

The fifth will be of those who accept Christ during the tribulation, and are killed for their faith before it is over (20:4 K43). They will be raised up soon after the second coming of Christ (19:11, 1:7 K38).

The sixth is of the Old Testament saints (Daniel 12:2, Ezekiel 37:9-14, see K43). It will be the reward that permits the faithful of Old Testament Israel to participate in the millennial kingdom (K44). It occurs at the same time as the resurrection of the tribulation martyrs. But this group of ancient believers is better counted as a separate resurrection, since they have been dead for over two thousand years.

The seventh resurrection will be of the believers who die during the millennium. Revelation does not specifically speak to their fate, but it must be assumed that at the end of the millennium they will receive glorified bodies (K46).

This resurrection at the close of the millennium, and the rapture that occurs before the tribulation, are two events very similar in nature. They involve not just resurrections from the dead, but also ascensions of living people into heaven. These ascensions have two biblical precursors: Enoch (Genesis 5:24) and Elijah (2 Kings 2:11). Those men also did not die, and were not resurrected. Instead, they were taken up into heaven and undoubtedly transformed into glorified bodies, never subject to decay. There is symmetry in number between those two ascensions that occurred long ago, and the two ascensions of living believers at the rapture and after the millennium.

These seven resurrections all involve believers. The eighth and final one is of all the unbelievers who ever lived. It occurs prior to the judgment of the great white throne (20:11-12 K46). It includes all who did not seek God, or who rejected his son Jesus to be their substitute for sin. They have been waiting in the intermediate location of *hades*. At the time of their judgment they will receive resurrected physical bodies (20:5 K46), appropriate to their future fate. They will appear in these bodies before the great white throne. Their destiny is to be cast into hell, the eternal lake of fire (20:15 K46). God leaves the unbelievers in the intermediate state for as long as possible, as one last kindness, but at the end of time, they must join Satan whom they willingly followed into deception.

How much better will it be for you to be in one of the resurrections of the believers, and not the eighth resurrection.

Again, there is a symmetry in number. There were eight temporary resurrections of individuals in Scripture. They are precursors. There are also eight glorified resurrections. Every man, woman, and child ever born, and every unborn child, will experience one of the eight glorified resurrections.

The number eight in the Bible represents new life. In the Old Testament, God commanded that boys be circumcised on the eighth day after birth. Circumcision of the body is meant to teach us about circumcision of the heart (Romans 2:28-29) and new life in Christ. The power of God's spirit works in us to become like Jesus (Ephesians 2:10, 4:23-24).

The number eight also represents resurrection, and new creation. That is because it follows from the numbers six and seven. God created the heavens and the earth in six days. His fourth commandment mandates that we thank him for his creation by resting on the seventh day (Exodus 20:8-11). After he was crucified, Christ spent the entire seventh day in the tomb. God then raised him from the dead on the eighth day, which was the first day of a new week (Matthew 28:1, Mark 16:9, Luke 24:1, John 20:1). Out of gratitude, the church worldwide moved the sabbath day for worshipping God to the first day of the week, Sunday. In this way it also celebrates the eighth day, when Christ was resurrected, the day of the new creation. Those in Christ are become a new creation (2 Corinthians 5:17).

It is awe inspiring that Christ came to glory on the eighth day, and that there will also be eight glorious resurrections from the dead. All of God's children who are raised up will praise his wisdom and majesty forever.

Appendix F: Final judgments before the throne of God

At some point after we die, every one of us will receive a final judgment before the throne of God (Hebrews 9:27). He takes an intense interest in each person, the billions and billions who ever lived. We are the pinnacle of his creation, created in his image. He will examine us one-by-one in public. We will give account of our lives before him (Romans 14:10-12), then he will make a formal pronouncement on each person's eternal destination: everlasting life in the new heaven and the new earth, or hell and the lake of fire. By his side will be the son of God, Jesus Christ.

When does this judgment happen? As in the previous appendix regarding resurrection, there is a common objection to literal interpretation of Bible passages on the topic of judgment. Many say that it would be easier to comprehend just one judgment event after the one resurrection of all the dead. A viewpoint of others is that there are multiple resurrections, but just one judgment event at the end of time.

However, the most consistent biblical interpretation is that there are multiple resurrections, according to the age in which the believer lives (see Appendix E), and that for each one there immediately follows a separate final judgment for that group of people.

Two of the separate judgments are explicitly prophesied in Scripture. The others proceed from theological deduction.

The first judgment described in the Bible is of the tribulation martyrs. It happens shortly after the second coming of Christ at the end of the seven-year period, when they will be granted glorified bodies. They come before the throne of God as the sheep of the judgment of the sheep and goats (Matthew 25:32-33, K43). Afterward, they assist Christ in the government of his thousand-year kingdom on earth. Then the martyrs will be with him for all eternity in the new heaven and the new earth.

The other judgment explicitly mentioned is of all the unbelievers. After the end of the millennium, they will receive new physical bodies appropriate to their fate, and will give their accounts at the great white throne judgment (20:11-12 K46). God will judge them for their sin and rebellion, and will send them to hell to join Satan and the devils. This is also the judgment that Paul spoke of to the pagan Greeks of Athens:

> Acts 17:31 Because he hath appointed a day, in the which he will judge the world in righteousness by that man whom he hath ordained; whereof he hath given assurance unto all men, in that he hath raised him from the dead.

Paul did not speak of *the day* of judgment, but *a day*. The lack of the definite article is not surprising for someone who prophesied the rapture and resurrection of all the faithful church saints (see K13), with an implied judgment for them before God's throne immediately thereafter. The judgment Paul speaks of to the Athenian Greeks is the great white throne judgment that will await them and the rest of the unbelieving world, unless they seek out Christ to be their savior.

The church saints who are raptured will receive glorified bodies. Then they will dwell in heaven with Jesus and God the Father for the time of tribulation. During the millennium that follows, they remain in heaven with the Father while Christ goes to earth as king. It is inconceivable that God would keep his children in suspense of *the day* of judgment over all that time, and make them wait in their glorified bodies until the great white throne judgment. Out of his love for the church, the bride of Christ, he would put them immediately at peace by conducting a day of judgment right after the rapture. He will hear all their testimonies as true believers. Whatever sins they committed are washed away in the blood of the Lamb, whom they trusted with their eternal life.

The final judgments of other groups of people are not portrayed in the Bible, but we know that they will occur. “For we must all appear before the judgment seat of Christ” (2 Corinthians 5:10).

A separate final judgment would be appropriate for the Old Testament saints at the close of the tribulation. Otherwise, they could not rightfully return to their homeland of Israel for the millennial kingdom (Ezekiel 37:12).

In section K42 we saw that God will enforce purity of entrance to his millennial kingdom, by putting to death all those who followed the beast and the woman of Babylon, those who scorned Jesus and his offer of salvation. This is a ruling by God, through Christ "with a rod of iron" (see 2:27, 12:5, 19:15 in K42). But it is not the final judgment of the rebels still alive after the battle of Armageddon. It only results in their physical bodies being put to death. Their souls will then wait in hades for the duration of the millennial kingdom. Afterward, they will be resurrected to face final judgment of both body and soul, before the great white throne of God.

I write to you from the church age. Ours is an age of grace. However, in recent decades, people worldwide no longer have fear of God. Our culture does not believe there is a hell anymore. They are more concerned with supposed global warming rather than the lake of fire; with expanding their sexual activities, instead of making their body a temple of the Holy Spirit (1 Corinthians 6:19). They think that since God has not struck them with lightning, he probably doesn't even exist, and if he does, he is a nice god who surely won't punish them with death. Recent generations have formulated a false gospel of "tolerance" that they insist God fall in with. Others want to identify infidels or fascists and liquidate them, instead of looking in a mirror for the enemy within.

But God's tolerance has limits. He has standards of righteousness. When we follow them, he blesses us through them. It is a joy to be conformed to the image of God, and to become more and more like Christ. God does not wish to punish. He is extending his offer of salvation as long as possible, until the fullness of his people are saved.

If you are reading this book, it is not too late to change your mind and accept Jesus Christ into your life. If you do, you can know for sure that you will be in one of the resurrections of God's children, and that you will go to heaven when you die.

How can you be sure of this eternal life?

God wants you to be sure. He wants you to "give diligence to make your calling and election sure ... for so an entrance shall be ministered unto you abundantly into the everlasting kingdom of our Lord and Saviour Jesus Christ" (2 Peter 1:10-11).

You can be sure because God is the one giving you a new spiritual birth. You are born again "not of blood, nor of the will of the flesh, nor of the will of man, but of God" (John 1:13). Your new life is in Christ. "Whosoever believeth that Jesus is the Christ is born of God" (1 John 5:1).

You can be sure because your new birth does not depend on you, or anything you have done, good or bad. It is by God's gift of faith to you, because he loves you. "For by grace are ye saved through faith; and that not of yourselves: it is the gift of God: not of works, lest any man should boast" (Ephesians 2:8-9). "For whatsoever is born of God overcometh the world: and this is the victory that overcometh the world, even our faith" (1 John 5:4).

You can be sure because you are adopted into God's family (Romans 8:15). You will always carry God's name, even if you sin against his way in future. When you sin again, "if we confess our sins, he is faithful and just to forgive us our sins, and to cleanse us from all unrighteousness" (1 John 1:9). We have earthly fathers who correct us, how much more shall we submit to our heavenly father and live.

Jesus said "I give unto them eternal life; and they shall never perish, neither shall any man pluck them out of my hand" (John 10:28). He will be yours forever.

Bible Index

Topic Index

About Matthias Key

As a laser physicist working at a world-famous laboratory, Matthias Key was unable to find the secrets of the universe. He then concentrated on his lifelong spiritual quest instead. At the age of 28, he experienced a profound turning point when he encountered the living Christ, known to others as Yeshua HaMashiakh, ʿIsa al-Maseeh, or Jesus the Messiah.

Born in the U.S. to persecuted Christians who had escaped Soviet communism, Matthias excelled academically and began his career in advanced physics. He also directed his analytical training toward messages found in different schools of thought: Marxism, New Age, mystical Islam, Judaism, Hinduism, Christianity and mainstream Islam. After his awakening, he proceeded to earn a Master of Divinity from a conservative, Bible-affirming seminary.

Professionally, Matthias transitioned to IT, eventually becoming a lead cybersecurity architect with a major U.S. federal contractor. In that role, he developed systems thinking and an eye for complex design — perspectives that now inform his prophetic teaching.

In parallel, Matthias helped start a Russian-speaking Messianic Jewish congregation in a large American city, and later trained for engagement with upper-caste Hindu immigrants. His work reflects both precision and compassion — the heart of a scientist and the soul of a servant.

Matthias Key has moved to devoting himself fully to the study of the Old and New Testaments, the Qur'an and the Hadiths, and the communication of prophetic truth which they contain. Through his writing, he helps other seekers who are on a spiritual journey to interpret the book of Revelation's "cyber patterns." He shows how they are the key to understanding divine order within end-time prophecies. His aim is to introduce others to the living Christ, who gave his life for them.

"Revelation isn't chaos—it's code.
Once you see its divine sequence, everything becomes clear."

www.ingramcontent.com/pod-product-compliance
Lightning Source LLC
LaVergne TN
LVHW090555110826
845146LV00001B/136

* 9 7 9 8 9 9 2 1 3 3 1 8 9 *